Recent Research in Developmental Psychopathology

Book Supplement to the Journal of
Child Psychology and Psychiatry No. 4

Series Editors M. BERGER and E. TAYLOR

Other Titles in the Series

Recent Research in Developmental Psychopathology

Edited by

J. E. STEVENSON

University of Surrey, Guildford

PERGAMON PRESS

OXFORD · NEW YORK · TORONTO · SYDNEY · PARIS · FRANKFURT

U.K.	Pergamon Press Ltd., Headington Hill Hall, Oxford OX3 0BW, England
U.S.A.	Pergamon Press Inc., Maxwell House, Fairview Park, Elmsford, New York 10523, U.S.A.
CANADA	Pergamon Press Canada Ltd., Suite 104, 150 Consumers Road, Willowdale, Ontario M2J 1P9, Canada
AUSTRALIA	Pergamon Press (Aust.) Pty. Ltd., P.O. Box 544, Potts Point, N.S.W. 2011, Australia
FRANCE	Pergamon Press SARL, 24 rue des Ecoles, 75240 Paris, Cedex 05, France
FEDERAL REPUBLIC OF GERMANY	Pergamon Press GmbH, Hammerweg 6, D-6242 Kronberg-Taunus, Federal Republic of Germany

Copyright © 1985 Pergamon Press Ltd.

First edition 1985

Library of Congress Cataloging in Publication Data
Main entry under title:
Recent research in developmental psychopathology.
A selection of papers presented at the 10th
International Congress of the International Association
for Child and Adolescent Psychiatry and Allied
Professions, held in Dublin in July 1982.
1. Child psychopathology — Research — Congresses.
2. Child psychotherapy — Research — Congresses.
3. Parenting — Congresses.   4. Child psychotherapy —
Congresses. I. Stevenson, J. E. (Jim E.)
II. International Association for Child and Adolescent
Psychiatry and Allied Professions.   International
Congress (10th : 1982 : Dublin)
RJ500.2.R43   1984   618.92'89   84–11078

British Library Cataloguing in Publication Data
Recent research in developmental psychopathology.
1. Child psychiatry
I. Stevenson, J. E.
618.92'89   RJ499
ISBN 0–08–030828–7

Printed in Great Britain by A. Wheaton & Co. Ltd., Exeter

Contents

v

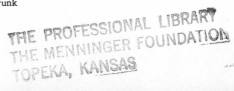

Introduction to the Series

The Association for Child Psychology and Psychiatry, a learned society, was founded in 1956 to further the scientific study of all matters concerning the mental health and development of children through the medium of meetings and the establishment of a journal. The *Journal of Child Psychology and Psychiatry and Allied Disciplines* was first published in 1960 in conjunction with Pergamon Press and this fruitful collaboration has continued over the years.

The Journal aims to enhance theory, research and clinical practice in child and adolescent psychology and psychiatry and the allied disciplines through the publication of papers concerned with child and adolescent development and especially developmental psychopathology and the developmental disorders. It is recognized that many other disciplines have an important contribution to make in furthering knowledge of the mental life and behaviour of children. The Editors have aimed to bring together knowledge from related fields of animal behaviour, anthropology, education, family studies, sociology, physiology and paediatrics in order to promote an eventual integration.

We can claim some success in this endeavour, but have been aware of the need to supplement the material in the Journal with a publication which would bring together, under one cover, research studies on one particular topic or the contributions to a symposium or conference on a particular theme.

In recent years the officers of the Association have considered ways and means of bringing such a publication to the membership and to a wider readership of professional workers in the various disciplines concerned with child health, development, education and care. The Association and Pergamon Press began publishing supplements to the Journal in 1978. These will appear from time to time under the general Editorship of the Editors of the Journal with the help of an Associate Editor when needed.

The Editors invite contributions of high quality from clinicians and research workers who wish to publish their studies in a single volume, as well as the proceedings of conferences and symposia on themes related to

child psychology, psychiatry and allied disciplines. All submissions
will be assessed through the normal refereeing process.

MICHAEL BERGER
ERIC TAYLOR

Joint Editors
*Journal of Child Psychology and
Psychiatry and Allied Disciplines*

Introduction to the Volume

The 10th International Congress of the International Association for Child and Adolescent Psychiatry and Allied Professions was held in Dublin in July 1982. An initial selection of the papers presented at the Congress was made by the Editors of the Yearbook of the International Association (E. James Anthony and Colette Chiland) for inclusion in a forthcoming edition. The papers in the present volume were chosen from the remainder.

The Dublin Congress was a very large affair with over 500 papers presented. It was also a very successful meeting which was a reflection of the effort put into its organization by Dr. Lionel Hersov (President of the International Association) and Dr. Richard Lansdown (Secretary-General). From the rich and diverse range of work assembled on the Congress theme of 'Children in Turmoil: tomorrow's parents' it would not be possible to select a representative collection of papers that would make a coherent single volume. There were for example two subject areas that warranted separate publications in their own right: 'Children as victims of war' and 'The impact on children of the civil strife in Northern Ireland'. There were other areas too where excellent collections of papers could have been made, e.g. depression in children, child abuse, treatment in adolescence and infant psychiatry.

In making a selection of papers for this volume I wanted to present a picture of where research in developmental psychopathology had been developing. This branch of the scientific study of disorders in childhood has recently emerged. Within psychology studies of children have been a major research interest over the past twenty years. Over this time also the scientific investigation of issues within child psychiatry has been established. Developmental psychopathology represents an area of research activity where child psychiatry and developmental psychology meet. It provides the investigation of topics of concern within child psychiatry with the methods and models of developmental psychology. At the same time research in developmental psychopathology affords a rich set of opportunities for the developmental psychologist to extend understanding of developmental processes with children and families with extreme or abnormal characteristics. This is analogous to the contribution made to cognitive psychology by neuropsychological investigations of information processing in patients with lesions. The importance of this emergent field of research can be highlighted by contrasts with other disciplines that are related to child psychiatry. In contrast to adult psychiatry, developmental psychology is primarily concerned with change in behaviour; in contrast to psychoanalysis it utilizes potentially falsifiable hypotheses; in contrast to experimental psychology it attempts to maintain ecological validity. This latter aspect is reflected in the extent to which the methods if not the theories of human ethology have been integrated into developmental psychopathological investigations.

The papers were eventually selected to present this picture of developmental psychopathology around three distinct themes. These are represented in the titles of the first three sections of the book: the fourth section comprises review papers.

The first section on Parenting the Preschool Child is based on a number of related studies on influences on differences between parents in the style of their behaviour towards their children. Two of these papers by Pound *et al.* and by Mills *et al.* discuss the effect of depression on mothers' interaction with their children. Dowdney *et al.* are concerned to relate current parenting to the individuals experience of less than adequate parenting in their own childhood. The importance of these topics for an understanding of developmental psychopathology has been established by work relating depression in mothers and disturbed behaviour in preschool children by, for example, Wolkind, who reviews his work on this and related topics in Chapter 18. Indeed the research studies in this section reflect a major development in research strategy: they are studies aimed at understanding processes underlying the associations previously established in epidemiological and other surveys. They thereby represent a move beyond associations to the understanding of the mechanisms whereby, for example, aspects of family functioning have an impact on the child. The implications for treatment and intervention of this type of research are more direct than in surveys and some of these implications are discussed in the thoughtful paper by Skuse and Cox.

The papers in the second section on Studies of Clinical Groups are more diverse than those in Section one. The first of these by Garrison and Earls links very directly with the papers in the section on Parenting the Preschool Child. The behaviour problems of young children have been shown to be related to the quality of parental care and the extent of their relation to later disturbance is relevant to the question of whether treatment for such problems is warranted. One behaviour that is sufficiently disruptive to family life to justify treatment in its own right is that concerned with sleep and waking at night. This is the topic of papers dealing both with the general population (Richman) and the visually handicapped (Kitzinger and Hunt). A link with paediatrics is seen in the next three papers. Mrazek *et al.* and Menzies provide rather different styles of study both of which however illustrate the complexities that arise when investigators attempt an integration of our understanding of psychological and physiological characteristics of children and their families. The paper by Smith *et al.* illustrates the

ways in which research centred on psychological processes can provide
very direct implications for the paediatric management of physical handicaps. The final paper in this section concerns a theme that was discussed in a number of symposia at the Congress; depression in children.
McConville and Rae-Grant provide a helpful summary of some of the issues
in this expanding but controversial field.

The third section of papers concerns Evaluation of Intervention. A
feature of these evaluation studies is that they are all concerned with
serious or traumatic events or problems. A variety of methods are used
in the evaluations, e.g. the controlled trial with random allocation to
treatment (Berg *et al.*), and the replicated single case study approach
(Nichol *et al*). Some of these evaluations involve changes to routine
care (Hawthorne Amick) and others the effectiveness of more specific
types of treatment (Forrest and Standish, Black and Urbanowicz). However, despite this diversity, these studies demonstrate the value of
evaluation studies in developing clinical practice. They can establish
the practical problems in implementing novel services and treatments but
also importantly they can provide the clinician with evidence about
effectiveness of treatment. Evaluation of intervention is one area that
highlights the importance of replication in developing our understanding
on the basis of research. In each of the papers in this section the
authors draw attention to the limitations and weaknesses of their own
studies: indeed it is impractical to attempt the 'perfect' treatment
evaluation. Any one study can only hope to cope with some of the potentially confounding influences on treatment. It is by cumulative
experience of a number of less than perfect studies that conclusions on
the best procedures for intervention can be reached. It is to be hoped
that the significance of the studies reported in this section will
encourage others to attempt this style of research that is so central to
the development of a coherent field of professional practice.

The final section, as indicated above, contains papers reviewing certain
central issues within developmental psychopathology. In the first of
these, Bradley summarizes some of the research that has utilized the
HOME Inventory developed by Caldwell and himself. Research activities
and the development of instruments are intimately linked, i.e. research
tends to be centred on those characteristics for which measures are
widely available. In general developmental research has had available
rather better measures of the characteristics of individuals whether they
be child or adult than of the environment. The measurement of the
child's environment has relied more on *ad hoc* indicators that have been
adopted for an individual study without necessarily making reference to
measures in other studies. This has meant that, with the exception of
crude environmental measures such as social class, it has been difficult
to integrate findings on influences on individual differences in development based on common measures of the environment. The HOME Inventory has
represented a singular exception to this trend, as is well illustrated in
Bradley's chapter. Wolkind's summary of work undertaken at the Family
Research Unit demonstrates the value of being eclectic in both technique
and theory and in combining information on biological, psychological and
social influences on the production and maintenance of disorders. The
last paper by Garmezy signifies an important part of the future research

programme in this field. The studies and reviews by Garmezy and others
such as Rutter have convincingly demonstrated the need to extend our
understanding of individual differences in developmental psychopathology.
Many of the main effects on psychopathology have now been established but
what is needed is to develop theories that can provide explanations of
the mechanisms of the interactions between main effects and other characteristics of the child, his family or experiences.

In this sense the Garmezy paper is appropriately placed at the end of the
volume in that it looks to future research activity. There is another
reason for so placing it here. Garmezy concludes his paper with a quote
from an Irish psychologist (Ken Heskin) about Ireland. Those who attended the 10th International Congress were very much aware of the typically
Irish conviviality of the occasion. It is therefore appropriate that the
Irish should have the last word.

                                                        JIM STEVENSON

PART ONE

Parenting the Pre-school Child

CHAPTER 1

The Impact of Maternal Depression on Young Children

Andrea Pound, Antony Cox, Christine Puckering and Margaret Mills

Department of Child and Adolescent Psychiatry, Institute of Psychiatry, London

Introduction

The work of Brown and Harris (1978), Kruk and Wolkind (1983), Richman (1978) and others has clearly demonstrated a high prevalence rate of depression among mothers of young children, and a strong association between maternal depression and disturbance in the children. Our study has set out to investigate in closer detail the interaction between the depressed mother and her child, and the factors which ameliorate or intensify the risk of childhood disturbance. In this paper we will present some interim findings from our study, which is still in progress, so we cannot at present do more than identify some trends in our data, and suggest further questions which we hope to be able to answer in the future when the full analysis is completed.

Our subjects have been recruited largely via the Health Visitors of the King's Health District, a predominantly working-class area of South London. We have asked them to contact all the mothers of 2-3-year-old children on their books who were British (or Irish) born, working-class by husband's occupation, stably married or cohabiting, and not working full-time. We initially excluded families with an unemployed husband, but as the study progressed a tragically large proportion of our potential sample has become unemployed, so we have recently begun to take in an unemployed sub-group.

The Health Visitors administered the Malaise Inventory, a brief questionnaire concerning the mother's physical and psychological health, and all high scorers plus a random sample of low scorers were interviewed at home using a structured interview schedule. High scorers on the Malaise Inventory who are not clinically depressed, i.e. those who are anxious, hypochondriacal or physically ill, or who have only mild symptoms with no significant degree of handicap, are excluded from further study. Depressed and control mothers are later observed at home for two 2-hour observation periods, and in a final session the child's intelligence, language development and temperament are assessed. If there is serious concern about either mother or child as a result of our observations the Health Visitor is informed with a view to her taking appropriate action.

A. Pound *et al.*

Six months after the first interview a follow-up interview is carried out and the child again observed at home and in nursery or playgroup if he attends one.

Characteristics of our Sample

We have not attempted a full-scale epidemiological study and have delib-erately excluded grossly disadvantaged families with children in day care, single parents and ethnic minorities, in order to reduce the num-ber of intervening variables. However, of the 267 questionnaires received to date 105 or 39 per cent were high scorers, a figure very close to George Brown's for a similar group. There are also very close similarities in terms of quality of marriage and severity of problems in the children between our data and Naomi Richman's group of depressed mothers (Richman, Stevenson and Graham, 1982), though we have fewer poor marriages in the control group, probably because we have excluded inter-mediate scorers on the Malaise Inventory from the study. The proportion of children of depressed mothers with behaviour problems is also very close to those reported by Kruk and Wolkind (1983) in their 42-month-old group. We were reassured to find that despite the differences in our sampling methods, we were working with a very similar population (see Table 1).

Table 1. Comparison of the association between child
behaviour problems and maternal depression
in three studies

Child behaviour problems	Present Study		Richman		Kruk and Wolkind
	Control %	Depressed %	Control %	Depressed %	Married controls %
None	57	38	57	33	58
Mild	24	18	25	29	29
Marked	19	44	18	39	13

Main Findings on Depressed Mothers

We are reporting here on the first 60 cases we have seen, of whom 39 were depressed and 21 controls. It was apparent that many of the depressed mothers in our sample were not only currently ill and unhappy but had long histories of deprivation and difficulty, and some of their life stories were very distressing to hear. They were likely to report poorer relationships with their own parents, with trends towards less warmth and harsher discipline than in the control group. Evaluation of their own mother's qualities as mothers was particularly important, with most con-trols seeing their own mothers as 'good' and a high proportion of the depressed group seeing theirs as 'indifferent' or 'poor' mothers (see Table 2).

Table 2. Comparison of early life histories in depressed and control groups

	Depressed N = 39	Controls N = 21	χ^2	P
Evaluation of Own Mother				
Good	15 (38%)	15 (71%)	3.17	< 0.05
Indifferent/Poor	24 (62%)	6 (29%)		
Separation from Parents				
None	26 (67%)	18 (86%)	2.53	n.s.
Some	13 (33%)	3 (14%)		
Truancy				
Regular	15 (38%)	2 (10%)	4.29	< 0.025
None/Occasional	24 (62%)	19 (90%)		

A third of the depressed group were separated from one or both parents for significant periods of time during childhood because of death, desertion or turmoil in the family, twice the rate found in the controls, and they tended to report unhappy parental marriages (Table 2). A quarter reported emotional difficulties during childhood and more than half truanted regularly from school during adolescence ($p < 0.025$, see Table 2). They then tended to marry very young, and to have their first child at a very early age ($p < 0.005$, Table 3).

Table 3. Age at marriage and at birth of first born in depressed and control groups

	Depressed N = 39	Controls N = 21	χ^2	P
Age at Marriage				
under 21	32 (82%)	9 (43%)	7.96	< 0.005
over 21	7 (18%)	12 (57%)		
Age at First Birth				
under 21	24 (62%)	4 (19%)	8.26	< 0.005
over 21	15 (38%)	17 (81%)		

It seems they were attempting to escape from long-standing personal difficulties and poor employment prospects by precipitate marriage and child bearing, only to find themselves faced by even greater demands which they

had few inner or outer resources to meet. Their marriages were likely to
be disastrous and marked by constant quarreling, unco-operativeness and
staying out on the part of the husband (Table 4). In some cases the
depressed wife was deeply preoccupied with the disappointment in the
marriage, which she saw as the major cause of her depression. However,
some wives felt they unfairly 'took it out on him', when the real cause
of their discontents lay elsewhere, and some of these husbands bore with
their wives' irritability with heroic tolerance and good humour. We were
also painfully aware that many of our subjects were labouring under very
difficult material circumstances, including low family income and poor
quality housing. Most of our sample lived in council accommodation, some
very old and poorly maintained, some new but in vast estates with high
rates of vandalism and violence. Many more of the depressed group were,
with good reason, dissatisfied with their housing, and a good proportion
saw it as the main cause of their depression.

Table 4. Quality of marriage and child problems in
depressed and control groups

	Depressed	Controls	Chi-square for Linear Trends	
	N = 39	N = 21	χ^2	P
Quality of Marriage				
good	14 (36%)	19 (90%)		
fair	8 (21%)	2 (10%)	17.26	< 0.005
poor	17 (43%)	0 (0%)		
Substantive Child Problems				
none	15 (38%)	12 (57%)		
mild	7 (18%)	5 (24%)	3.64	< 0.05
marked	17 (44%)	4 (19%)		

Effects on the Children

We will next examine the effects of all this cumulative disadvantage on
the next generation. As other studies have found there were indeed more
substantive child problems in the depressed group (Table 4, p < 0.05),
although a not inconsiderable number of control children also had substantive problems, particularly in sleeping. It was also clear that
there were fewer child problems where the depression had improved at 6
months follow-up, as well as less marital disharmony. Within the
depressed group child problems were far more common when the mother had
personality problems (16 in all) or a long-standing history of previous
depression (Table 5). Brief depressive episodes, which often arose in
the context of clear precipitating events, like recent bereavement, have
relatively little impact on the children compared to the more serious
hazard of long-standing psychiatric disturbance in the mother.

Table 5. Child problems related to mother's psychiatric
          history, quality of marriage and evaluation
          of own mother in the depressed group only

	Child Problems			Chi-square for Linear Trends	
	None	Mild	Marked	χ^2	P
Mother's History					
No personality disorder and little previous depression	9(60%)	4(27%)	2(13%)		
				8.00	< 0.005
Personality disorder and/or extensive periods of depression	6(25%)	3(12.5%)	15(62.5%)		
Quality of Marriage					
Good or fair	12(55%)	4(18%)	6(27%)		
Poor	3(18%)	3(18%)	11(65%)	6.48	< 0.01
Evaluation of Own Mother					
Good	7(47%)	5(33%)	3(20%)		
Indifferent/Poor	8(33%)	2(8%)	14(58%)	3.01	< 0.05

However, we already know that many of the depressed women had poor
marriages and difficult relationships with their own parents. Does the
depressed mother's style of relating to her child produce disturbance in
him, or does the poor quality of family relationships mediate his disturbance? There was indeed a strong association (p < 0.01) between substantive child problems and marital difficulties (see Table 5), but there
seemed to be no interaction between the factors, which were additive, so
that of the children with both chronically ill mothers and unhappily
married parents 77 per cent had two or more substantive problems. Low
evaluation of own mother was also strongly associated with child problems
(Table 5, p < 0.05) even though most women's *current* relationship with
their mothers was quite friendly, and they had, as it were, forgiven them
for their past shortcomings.

It might be expected that where family relationships were in turmoil the
children have poor models for their behaviour to others and therefore
have relationship problems. There are in fact many such problems with
parents and peers in the depressed group, and within the group there was
also a strong linear relationship (p < 0.005) between poor marriage and
relationship problems (Table 6). A less expected finding was that eating
problems in the children was equally strongly related to marital problems
(p < 0.005, see Table 6).

A. Pound *et al.*

Table 6. Quality of marriage and type of child problems
          in the depressed group only

	Quality of Marriage			Chi-square for Linear Trends	
	Good	Fair	Poor	χ^2	P
Relationship problems	3	4	12	7.24	< 0.005
No relationship problems	11	4	5		
Eating problems	4	5	12	7.24	< 0.005
No eating problems	11	3	5		

Conclusion: Implications for Services

We have not yet analysed the data on women's contact with their family
doctors or psychiatric facilities, nor on the group who had been admitted
to hospital following suicidal attempts. We can therefore only address
ourselves to the clinical issues as they have impinged upon us during
long hours of talking with and observing mothers and children at home.
The first and most powerful impression is of the size of the problem, and
the paucity of resources to deal with it. It is also a very private and
largely invisible problem - most depressed women are at home almost all
the time. Very few of our depressed mothers had come to the attention of
any psychiatric or social service, but a considerable number had consulted their GPs, and some had received medication from them. Many had felt
misunderstood by their doctors, who they felt had made light of their
problems, though some were deeply appreciative of advice they had
received on children's management or simply being *listened* to in a sympathetic way. Medication had rarely been found very useful - women were
either afraid of becoming addicted to valium, if that were given, or
found that anti-depressants made them drowsy and lethargic, so they could
not wake up in the night to see to their children. Health Visitors,
where they were still in close contact with the mother, had again been
very helpful to some of them in giving advice on sleeping and eating
problems, or in several cases transforming isolated lives by introducing
them to another local mother. However, a surprising number of women had
not confided their problems to anyone, and seemed to accept their depression fatalisticaly. The few who had received psychiatric treatment were
highly anxious women who had been treated behaviourally for agorophobia.
Almost no depressed women had received psychiatric treatment, and even
those who had been admitted to hospital following overdoses were all discharged with no psychiatric or social follow-up

The second major impression is of the poverty and stress of many young
mothers' lives. Mothering is a delicate and difficult task which
requires good conditions to do it well. As we have shown, many of our
subjects lived in substandard housing on large estates where the sheer
numbers of people militated against a satisfying community life. The
effect of housing design on family life cannot be over-estimated, and

where we have come across good quality, small-scale developments, careful
management (by housing associations rather than local authorities) or
measures like the use of door phones to prevent vandalism, the effects
have been much appreciated by tenants. Low family income, unemployment
and the fear of unemployment, are further spectres which haunt many young
families. As Townsend (1979) has shown, families with young children are
among the poorest in the country, and anxiety about money figures in many
women's depressive preoccupations. Even among those with a husband in
secure employment, a high proportion could afford no entertainment or
outside leisure activity, which bound them even more closely to home and
the domestic routine.

Finally, and possibly most important, is the social context of their
daily lives. The mothers in our sample were *not* extremely isolated.
Many had mothers or sisters who lived near and some had one or more close
friends with whom they could confide; and there was little difference
between the depressed and control groups in this respect. Nevertheless
most women were alone with their children for the better part of each day
and each week. As Ann Dally (1982) says in a recent book, this isolation
of mother and child is a very recent phenomenon, without precedent in any
other age or society. Many manual workers still work long hours, so even
the most supportive husbands cannot help out to any great degree. However, as George Brown has shown, and we have confirmed, a good marriage
is the best antidote to depression and many of the control women were
clearly aware of their good fortune in this respect. In some of the poor
marriages (which were all in the depressed group) it was clear that the
husband had a long history of personality disturbance with an aggressive
attitude to life and a record of anti-social behaviour. In others, it
seemed most likely that the couple had got into a vicious circle of poor
communication and minimal co-operation, so that both felt unappreciated
and unsupported. None of our subjects had ever consulted a marriage
guidance counsellor, and neither GPs nor Health Visitors seemed to have
considered the possibility of seeing couples together with a view to
helping the marriage. There would, in many instances, be strong cultural
resistance to such a procedure, but for some it would almost certainly be
the most economical and effective intervention, especially if counselling
were more widely available within general practice settings.

However, in the face of such widespread psychiatric disturbance in young
mothers, with its associated childhood problems, any form of *individual*
intervention is likely to be too little, and too late, and to reach only
a small proportion of those at risk. Prevention probably is the only
adequate cure, and will require radical changes in our educational and
social structure. Few contemporary mothers have ever cared for a child
before the arrival of their own first-born, and most have no knowledge of
child care apart from their memories of their own childhood. In general,
the physical care of the children we have seen has been more than
adequate, but the provision of play materials, and the management of the
child's day so that both mother and child have pleasure with each other
has been indifferent to poor. It is clearly not lack of interest or
desire, but lack of knowledge, which middle-class women probably compensate for by reading books on child development and play. Education for
marriage and parenting should obviously start in school, but needs to

continue over the period of early married life when people are actually grappling with the problems. The admirable playgroup movement has made a major impact on the 3+ group and their families, but at present the under 3s and their mothers are left to fend for themselves. Could there not be small-scale mother-toddler clubs in every estate and housing area, which would provide companionship, emotional support in hard times, and covert education for parents? A way must be found to compensate for the major social changes which have occurred over the past couple of generations, and which have borne heavily on mothers and young children, or we will reap a bitter harvest of insecure and disturbed children on a hitherto unexampled scale.

References

BROWN, G. W. and HARRIS, T. O. (1978) *Social Origins of Depression.* London, Tavistock.

DALLY, A. (1982) *Inventing Motherhood. The Consequences of an Ideal.* London, Burnett Books.

KRUK, S. and WOLKIND, S. N. (1983) A longitudinal study of single mothers and their children. In N. Madge (Ed.), *Families at Risk* (p. 130). London, Heinemann.

POUND, A. (1982) Attachment and maternal depression. In C. M. Parkes and J. Stevenson-Hinde (Eds.), *The Place of Attachment in Human Behaviour.* London, Tavistock.

RICHMAN, N. (1978) Depression in mothers of young children. *Journal of the Royal Society of Medicine*, 71, 489–493.

RICHMAN, N., STEVENSON, J. and GRAHAM, P. (1982) *Preschool to School: A Behavioural Study.* London, Academic Press.

TOWNSEND, T. (1979) *Poverty in the United Kingdom. A Survey of Household Resources and Standards of Living.* Harmondsworth, Penguin.

CHAPTER 2

What is it About Depressed Mothers that Influences Their Children's Functioning?

Maggie Mills, Christine Puckering, Andrea Pound and Antony Cox

Department of Child and Adolescent Psychiatry, Institute of Psychiatry, London

There are considerable individual differences in the way mothers cope at home with the emotional and cognitive needs of pre-school children. This study describes patterns of maternal responsivity, particularly where mothers are depressed. It also attempts to assess the implications of differences in parenting style for satisfactory cognitive functioning in 2-3 year old children.

Day in, day out, 24 hours each day, women in South London are responsible for the care and raising of young children. The mothers that we, of the South London Under-Fives Project, have been visiting, live in families that are not seriously disadvantaged. Of British or Irish parentage, they are stably cohabitating, with most of the menfolk in working class employment. None of their children is in care or full-time day nursery since, for inclusion in the study, mothers and children must spend at least 50 per cent of their day together.

But these young mothers are presented with intolerable hazards during the process of bringing up young children. Our families do not have cars. There is no Underground Railway in South London. They cannot get a pram on a bus. These mothers are limited in their mobility to the distance they can push the pram carrying heavy shopping. At home there are few places to play, which are safe and salubrious, and a mother needs constant vigilance, particularly in high-rise blocks, where many of our mothers live. Many of these women live in a very restricted social network, seeing usually only close family, lacking telephones, cars and often financial resources and, in any case, preferring to keep themselves to themselves in what they regard as a hostile environment.

The question we have asked is: how in this setting are mothers coping with the emotional and cognitive needs of a 2-3 year old child? Observations were made during two morning visits to the home at a time when it was expected that no other family or friends would be present. Observations were structured using a 10-second time interval and on the spot recording of pre-coded sampled categories, with an audio tape for later editing (Dowdney *et al.*, 1984).

Out of the three hours of data that has been analysed from coded observations on each of 60 mother/child pairs, mothers were willing to sustain
joint activity or chat with their child at a level that made possible
reciprocal contributions from them both for at least one hour. We are
not talking here about play alone; a phenomenon grossly over-represented
in psychological studies of pre-school children, but a set-up where
mother incorporated the child into her household activities. These may
include peeling potatoes together (although the child may be more inter-
ested in getting wet); watching interesting happenings together out of
the window and making comments; watering mum's plants - an activity once
seen turned into a game with mother and child watering each other as
well - or, the mother may set up the child with child-appropriate activities, peel the potatoes herself but monitor the child and continue to
contribute - thus as the child is riding his toy car round the kitchen
she may ask, "Do you need some petrol?"

It should be clear that joint involvement does not include desultory chat
or time when the parties are primarily engaged in their own activities,
but would include play, conventionally defined. Half the mothers set up
their child in this way. And whether or not mothers were depressed (for
a fuller clinical description see Pound *et al.*, Chapter 1) or their child
was rated a behaviour problem made no difference to the time they spent
in joint involvement.

During joint involvement reciprocal contributions to mother or child
behaviours were coded. Where they added to the partners' activity or
talk this measure was called a *Link*. It could be verbal or non-verbal,
and consisted of two components: content - the introduction or expansion
of conceptual material; and context - the material must be relevant to
the child's ongoing behaviour. The Link and its potential for subsequent
response can be seen as a measure of successful meshing between mother
and child for at least three alternating 'turns'. Thus, if the child
says, as they look at a book together, 'That's a cow', possible maternal
links might be, 'Yes, it says moo', or, 'Yes, there are two, do you see
the other one?', or, 'The other one's smaller, perhaps it's a baby'. The
child in turn may respond to the mother's link by saying, 'Nice cow', or
might produce the sound 'moo', or pat the picture and say, 'That's not a
cow, that's a dog'.

A frequency count can be made of the number of Links made by one party
whick are followed by the other. In addition, since it is possible for
two mothers to have similar *numbers* of Links with responses but very different *proportions* of Links followed (e.g. (a) 10 Links followed, 0 Links
not followed, (b) 10 Links followed, 90 Links not followed) we have
included a proportion measure of mother Links not responded to.

So we can talk about the number of mother Links which are responded to by
the child, during joint involvement. This measure differentiates depressed from non-depressed mothers. Depressed mothers have fewer Links that
their child responds to which is associated with increasing behaviour
problems (see Table 1). Depressed mothers in the 3+ behaviour problem
group are doing particularly badly. If we look at mother Links which
the child does *not* respond to, then fewer Links that depressed women

make are responded to than for control mothers (see Table 2) and
depressed mothers are equally impaired relative to controls whether
their child has a behaviour problem or not.

Table 1. Mean mother Links responded to in depressed
          and non-depressed groups

	Child Problems		
	0-1	2	3+
Depressed	63	45	25
Non-depressed	89	52	70
Significance of differences in means	n.s.	n.s.	p < 0.05

Table 2. Mean proportion of mother Links not responded
          to in depressed and non-depressed groups

	Child Problems		
	0-1	2	3+
Depressed	0.30	0.32	0.41
Non-depressed	0.11	0.10	0.21
Significant differences in proportions	p < 0.025	p < 0.02	p < 0.01

A special kind of Link we code - the World Link, is one that situates the
child in his own family and social context and makes experiences relevant
to him. So that if the child said, 'That's a cow', Mother might say, 'Do
you remember the weekend when Daddy took us on the picnic and the cow ate
your hat?' or, 'It's like the cow who fell in the canal, you used to love
that story when you were little'. This measure does not differentiate
depressed from non-depressed mothers but significantly more of the mothers
in the 3+ behaviour problem group make no World Links to their children
(see Table 3).

Table 3. Relationship of World Links to child problems

	Child problems		
	0-1	2	3+
Make World Links	18	7	3
Making no World Links	7	5	16

$\chi^2 = 14.07$ (2 d.f.) p < 0.001.

Why do depressed women fail to mesh?   If it is something to do with the
child, all we can say at this stage is that language comprehension and DQ
(Merrill Palmer) do not differentiate our groups.   It may be that
depressed mothers get the timing of their intervention wrong, e.g. if a
child is exploring a new toy it might be intrusive to intervene too soon
or too often, or a depressed mother's attention may lapse momentarily so
that she fails to register the child's change of focus. We should
mention here that depressed mothers spend longer staring vacantly into
space and doing nothing during observations.

One can explain maternal Links not being responded to because, although
the mother seems to be introducing material of the right developmental
level for a 2-3 year old child, it might not be right for that particular
child, and our measure is too gross to pick this up. Lastly, depressed
mothers may discourage responsiveness in other ways (Gotlib and Robinson,
1982). Certainly depressed mothers *can* respond to the Links their
children make. They do as well in picking up child contributions as
non-depressed mothers do (see Table 4) but their children make fewer
links. Children with behaviour problems also make fewer Links that are
responded to.

Table 4.   Mean child Links responded
to in depressed and non-
depressed groups

	Child problems		
	0-1	2	3+
Depressed	26*	20	11*
Non-depressed	39	27	24

*p < 0.02 between 0-1 and 3+ problems
within depressed group.

The impaired performance of Links we report for the depressed mother has
implications for child cognitive functioning with regard to the building
of vocabulary and semantic understanding, the use of relational information and the acquisition of real-world knowledge for long-term memory
store. But we would like to argue that the poor meshing, evidenced by
Links, could be interpreted as a failure on the mother's part to recruit,
sustain and expand the young child's attention and concentration.

Richman, Stevenson and Graham (1982) report that 75 per cent of children
with IQ-corrected reading retardation at 8 years of age have mothers who
were depressed when the children were aged 3. Neither class, behaviour
problems, social factors or early language delay fully explains why the
children of mothers who have been depressed fail to read. Perhaps the
existence of depressed mothers who neither recruit nor practise the
child's attention throughout the pre-school years can help to explain the
relationship.

Not making reading progress in primary school is often plausibly attribu-

ted to the language delay some at least of these children have experienced. We can report on the cognitive outcome in the child of expressive
language as measured by the Reynell Developmental Language Scales
(Reynell 1969). We have the typical pattern so that children with many
behaviour problems have the most expressive language delay, but as can be
seen from Table 5 it is really the 3+ problem children who have depressed
mothers, that are retarded by 9 months or so on expressive language.
While these children do not show general developmental delay, it is particularly these mothers and children who have fewer mother Links with
child responses. Expressive language delay may thus in part explain the
poor meshing as evidenced by Links between depressed mothers and children
with many behavioural problems, but it cannot explain depressed women's
impaired performance on Links where the children have no or few behaviour
problems. Here, an attentional mechanism still seems a likely candidate
to mediate between maternal state and child cognitive functioning.

Table 5. Means of cognitive test data in depressed
and non-depressed groups

(standard scores, adjusted to mean = 0, s.d. = 1)

	Depressed			Non-depressed		
Child problems	0-1	2	3+	0-1	2	3+
Merrill Palmer DQ	1.13	1.21	0.13	0.53	0.45	0.58
Reynell Language Expression	0.15	1.10	-0.84*	0.32	-0.31	-0.28
Reynell Language Comprehension	0.44	0.85	-0.38	0.36	0.10	-0.45

*Significance of differences in means within depressed group on Reynell
Language Expression $p < 0.02$.

At the outset we asked how mothers cope with the emotional and cognitive
needs of their children. Since Patterson (1980) has described early
child rearing as a time of 'maximum dysphoria' for mothers, we asked the
question 'Do our mothers and children have fun together?' We have looked
at mutual positive affect - that is, the co-occurrence within a 10-
second interval of child smiles, laughs, affectionate touches etc. with
maternal positive affect - tone of voice, verbal behaviour and physical
affect. There is no main effect of depression and Table 6 shows why this
is. If you do not have fun, i.e. low mutual affect as defined by a
median split, and you are depressed, you do not make many Links with a
child response. If you are depressed, but have fun you do make Links
that the child responds to. If you do not have fun but are not depressed, you still make Links. The only group who have trouble with Links
are those who are both depressed and low on mutual affect.

If a depressed mother is having fun then the gratification she gets may
sustain her in her attempts to guide the child's attention and understanding. Certainly, mutual positive affect most spontaneously occurs

during play and joint activities. Also, the child who is having fun
may be more open and alert to the depressed mother's initiatives when
they come. Whatever the mechanism, it is clear that the emotional containment of the young child cannot be seen as separate from cognitive
functioning. Indeed, clinicians usually assume that a child who can sustain activity on a task alone or jointly is emotionally contained.

Table 6. Relationship of depression, mutual positive affect,
and mean Links followed

	High mutual affect	Low mutual affect	Significance of difference in means
Depressed	72	28	p < 0.001
Non-depressed	76	75	n.s.
Significance of difference in means	n.s.	p < 0.001	

Within our depressed sample we have at least three different groups of
women and very possibly more. One sub-group is composed of children with
3+ behaviour problems and women with a history of personality disorder
and/or extensive previous depression. These depressed women are impaired
on *more* areas of child handling. The adverse pattern is that they score
highly on the amount of time spent controlling the child, they do not
have fun, the mother stares into space and the child is unoccupied, and
they have fewer Links with child responses, more Links not responded to
and they make no World Links.

Our second sub-group is just the opposite. They score very well on all
our measures. We rated them among the most sensitive mothers we saw, and
they spent a great deal of time in 'pretend' play, often modelling
mothering behaviours to their child through dolls, baby siblings, etc.
In providing emotional containment they often indirectly met the
cognitive needs of their children. We had expected a group of mothers
who, because they were sensitive, would be vulnerable to stressful
experience, but in whom parenting would be preserved.

In our third sub-group we had mothers, some of whom showed a pattern similar to the first group described, although their children were not
behaviour problems. Anecdotally, it is clear from follow-up interviews
and observational data which is not yet analysed, that these children
have become more disturbed over the follow-up period. We would argue
that the unoccupied 2 year old who mills around the house will soon get
into hot water. He simply cannot keep himself safely and appropriately
employed, or emotionally controlled without maternal support. And he
gets bored. He will fiddle with gas taps and pull stuff out of cupboards
and get into bouts of control with his mother which are likely to
escalate. The more control there is the less there becomes opportunity
for constructive activity, and the bored, messing-about, slightly
miserable 2 year old becomes, over time, skilled in battle - at least
that way he has his mother's attention, and it is something to do, and

by 3 years of age he is deliberately challenging and provoking his mother and set on the path of being a proper tyrant.

Our observations cover only a minute slice of family life. We have not mentioned the importance and involvement of fathers, grannies, siblings, etc. We set up observations in the home to try to see mothers and 2-year olds in their natural environment, where they are most likely to interact in their normal mode. But we are aware that our presence changes what we see and that in trying to standardize the situation to exclude other family members we may create unusual conditions for some mother/child pairs. One depressed mother with four children regarded the morning she spent alone with the index child as a holiday. Even standardized situations are less than perfect.

We code only observable events, and we know we miss the subtlety of the idiosyncratic meaning of events for the children, because we have no access to their internal representation of their own family and world. Our measures describe bad parenting but really subtle aspects of good parenting may elude our system. For instance, it may look as if a control issue is brewing but mother diffuses it - our coding sheet remains blank and we are not quite sure how she did it. Temperament measures, sex differences, follow-up and play group observations await analysis and we have not looked at the sequential data at all but only at the measures of joint activity and involvement taken within that framework. We are impressed with the many individual differences between families and the extraordinarily good parenting that we see from many mothers in the difficult circumstances we have described. This preliminary report does not do justice to the subtlety of mothering or the richness of our observational data. We hope you will bear with us and await future reports.

References

DOWDNEY, L., MRAZEK, D. A., QUINTON, D. and RUTTER, M. (1984) Observations of parent-child interaction with two to three year olds. *Journal of Child Psychology and Psychiatry*, 25, 379-409.

GOTLIB, I. M. and ROBINSON, L. R. (1982) Responses to depressed individuals: discrepancies between self-report and observer rated behaviour. *Journal of Abnormal Psychology*, 91, 231-240.

PATTERSON, G. R. (1980) Mothers: the unacknowledged victims. *Monographs of the Society for Research in Child Development*, 34, No. 6, 1-54.

REYNELL, J. (1969) *Developmental Language Scales, Experimental Edition*. Windsor, N.F.E.R.

RICHMAN, N., STEVENSON, J. and GRAHAM, P. (1982) *Preschool to School: A Behavioural Study*. London, Academic Press.

CHAPTER 3

Parenting Qualities: Concepts, Measures and Origins

Linda Dowdney, David Skuse, Michael Rutter and David Mrazek

Department of Child and Adolescent Psychiatry, Institute of Psychiatry, London

Introduction

Knowledge on the skills and qualities of parenting is of obvious importance to everyone concerned with the care and upbringing of young people.
We assume that the particular patterns of parenting employed are likely
to influence the growth and development of the children and there is substantial empirical support for that assumption (Rutter, in press). This
appreciation of the importance of parenting is reflected in the day-to-
day practice of everyone concerned with the treatment of children showing
disorders of their emotions, behaviour or relationships. But, the importance of parenting extends far beyond the child psychiatry clinic. As
the CCETSW (1978) report on 'Good Enough Parenting' emphasized, crucial
judgements on the essentials of care-giving are involved in decisions on
whether or not children should be taken away from their parents into some
form of fostering; and, clearly, they are implicit in decisions on the
types of alternative care provided by foster parents, residential nurseries or Children's Homes. Also, concepts of what is meant by good parenting underly the growing field of parent education (Harman and Brim, 1980)
and occupy an important place in many views on approaches to the primary
prevention of child psychiatric disorders (World Health Organisation,
1977; Rutter, 1982a). Of course, too, parenting issues are crucial in
our understanding of children's social development. As Maccoby (1980)
pointed out, no one doubts that parents influence their children, but the
elucidation of just what these influences are and how they operate has
proved to be a complex and difficult enterprise. Therapeutic approaches
used with troubled children rightly cover a wide range, but usually
attention to the qualities of parenting constitutes a major focus in the
counselling of families (Rutter, 1975).

Numerous issues arise in any consideration of the topic of parenting but,
perhaps, two matters are of prime importance. First, there is the question of what is meant by good parenting; and second there is the question
of which factors or influences determine whether or not parenting is of a
high quality. These two issues constitute the main focus of this paper.

Concepts of parenting

Concepts of the requirements of good parenting have changed a good deal
over the years. Of course, the debate started by Locke and Rousseau in
the 17th and 18th centuries on whether children should be allowed to grow
with as little pressure or guidance from adults as possible or, rather,
whether good upbringing consists of deliberate and careful structuring of
the environment from infancy onwards, continues - although the language
and the emphasis have altered. But, the focus of discussions has shifted
from arguments over types of discipline or toilet-training or schedule
versus demand feeding to considerations that emphasize relationships and
reciprocity, doing things *with* children rather than *to* them, patterns of
communication and of problem-solving, and, of course, security and continuity in parent-child relationships. These concerns have forced the
development of new methods of measurement. Interviews have had to be
devised to assess, in detail, *how* parents deal with their children in
terms of play, discipline and response to distress - not just whether
they employed this technique or that. But, also, there has been the need
to devise observational schemes that permit the assessment of *styles* of
parent-child interaction and of the *sequential* flow of such personal
interchanges.

Determinants of parenting

At the same time as clinicians and researchers have been re-thinking what
is involved in parenting, there has been a similar resurgence of interest
in the factors that determine *why* parents behave in the ways that they do
(Rutter, 1981). There has been a growing awareness of the effects of the
child himself - children influence parents just as parents influence
them. Also, it has been shown that the very experience of bringing up
one child influences how the next one is dealt with. Recent years have
seen the emergence of an interest in the possible effects of events in
the immediate post-partum period - an awareness that parents have to
develop relationships with their infants. In addition, it has become
apparent that parenting may be influenced both by the immediate social
context and also by the wider social environment. However, evidence has
also begun to accumulate showing that parenting may be shaped both by
childhood experiences in the past and by parental depression in the
present. The focus of the present study was on the first of these -
namely, the role of patterns of rearing as a possible influence on later
patterns of parenting.

Study Design

Sample

Our study of the childhood antecedents of parenting involved a
follow-up into early adult life of two groups of girls who had been
previously assessed during the mid-1960s (see Rutter, Quinton and
Liddle, 1983). The first group, the 'ex-care' sample, comprised
girls who spent much of their childhood in residential institutions
run on group cottage lines. The girls had been admitted to institutional care because their parents could not cope with child-rearing,

rather than because of any type of disturbed behaviour shown by the
children themselves. Over a third had been admitted before the age
of 2 years and over two-thirds before 5 years. The information
available on their childhood experiences indicate that they involved
a mixture of severe discord and disharmony in the girls' own families, together with the more harmonious, but rather impersonal, multiple caretaking of the institution.

The 'comparison' group comprised a quasi-random general population
sample of girls of the same age, never admitted to institutions or
experiencing foster care, living with their families in the same
general area in inner London, and whose childhood behaviour while at
school was assessed at approximately the same age by means of the
same questionnaire.

Thus, this latter group represented a sample of ordinary inner-city
girls experiencing a generally average sort of upbringing for children reared in a socially disadvantaged section of a large indus-
trialized city. The former, 'ex-care' institutional group came from
the same area but, in contrast, experienced a seriously adverse
upbringing. Accordingly, a comparison of the parenting of these two
groups of women when adult allows a determination of the extent to
which seriously adverse childhood experiences predispose to parenting
difficulties.

Parenting sample

In total, 94 ex-care women fulfilled the criterion for selection into
the study (Quinton, Rutter and Liddle, 1984). Of the 89 still
alive at the time of follow-up, 81 were traced and interviewed. In
the comparison group, 41 women out of a potential 51 subjects were
traced and interviewed.

Of the ex-care women, 49 had given birth to live children. Only 16
comparison women had become mothers, 13 of whom were successfully
interviewed. In order to provide a group large enough for a comparative assessment of parenting, this group was expanded by the inclusion of 14 women who were the wives of male controls (these comprised
only wives with children in the age group used for observations of
parent-child interactions). The interview findings for the comparison women and the female spouses were generally similar (Quinton,
Rutter and Liddle, 1984).

The observation sample consisted of 23 ex-care and 21 comparison
mothers with children between the ages of 2 and 3½ years. This age
range was chosen as the period of development during which children
become more oppositional and negative, and place demands upon
parental strategies of management. Two years was chosen as the lower
limit because most children have acquired some language by that age,
allowing relatively greater reliance on verbal communication as a
basis for observational recording. Choosing an upper limit of 3½
years meant that it would be unusual for the children to have entered
playschool. Thus, they would have had relatively little experience
outside the nuclear family, and would probably still have such

dependence on their mothers that interaction between them would be
frequent during a restricted period of observation.

Recognition of the different strengths of both interview and observational techniques in the study of parenting has led to their combined use (see, for example, Dunn and Kendrick, 1982; Lytton, 1973).
The same procedure was adopted in this study.

Assessment of parenting by interview

Interviews conducted with subjects lasted $2\frac{1}{2}$-4 hours and used a non-
schedule standardized approach based on methods established in
earlier investigations (Brown and Rutter, 1966; Graham and Rutter,
1968; Quinton, Rutter and Rowlands, 1976; Rutter and Brown, 1966).
The interview covered the person's recall of their childhood, their
later family, peer and work experiences, and their current circumstances, functioning and adjustment. Parenting skills (with respect
to children aged 2 years or older) were assessed on the basis of
maternal report. The mothers were encouraged to talk freely about
the child's daily routine, including the regularity and timing of
waking, of mealtimes, and of bedtimes, as well as the parental handling of any problems associated with daily routines. Detailed
accounts were obtained of disruptive and oppositional behaviour, peer
and sibs disputes, fears and anxieties, together with the mother's
response and handling of these issues. For each type of issue the
mother was asked for a detailed account of the most recent incident.
The frequency and typicality of such interactions were established as
well as the frequency of less often occurring parenting issues or
parenting techniques. In addition, questions were asked on the
amount of and nature of parental involvement in play. Summary
ratings on current parenting included those on overall style of
parenting, effectiveness and consistency in control, parental sensitivity to the child's needs, and the amount of expressed warmth
towards and criticism of the child.

The overall assessment of parenting outcome includes both historical
evidence (such as receptions into care, long parent-child separations, infanticide or abuse) as well as the current interview
parenting measures. The historical data are relevant when considering the overall picture of the transmission of parenting problems
across generations, but they are omitted when the assessment of
current parenting is being considered.

Observational measures

All observations were undertaken in the family's own home in order to
assess mother-child interactions as they ordinarily occurred (see
Dowdney *et al.*, 1984a; Mrazek, *et al.*, 1982). We endeavoured to
make the observation period as natural as possible by allowing the
family to become familiar with the observers through a lengthy preliminary visit; by explaining to mothers that they should get on with
their regular activities in the usual way; by making it clear that
there was no expectation that they deliberately do anything particular with the child; and by not interacting ourselves with either

mother or child during the period of observation. We went to some
trouble to select periods for observation when the mother would be
free of other commitments and when it was least likely that friends
and neighbours would be dropping in. So far as possible, too, we
chose times when the mother and child would be alone together without
either the father or other children.

Because numerous studies have shown the major variations in patterns
of behaviour between different situations and from day to day, we
observed families on two different days for two separate two-hour
periods of observation - making 4 hours of observations in all.

Unrestricted, unstandardized interactions have the advantage of getting closest to what might take place in the absence of observers.
However, for this very reason they involve the disadvantage of
relative non-comparability across families. Maternal *styles* of
interaction will be influenced by the *content* and *context* of the
interactions (Dunn, Kendrick and MacNamee, 1981). Different affective responses and different degrees of maternal control are likely
to be induced by rough and tumble play, by a teaching situation, or
by having to cope with the child in the middle of trying to prepare a
meal or clean the house. Accordingly, towards the end of each of the
two observation periods we introduced a standard stimulus for joint
play - a toy cash register in the first session and a picture book
that tells a simple story without words in the second.

Three different systems of measurement of mother-child interaction
were employed. First, 10-second *time-interval sampling* was used to
provide a basic frequency count of specified behaviours (any particular behaviour could be recorded once only in each time interval).
This gave rise to measures of the duration and form of mother-child
interaction. There was also recording of positive or negative
expressions of affect by the mother (such as affectionate contact or
smacks); maternal initiations of interaction; the proximity of mother
and child in terms of whether or not they were in the same room; and
the frequency and duration of independent activities on the part of
the mother or child.

Secondly, *sequential* measures were used to assess how mothers responded to each of three different sets of circumstances: a) episodes
involving discipline or control; b) situations in which their child
showed distress; and c) their child's attempts to gain attention or
initiate an interaction. For each of these, there was specification
of the 'key' events that served to initiate sequential recording (see
Dowdney *et al.*, 1984a). For example, in the area of control,
sequential recording began if a child showed opposition to or non-
compliance with a maternal instruction. Pre-specified 'outcomes'
determined the termination of sequential recording. For instance, in
the case of control episodes, the sequence continued until either the
child complied or the mother ceased attempting to assert control.
Time intervals were abandoned while sequences were being noted;
rather, single or multi-element maternal and child behaviours were
recorded in turn-taking fashion without concern for the precise
duration of each behavioural event. However, as an audiotape

recording was made of the entire observation, the duration of
sequences could be obtained later.

The third system of measurement concerned the mother's *verbal interactions* with her child. The measures were obtained from a detailed
analysis of the audiotape recording of the observation period; the
mode of coding was primarily oriented to the social functions of
maternal communications. The mother's contribution to the dialogue
was coded according to a scheme consisting of eight categories of
social communication.

The inter-observer reliability of the measures obtained was tested
and found to be high - both with respect to the individual elements
and with regard to sequences of elements (Dowdney *et al.*, 1984a).

However, ultimately, the issue of validity is more important than
that of reliability. Most observational studies have tended to take
validity for granted. Of course, in a sense, observational data *do*
have an intrinsic face validity in that the behaviours have been seen
to take place and in that there is no problem of biased or selective
reporting. Nevertheless, validity cannot be assumed. It is necessary to ask whether the behaviour observed during the specific observation session is representative or characteristic of the pattern of
parent-child interaction as it occurs at other times; how far the
measures provide an adequate differentiation of families; and the
extent to which they relate to or predict other aspects of family
functioning.

Perhaps, the first issue in this connection is whether the observation period tapped the parental behaviours that are relevant to
measures of the quality of parenting. After all, 4 hours is a very
brief period in the life of a child and it is likely that many
aspects of child care will not arise during the period of observation.

Table 1. Agreement between global ratings of observers
and interviewers

		Observers' ratings of parenting		
		Good	Intermediate	Poor
Interviewers' ratings of parenting	Good	9	4	1
	Intermediate	1	15	2
	Poor	1	3	8

$$\chi^2 = 30.99, \text{ d.f.} = 4, p = < 0.001$$

We examined this matter by getting the observers to make an overall
global rating of the quality of parenting as they observed it over
the 4-hour observation period; these ratings were then compared with

the broadly comparable summary of parenting ratings based on interview data. The interviewers rated current parenting as 'poor' where
there was evidence of marked lack of warmth to the children (score of
0 to 2 on a six point scale) *and* difficulties in at least two out of
three areas of disciplinary control (consistency, effectiveness or
style). Conversely, 'good' parenting was rated if there were no
difficulties on any of the scales of current parenting. An intermediate ranking indicated some current problems.

The observers made entirely independent global ratings of the quality
of parenting of all observed mothers, based on the total observation
period of 4 hours. The three categories of parenting that were
used – 'good', 'intermediate' and 'poor' – corresponded to the interview summary ratings of parenting.

The findings are shown on Table 1. Two points emerge from this comparison. First, mothers varied greatly in their styles of interaction during the observation period and, in most cases, observers
had no difficulty in making an overall rating on parenting. Second,
there was a generally high level of agreement, significant at the
0.1 per cent level, between the interview and observation measures
(χ^2 = 30.99; 4 d.f.; p < 0.001). We may conclude that 4 hours of
home observation *does* tap important dimensions of parenting. Of
course, perfect agreement between these two methods of assessment of
parenting is not to be expected. In the first place, the interview
is based on a much wider sample of parental behaviour (albeit, subject to the vagaries of mother's reporting), including features such
as the response to altercations with siblings or peers, of the manner
of coping with mealtimes or bedtimes, that could not have occurred
during the observation period. Secondly, the interview assessed
parenting as it took place in the ordinary conditions of family life
in which the care of one child had to compete with that of the other
children, not to mention the demands and attention of the mother's
spouse. In contrast, the observation assessed parenting as it
occurred in the more optimal circumstances of a dyadic interaction in
a context relatively free of other pressures. It is clear that the
two types of measures serve rather different purposes. Nevertheless,
it is important for the assessment of validity that there is very
substantial overlap between them.

The next issue with respect to validity is whether or not the individual quantitative measures of molecular aspects of mother–child
interaction reflect the overall qualities of parenting as assessed by
observers. The next four figures provide evidence on this point. In
each case the quantitative observation measures are related to the
observer's global rating on a four-point scale – good, adequate,
mediocre and poor, the vertical lines showing the spread of scores in
terms of one standard deviation above and below the mean. Figure 1
gives the findings for the number of episodes in which the child
showed distress – as shown by whining, crying or hurting himself. It
is apparent that distress episodes were much more frequent in the
observation sessions that gave rise to an overall rating of 'poor'
parenting (Kruskall-Wallis ANOVA, H = 20.76; 3 d.f.; p < 0.001).

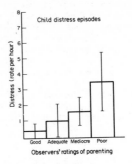

Figure 1.

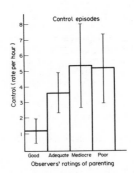

Figure 2.

Figure 2 provides the same type of comparison with respect to
episodes involving control – that is child behaviours involving
opposition to the mother, non-compliance with a maternal prohibition
at instruction, or repetition of a behaviour previously forbidden.
Again, there is a significant association with the global ratings –
control sequences being more frequent when parenting was rated as
mediocre or poor (H = 30.21; 3 d.f.; p < 0.001). Both this finding,
and the last one, emphasize that judgements on parenting tend to take
into account parental skills in *avoiding* distress or confrontation,
as well as effective and appropriate responses once the episodes have
occurred.

Findings on the amount of negative effect shown by the mother are
illustrated in Fig. 3. This rating was made for each of 10-second
time periods throughout the observation according to whether or not
there was negative maternal physical behaviour (such as smacking or

shaking the child); verbal behaviour (threats, teasing or statements
of disapproval); or tone of voice. The rate of negative affect per
hour was strongly associated with the observers' global ratings of
parenting (H = 52.59; 3 d.f.; p < 0.001.

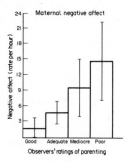

Figure 3.

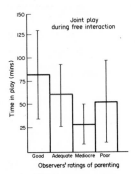

Figure 4.

The last comparison of this type to be mentioned concerns the amount
of joint play between mother and child during the free interaction
periods of the observation sessions (Fig. 4). That is, the data refer
to the number of 10-second time periods, outside the standardized
periods following presentation of the cash register or book, during
which the mother and child played together. The association with the
global ratings was statistically significant (H = 18.9; 3 d.f.;
p < 0.001) although not as consistent as that shown by the other
measures.

We may conclude that our measures of parenting were both reliable and
effective for the purposes for which they were designed.

L. Dowdney *et al.*

Results

We need to turn now to the substantive findings stemming from our comparison of the 'ex-care' and 'comparison' groups. Before considering
parenting, it is necessary briefly to note the overall pattern of outcome
for these two groups of women. If we are to understand the possible
mechanisms underlying the links between childhood experiences and
parenting, we have to ask whether any continuities found apply to parenting *as such* or rather whether they reflect some type of intergenerational
persistence of overall personality integrity of which parenting constitutes but one part.

Overall psychosocial functioning

Table 2. Current psychosocial functioning (women)

	Ex-care	Comparison	Statistical significance		
	N = 42	N = 27		d.f.	p
	%	%			
Current psychiatric disorder	26	7	2.66	1	n.s.
Personality disorder	17	0	3.35	1	n.s.
Criminality (self-report)	26	0	6.57	1	p < 0.02
Criminality (official records)	33	8*	2.12	1	n.s.
One or more broken cohabitations	40	11	5.33	1	p < 0.01
Marked marital problems (of those cohabiting)	31	7	4.06	1	p < 0.01
Substantial difficulties in love/sex relationships	19	0	4.11	1	p < 0.01

*Data available only on subjects n = 13 (i.e. not spouses)

Individual measures of psychosocial functioning showed marked differences, between the 'ex-care' and comparison groups. Table 2 shows that
many more of the former showed current psychiatric disorder, or had a
criminal record, or had substantial difficulties in their sexual or love
relationships. Overall, 17 per cent were rated as showing a personality
disorder as evidenced by persisting handicaps in interpersonal relationships since their early teens or before. In contrast, only 7 per cent of
the comparison group had a psychiatric condition and none of them was
rated as having a handicapping personality disorder.

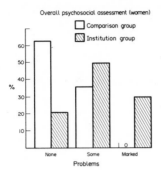

Figure 5.

An overall assessment of psychosocial outcome was obtained by combining these various specific measures. A 'poor' outcome (i.e. marked problems) was rated if there was a personality disorder or severe and longstanding difficulties in sex/love relationships, or if there were definite current problems in *at least* 3 of six areas of marriage, broken cohabitation, social relationships, criminality, psychiatric disorder or living in hospital/hostel/or sheltered accommodation. A good outcome was rated if there were no problems on any of these measures. Nearly a third (30 per cent) of the women reared in institutions had a poor outcome, whereas this rating applied to none of the controls. In contrast, over three-fifths of the comparison group showed 'good' functioning, a rating made for only just over a fifth of the 'ex-care' group. It is clear that the 'ex-care' women had a substantially worse psychosocial outcome. But, equally, it is apparent that within this group with seriously adverse experiences in childhood some had done well and were functioning adequately in all areas of their lives.

History of parenting

The findings so far underline the importance of the issue of *resilience* and of resistance to the ill-effects of stress, deprivation and disadvantage – a matter to which we shall return. But before doing so, we need to examine the findings with respect to parenting, turning first to the women's history of parenting. The findings show marked differences between the groups (Table 3). Firstly, nearly twice as many of the 'ex-care' women had become pregnant and given birth to a surviving child by the time of the follow-up interview; moreover, whereas only 5 per cent of the comparison group had become pregnant before their nineteenth birthday, two-fifths of the 'ex-care' sample had.

L. Dowdney *et al.*

Table 3.   Parenting history: women

	Ex-care women	Comparison group	Statistical significance		
	N = 81	N = 42	χ^2	d.f.	p
	%	%			
Ever pregnant	72	43	8.50	1	0.01
Pregnant by 19	42	5	16.75	1	0.001
Had surviving child	60	36	5.85	1	0.02
Of those with children	N = 49	N = 15			
	%	%			
Without male partner	22	0	Exact test p = 0.039		
Any children ever in care/ fostered	18	0	Exact test p = 0.075		
Any temporary or permanent parenting breakdown	35	0	Exact test p = 0.02		
Living with father of all children	61	100	6.52	1	0.02

However, it was not just that more of the institution-reared women had
become mothers rather early; also, their parenting had worked out less
well. To begin with, the 'ex-care' group were less likely to be living
in a stable cohabiting relationship at the time of follow-up. Only 61
per cent were living with the biological father of all the children, compared with 100 per cent in the comparison group; and 22 per cent were
without a current male partner compared with none of the comparison
sample. In addition, serious failures or breakdowns in parenting were
evident only in the institution-reared women. Of the 49 'ex-care' women
who had given birth, 9 (or nearly a fifth) had children who, for one
reason or another, were no longer being looked after by them, with no
apparent likelihood of their being returned. This included one case of
infanticide, two infants who were given up for adoption, three taken into
care for fostering or institutional placement, and three subsequently
looked after by the biological father. Moreover, just over a third (35
per cent) had experienced some form of transient or permanent parenting
breakdown with at least one of their children; this occurred with none of
the comparison group mothers. In most cases the women had left their
children to the care of others because they could not cope with the
demands of life as they faced them at the time, rather than because the
children had been compulsorily removed as a result of gross neglect or
physical abuse.

Interview assessments of parenting

Table 4. Current parenting outcome
(Overall interview findings)

	Ex-care	Comparison group*	
	N = 42	N = 27	Residuals
	%	%	
Good	31	48	1.44
Intermediate	29	41	1.05
Poor	40	11	-2.62

$*\chi^2$ = 6.91, d.f., p < 0.05

An interview assessment of parenting was made according to the criteria
outlined above. Over two-fifths of the ex-care mothers had a current
rating of poor parenting compared with one in ten of the comparison
group – a fourfold difference (Table 4). On the other hand, nearly one
third (31 per cent) of the women reared in institutions showed good
parenting, a rating made on just less than half of the comparison group.
It is clear that in spite of the fact that *all* of the ex-care group had
experienced an institutional rearing for part of their childhoods and
that most had experienced poor parenting when with their own families,
there was great heterogeneity of outcome in the ex-care sample, with a
substantial minority showing *good* parenting. It is evident also that a
surprisingly high proportion (just over half) of the comparison group
mothers showed some problems in parenting, although far fewer showed
severe difficulties.

The next point to consider is how far the problems in parenting formed
part of a broader impairment in overall psychosocial functioning (Figure
6). The striking finding here concerned the marked difference in pattern
between the two groups (see Rutter *et al.*, 1983). In the 'ex-care'
group, poor parenting was *usually* associated with generally poor psychosocial functioning. We may conclude that the link between childhood
adversity and parenting largely applied to poor parenting that constituted one element in a more pervasive pattern of psychosocial difficulties
incorporating psychiatric disorder, criminality and personality impairments. In sharp contrast, there was little overlap between parenting and
psychosocial functioning in the comparison group. The parenting difficulties experienced by those women often occurred in the context of generally good social adaptation. The inference is that the explanation for
isolated parenting difficulties of mild to moderate degree may well be
different from that for severe and generalized psychosocial problems
which include parenting difficulties as one of many areas of concern.

As we have seen, in some cases the problems in parenting experienced by
the 'ex-care' women were so great that they abandoned their children.
But, in most cases they did not. Moreover, among the 9 women who had

permanently given up a child, 5* had given birth to a second child which
they had succeeded in keeping and looking after. Accordingly, we need to
consider in greater detail the particular types of difficulties in
parenting experienced by the 'ex-care' women. Were they generally rejecting or neglectful or punitive mothers or were the problems in parenting
of a more subtle kind?

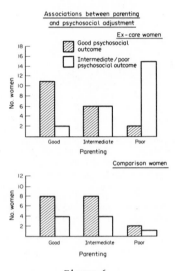

Figure 6.

Tables 5 and 6 show some of the findings on the specific molecular interview measures of parenting. The first point to note is that many of the
measures did *not* show substantial inter-group differences. Thus, the
amount of joint play between mother and child showed no significant difference. In both groups, there was a good deal of inconsistency in disciplinary control but this was just as frequent in the comparison group
as in the 'ex-care' sample. There was a tendency for the 'ex-care' women
to include a higher proportion with less effective disciplinary control
('ineffective' meaning that the disciplinary act did not result in the
intended change in the child's behaviour) but the overall difference between the groups fell short of statistical significance. The same applied
to unreconciled disputes – meaning that the episode of control failed to
result in harmony or any attempt to 'make-up' or restore the relationship.
Similarly, most of the women in both groups were warm to their children

---

*Two of these had babies that were too young for inclusion in our
measures of parenting – which were restricted to children aged 2 years
or older.

although markedly low warmth was rather more frequent in the 'ex-care' group. On all of these measures, there was great heterogeneity in both groups and major overlap between the two samples, although a slight tendency for more of the extremes to occur among the institution-reared women.

Table 5. Interview measures of affection and play

(a) Expressed warmth	Ex-care	Comparison group	Statistical significance		
	N = 42	N = 27	χ^2	d.f.	p
	%	%			
Low	24	7			
Moderate	21	37	3.998	2	NS
High	55	56			

(Low vs. Rest; Exact test − p = 0.146)

(b) Daily play with child	Ex-care	Comparison group	Statistical significance		
	N = 25*	N = 21*	χ^2	d.f.	p
	%	%			
Type (i)					
Let's pretend games	24	38			NS
Constructional games	28	43			NS
Drawing, writing, reading	56	67			NS
None of the above	40	19	1.48	1	NS
Type (ii)					
Watching T.V.	28	33			NS
Rough and tumble	36	19			NS
Help with housework	56	48			NS

*Comparison based on 2-3½-year-old children only.

N.B.   Throughout this chapter all exact tests are two-tailed.

L. Dowdney *et al.*

Table 6. Interview measures of sensitivity and of control

	Ex-care	Comparison group	Statistical significance		
	N = 42	N = 27	χ^2	d.f.	p
	%	%			
(a) Consistency of control					
Somewhat/very inconsistent	50	44	0.04	1	NS
(b) Reconciliation of disputes					
0-4/10 reconciled	26	8			
5-7/10 reconciled	21	8	6.62	2	0.05
8+/10 reconciled	54	85			
(c) Control style					
Indulgent	12	7			
Firm - not aggressive	26	41	3.95	3	NS
Mildly aggressive	29	37			
Definitely aggressive	33	15			

Definitely aggressive v. Rest; Exact test - p = 0.148

(d) Frequency of smacking					
Once a fortnight or less	24	33			
1-6 times per week	36	48	3.65	2	NS
Daily or more often	40	19			

Daily v. Rest; Exact test - p = 0.096

(e) Effectiveness of control					
Ineffective	26	4			
Some control	21	22	4.29	1	NS
Moderate control	29	41	(χ^2 for trends)		
Firm control	24	37			

Ineffective v. Rest; $\chi^2 = 4.33$, 1 d.f., p < 0.05

(f) Sensitivity					
Low	42	7			
Moderate	19	22	10.58	2	0.01
High	38	70			

The three measures that significantly differentiated the groups are shown
on Table 6. According to the mothers' reports, twice as many of the 'ex-
care' women smacked their children at least daily - the difference just
reached the 5 per cent level of significance. The difference with respect to aggressive methods of control (meaning a tendency to use shouting,
smacking or other approaches involving negative effect), was rather
greater. However, the greatest difference between the groups was found
for 'insensitivity'. This rating was based on the interviewers' judge-
ment of the mother's overall handling of the child. 'Insensitivity' was
rated, for example, when mothers seemed unable to perceive reasons for
their children's distress ("He's always crying without there being any
reason for it"), or when they moved excessively rapidly into control
without first sorting out what was happening. 'Sensitivity', on the
other hand, meant that the mothers showed some appreciation (in overt
behavioural terms) of why their children behaved in the ways they did,
that they made differential responses according to the specifics of the
child's behaviour, and that, in general they showed a flexible and adaptive approach to child-rearing with an appropriate variation according to
what was going on and according to the child's response and whether the
parental action 'worked' in doing whatever it was intended to do.

Taken as a whole, the interview assessments of parenting suggest both
negative and positive aspects. Thus, for the most part, the 'ex-care'
women were both affectionate to their children and involved with them.
Accordingly, it would be quite *wrong* to regard them as generally rejecting or neglectful. Also it would be misleading to describe them as cruel
or punitive although it is true that they were more prone to exhibit
negative affect to their children. Rather, the picture suggested that
the women were caring and were trying but that they were *not* particularly
skilful or adept in picking up their children's cues or in responding to
their children's needs in ways that circumvented difficulties through an
appropriate recognition of what was required to sort things out, rather
than just provide immediate control.

Observation measures

So far, the findings have been derived from interview measures that
relied on mothers' reports. We need to turn now to our detailed quantitative observational measures of what actually went on in the home.
These are based on a smaller sample (23 in the 'ex-care' group and 21 in
the comparison group) both because observations were restricted to
mothers with 2- to 3½-year-old children and because, necessarily, they
were confined to families in which the mothers were looking after their
children. This last requirement meant that some of the most seriously
impaired 'ex-care' women could not be included in the observational
measures; thus, only 3 of the 9 women who had had children who were no
longer living with them had further children of the appropriate age group
at home.

As with the interview assessments, it is appropriate to consider the
observation findings first of all in relation to the overall picture of
parenting provided. Figure 7 shows the results in terms of the proportion of women in both groups who fell into the lowest quartile on the
seven frequency measures that were thought by the observers to be most

likely to reflect the overall quality of parenting. The seven measures
included assessments of maternal affect to the child, the overall
frequency of distress and control, measures of responsiveness and the
amount of joint play between mother and child. As with the interview
measures, it is apparent that more of the 'ex-care' women were experiencing more difficulties. Thus, over a third of the 'ex-care' women, but
none of the comparison group, fell into the lowest quartile on at least
4 out of the 7 areas of parenting. Conversely, nearly half the comparison group but only one in 9 of the 'ex-care' women fell into the lowest quartile on *none* of the areas. The difference between the groups was
highly significant (χ^2 = 11.75, 2 d.f.; p < 0.01).

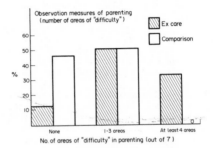

Figure 7.

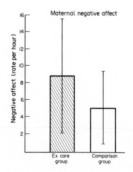

Figure 8.

Again, we need to turn to the specifics of the parenting shown by the two
groups. The next 4 figures show some of the main frequency observation
measures with statistically significant between-group differences. Figure 8 demonstrates that the 'ex-care' women exhibited higher levels of
negative affect (t = 2.12, d.f. 40, p < 0.05). This was assessed in
terms of the number of 10 second time intervals per hour of observation

in which the mother showed negative affect directed towards the child in
terms of physical behaviour (smacking, shaking, etc.), verbal content
(disapproved, threats, etc.) or critical or hostile tone of voice.*

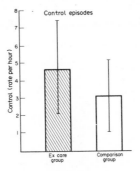

Figure 9.

Figure 9 presents the frequency with which control episodes arose during
the observation period. In the 'ex-care' group, incidents in which the
child was aggressive, destructive, oppositional or non-compliant occurred
at a mean rate of nearly 5 per hour whereas the rate in the comparison
group was only just over 3 (t = 2.24, d.f. 42, p < 0.05).

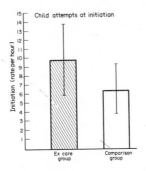

Figure 10.

*The data in Figure 8 exclude two women in the comparison group with
rates of negative affect several standard deviations outside the range
of both groups. Both observations included prolonged episodes of an
atypical type. The exclusion therefore was both for that reason
and the fact that statistically speaking the two cases could not be
pooled with the others.

Figure 10 shows the findings in the two groups for the frequency with which the children attempted to initiate an interaction with the mothers. Initiations included both verbal and physical approaches but they were counted only if they followed at least 20 seconds of non-interaction. It may be seen that the children in the 'ex-care' group attempted to initiate interactions at a much higher rate than those in the comparison group – 10 initiations per hour as against 6½ (t = 3.1, d.f. 42, p < 0.01).

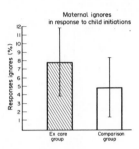

Figure 11.

The mother's responses to these initiations also differentiated the two groups (Figure 11). In the 'ex-care' group, 15 per cent of the mothers' first responses to child initiations involved ignoring the child's overtures; whereas in the comparison group only 10 per cent of first responses involved ignoral (Mann Whitney U test: z = 1.98, p < 0.05).

Table 7. Observation measures of parenting

	Ex-care Group	Comparison Group	Statistical significance
	N = 23	N = 21	
Maternal initiations (No. of 10-sec intervals)	36.8	30.6	NS
Joint play (No. of 10-sec intervals)	289	391	NS
Positive affect (No. of 10-sec intervals)	221	271	NS
No. of episodes of distress	9.6	8.0	NS

In order to attach meaning to these findings, we need also to consider the observational measures that did *not* differentiate the two groups. Table 7 shows that the overall amount of interaction between mothers and their children was closely similar in the two samples. The 'ex-care' women were just as likely (actually slightly more likely) to initiate

interactions and the two groups did not differ in the amount of joint
play. Also, the 'ex-care' women showed positive affect (meaning approv-
ing statements, cuddles, affectionate touching, warmly expressed comments
and the like) about as often as the comparison women. In addition, the
two groups did not differ in the frequency with which episodes of distress occurred.

Table 8. Characteristics of control episodes

	Ex-care women		Comparison women		Statistical significance
	N = 23		N = 20		cance
	Mean	(S.D.)	Mean	(S.D.)	p
% control episodes associated with distress	14.50	(14.75)	18.05	(23.24)	NS
% child compliance with maternal control	75.74	(15.12)	73.30	(21.31)	NS
% repeated confrontations	23.61	(18.27)	27.20	(22.45)	NS

The sequential data were analysed to determine whether the mothers in the
two groups differed in the ways in which they exercised disciplinary control (Table 8). The analyses showed a number of similarities. Both
groups of mothers were equally efficient in certain aspects of their
discipline. For example, they were both as likely to achieve child compliance, and the same disciplinary issue was no more likely to recur in
one group than the other. Similar proportions of control issues were
associated with the child becoming distressed in both groups. There were
no differences found between the groups in the total proportion of each
observation spent in confrontation. However, episodes of confrontation
varied greatly in duration and it was found that women from the ex-care
group experienced rather more brief control encounters. The implications
and details of this finding are discussed in detail in Dowdney *et al.*
(1984b).

It is apparent that the observational data give rise to a broadly comparable picture of parenting. The 'ex-care' women were generally warmly
involved with their children and the observation periods were *not* particularly characterized by distress. Moreover, the institution-reared women
seemed to be equally competent in their discipline as judged by what they
did in terms of an immediate response to their child's misbehaviour.
But, the 'ex-care' group did stand out as different in four other
respects. Firstly, the children made more attempts to gain their
mothers' interest, attention, and involvement; secondly, the mothers were
more likely to ignore their children's overtures; thirdly, the children

were more likely to behave in ways that required parental control; and
fourthly, the mothers were more likely to exhibit negative effect.

The findings emphasize that there is more to discipline than how you deal
with misbehaviour. Discipline involves *anticipatory* as well as reactive
elements (see Radke-Yarrow and Kuczynski, 1983). Occasions for
discipline may be averted by the prior statement of rules, prompts,
cautions and lessons. Also it appears that the emotional context of
interactions may have implications for control. Hostile or critical
expressions of feelings by the parents may precipitate or prolong the
child's misbehaviour - bringing about what Patterson (1982) has described
as cycles of coercive interchange. Of course, too, the frequency with
which parent-child confrontations arise is likely to be influenced by the
parent's skill in responding to the child's needs and in helping the
child acquire effective approaches to problem-solving. The interview
findings on the greater insensitivity of the 'ex-care' mothers suggest
that they may have less skills of this kind. But, in addition, it may be
that parents need to acquire a disciplinary 'currency'. That is to say,
if the children are going to comply with parental demands it is necessary
that parents first show that they are willing to comply with the children's
demands. Perhaps, it is in that connection that the 'ex-care' mothers'
greater tendency to ignore or rebuff their children's overtures may have
been influential. It was not that the mothers didn't play or talk with
their children - they did so as much as the comparison group. Nor was it
that the mothers didn't initiate interactions - again they did so as often
as the comparison group. Rather, the difference lay in the fact that the
interactions were less likely to have arisen as a prompt to the *child's*
demands. The picture was *not* one of generally maladaptive parenting but
rather of differences in subtle but crucial aspects of parent-child
interaction.

Conclusions

For a substantial minority of the women raised in institutions their
adverse early experiences were associated with significant later problems
in their relationships with their own children. For a proportion the
relationship itself could not be sustained. Of those women with a surviving child, a third had experienced a permanent or temporary breakdown
in parenting, often because they could not cope with the demands of life
at the time. Serious failures in parenting occurred only in the
institution-reared women.

Nevertheless, few of the women showed gross abnormalities in their current
parenting. For the most part, the significant differences from the comparison group concerned important, but often quite subtle features. Thus,
the ex-care women's discipline tended to be less effective, with more
frequent irritability and greater use of smacking. Women reared in institutions were much more likely to lack sensitivity and to be initially
unresponsive to demands for attention. In addition, there was some tendency for less playful activities of a kind that encouraged the children's
creativity, initiative and independence.

However, in many respects the parenting of the institution-reared women
was broadly similar to that shown by the comparison group. The great
majority of ex-care women were affectionate and actively involved with
their children. Only a few lacked warmth in their interactions, and
cruelty and punitiveness were rare.

In conclusion, the picture that emerges from these findings is that of a
group of women who were attempting to parent well and meeting with some
degree of success. However, they seemed to lack a certain perceptiveness
of their children's cues. Their failure to respond promptly and appropriately led to difficulties that might otherwise have been circumvented
so that they were frequently faced with behaviours that necessitated
immediate control. In addition, the women both faced greater social disadvantage and personal stress than was faced by those in the comparison
group, and they were more likely to experience difficulties in their
parenting in these adverse circumstances.

In short, the main differences between the groups concerned a vulnerability to psychosocial adversities in adult life, together with some
lack of awareness and of sensitivity to children's needs, plus an impaired
ability to anticipate and avert confrontation. Children who receive less
than adequate parenting themselves have an increased rate of difficulties
in adult life when bringing up their own families. However, the consequences are far from inevitable and it seems that the parenting difficulties may be of a kind that are potentially modifiable.

References

BROWN, G. W. and RUTTER, M. (1966) The measurement of family activities
    and relationships: a methodological study. *Human Relations*, 19,
    241-263.
CENTRAL COUNCIL FOR EDUCATION AND TRAINING IN SOCIAL WORK (1978)
    Good enough parenting. CCETSW Study No. 1. London: CCETSW.
DOWDNEY, L., MRAZEK, D., QUINTON, D. and RUTTER, M. (1984a) Observa-
    tion of parent-child interaction with two- to three-year-olds.
    Journal of Child Psychology and Psychiatry, 25, 379-407.
DOWDNEY, L., SKUSE, D., RUTTER, M., QUINTON, D. and MRAZEK, D. (1984b)
    The nature and qualities of parenting provided by women raised in
    institutions. *Journal of Child Psychology and Psychiatry* (in
    press).
DUNN, J. and KENDRICK, C. (1982) *Siblings: Love, Envy and Understanding*.
    Grant McIntyre: London.
DUNN, J., KENDRICK, C., and MACNAMEE, R. (1981) The reaction of first-
    born children to the birth of a sibling: mother's reports. *Journal of
    Child Psychology and Psychiatry*, 22, 1-18.
GRAHAM, P. and RUTTER, M. (1968) The reliability and validity of the
    psychiatric assessment of the child: II. Interview with the parent.
    British Journal of Psychiatry, 114, 581-592.
HARMAN, D. and BRIM, O. G. (1980) *Learning to be Parents: Principles,
    Programs and Methods*. London: Sage Publications.
LYTTON, H. (1973) Three approaches to the study of parent-child inter-
    action: ethological, interview and experimental. *Journal of Child
    Psychology and Psychiatry*, 14, 1-17.
MACCOBY, E. E. (1980) *Social Development: Psychological Growth and the
    Parent-Child Relationship*, New York: Harcourt Brace Jovanovich.

MRAZEK, D., DOWDNEY, L., RUTTER, M. and QUINTON, D. (1982) Mother and pre-school child interaction: A sequential approach. *Journal of the American Academy of Child Psychiatry*, 21, 453-464.
PATTERSON, G. (1982) *Coercive family process*. Eugene, Oregon: Castalia Press.
QUINTON, D., RUTTER, M. and ROWLANDS, O. (1976) An evaluation of an interview assessment of marriage. *Psychological Medicine*, 6, 577-586.
QUINTON, D., RUTTER, M. and LIDDLE, C. (1984) Institutional rearing parenting difficulties and marital support. *Psychological Medicine*, 14, 107-124.
RADKE-YARROW, M. and KUCZYNSKI, L. (1983) Perspectives and strategies in childrearing. Studies of rearing in normal and depressed mothers. In D. Magnusson and V. Allen (Eds.), *Human Development: Interactional perspectives*. New York and London: Academic Press.
RUTTER, M. (1975) *Helping troubled children*. Harmondsworth, Middx: Penguin Books.
RUTTER, M. (1981) Stress, coping and development: some issues and some questions. *Journal of Child Psychology and Psychiatry*, 22, 327-356.
RUTTER, M. (1982a) Prevention of children's psychosocial disorders: Myth and substance. *Pediatrics*, 70(6), 883-894.
RUTTER, M. (in press) Family and school influences: Meanings, mechanisms and implications. In A. R. Nicol (Ed.), *Practical Lessons from Longitudinal Studies*. Chichester: Wiley.
RUTTER, M. and BROWN, G. W. (1966) The reliability and validity of measures of family life and relationships in families containing a psychiatric patient. *Social Psychiatry*, 1, 38-53.
RUTTER, M., QUINTON, D. and LIDDLE, C. (1983) Parenting in two generations: Looking backwards and looking forwards. In N. Madge (Ed.), *Families at Risk*, pp 60-98. London: Heinemann Educational.
WORLD HEALTH ORGANISATION (1977) *Child Mental Health and Psychosocial Development: Report of a WHO Expert Committee*. WHO Technical Report Series No. 613. Geneva: W.H.O.

CHAPTER 4

Parenting the Pre-school Child: Clinical and Social Implications of Research into Past and Current Disadvantage

David Skuse and Antony Cox

Department of Child and Adolescent Psychiatry, Institute of Psychiatry, London

Parenting is an exacting task with any child, but perhaps never more so than with the nursery-aged toddler of 2 or 3 years who is learning to exert his independence. Previous research in England and the United States has shown that mothers of normal pre-school children are subject to considerable stress because of their children's oppositional and difficult behaviour. The twin investigations presented in Chapters 1-3, of women who have been brought up in care and women who are depressed, have demonstrated that there are particular groups of mothers who are having more difficulty than the general population.

We wish to emphasize four major findings. The first point to emphasize is that the studies show that whilst poor parenting is found amongst perhaps one in ten of the general population, almost half those mothers who were depressed or who had been brought up in care were experiencing severe parenting difficulties. Nearly half of the general population surveyed had no parenting problems at all, by interview or by observation, but this was true for less than one in four of the ex-care group. Nevertheless a surprisingly high proportion, well over a third, of mothers drawn from the general population have *specific* areas of difficulty. For instance, they may find it excessively hard to deal with those times when their child is distressed and fail to bring about an early resolution.

Secondly, the aspect of parenting which distinguishes ex-care mothers and those in the depressed sample with long-standing relationship difficulties and/or emotional vulnerability has to do with responsivity. This is a quality which potentially operates in many areas of parenting. However these deficiencies in responsivity do not appear to be specific in the sense of being characteristic *only* of ex-care or depressed mothers. The only connection which could be specific for depression, on what has so far been analysed, is evidence of poor meshing of mother and child and expressive language delay. These findings must be viewed with caution because much analysis remains to be done, including more careful comparison between the two studies.

Thirdly, in the ex-care group these parenting problems were often associated with serious personal, social and economic difficulties. There

was not such a multiplicity of adversities in the general population,
where moderate or severe parenting disorder usually occurred unaccompa-
nied by psychosocial or other disadvantage. The depressed sample were in
many respects intermediate.

The fourth major finding from both studies is of the strongly protective
effect of a good marriage. Nearly a third of those women who had been
brought up in care became adequate parents but many became poor or
inadequate. One of the crucial points bearing on outcome and later
functioning concerned the role of the spouse in the relationship. We
know from previous studies, such as those of Brown and Harris, how important an intimate confiding relationship is to a *mother* of small children,
and that the lack of such a relationship greatly increases her risk of
succumbing to depression. Gerald Patterson has demonstrated in his
research that there is a structural problem in the families of out-of-
control *children*; fathers in these cases are not giving the kind of
support to the mother that one finds in the families of normal children.
In our studies totally unsupported mothers were encountered exclusively
amongst those who had been brought up in care. These women functioned on
the whole significantly *less* well than those who had a male cohabitee.
In all samples where the mother *was* cohabiting the quality of that relationship had an important bearing on the quality of parenting exhibited
by those women. It was more likely to be poor if the man was deviant, in
the sense of being himself psychiatrically disordered, criminal or addicted to drugs. Conversely, if his good qualities predominated, the mother
was more likely to be deemed a good parent, whatever her background.
Unfortunately, on the whole, girls brought up in care were as likely as
not to choose to cohabit with or marry a deviant man. How does the
marital relationship mediate in maternal parenting? Is the mother more
emotionally resilient and responsive because she can share her problems
or are two heads better than one in devising handling strategies; does
the more competent parent teach the less competent? Or does the child
react directly to the tension and in turn influence the mother's
behaviour? A related and important question is to what extent did parenting failure in any particular case reflect a lack of management and
caretaking skills and to what extent was parenting inadequacy exemplified
by a poor emotional climate in the mother-child relationship? By a poor
emotional climate is meant that the mother did not seem to value the
child and was critical rather than warm towards him; the tone of the
emotional relationship was predominantly negative.

An important corollary to this finding about the importance of a supportive marital relationship must be emphasized. Lack of support had a
greater association with poor parenting amongst those who had been placed
in institutions as children than it had in the general population
samples. The same contrast is found within the depressed sample between
those with and without long-standing emotional and relationship difficulties. The implication is that the women with such difficulties and the
ex-care women suffer a relative vulnerability, lacking the inner resources which could enable them to cope in the face of later adversities
within the context of their adult sexual relationships. The evidence is
very suggestive that the important variable here is their early childhood
experiences. The model that emerges is of each disadvantage raising the
risk of entering a disadvantaged or deviant group in the next stage of

life, but that in addition certain early disadvantages mean that the
individual, when they enter that next stage, will be less able to cope
with any stresses or difficulties that arise. In other words the disadvantages such as being in care or living in a tense, discordant home
act in at least two ways: a) by increasing the likelihood of entering a
more vulnerable group, such as being a young mother, or entering a poor
marriage, and b) by reducing personal resilience or coping capacity.
However at every stage there are *discontinuities* as well as *continuities*:
because you have experienced a disadvantage, because you are in a disadvantaged group, you will not necessarily function badly.

Fascinating questions arise here about the influence of the environment,
both past and current, upon the development of personality. Would girls
with disrupted early life who function well whilst in supportive relationships, with financially reasonable circumstances and adequate living conditions, continue to do so if those favourable conditions changed? In
other words, to what extent are 'personality traits' malleable and
responsive to change in life situations? What are the social and clinical implications?

There are clear implications for social policy, in at least three areas:

(1) Women who were admitted to an institution in infancy and remained
there for the rest of their childhoods included the highest proportion
with poor parenting as adults of all ex-care mothers surveyed. Additionally three quarters of those admitted before the age of two years showed
less than good psychosocial functioning in adulthood. Psychosocial outcome was also poor for those children admitted in later childhood, following discordant and disruptive home experiences of relatively longer
duration.

Some children will need to be removed from their homes. How can the
quality of care be improved? Firstly, of course, by the use of adoption
where possible and appropriate. Secondly, there are several pointers to
the need to make childhood experiences more intimately personal - continuities in care are important in contributing to this. Although the
ex-care mothers had been in quite good quality children's homes their
memories were often negative and they had many caretakers. In the
depression study membership of the depressed group and having a disturbed
child were both strongly associated with mothers having, as a child, less
than positive evaluation of their own mother. It is also interesting
that in this study mothers with disturbed children less frequently
personalized experiences for their children. Perhaps it was this very
quality of being valued in an intimately personal way which constituted
the healing element in the good marriages of ex-care mothers. How might
the findings guide policy on returning children from institutional care
to their families? Where children were returned to homes in which there
was continuing disharmony their social competence as an adult was remarkably poor and would seem rather worse than if they had stayed in care. A
return to a now harmonious home did seem to be associated with a better
progress. Many mothers reported that they had been returned home without
preparation and with no follow-up. The implications are clear.

(2) Secondly, social circumstances do matter. If people live in poor
conditions we can expect more poor parenting and more disturbed children.
Improving the physical circumstances of families is worthwhile.

(3) Thirdly, more facilities are required for mothers with young
children. They need places to meet for mutual support. In England
'Toddler Groups' sponsored by the Preschool Playgroups Association, and
'One o'clock' clubs are examples. However the high rates of depression
and children's problems point to the need for ready accessibility of professional support, assessment and advice. Numerically the problems are
vast in urban areas. Professionals could not help all parents directly.
The groups need members who know how to listen and when to prompt contact
with professionals. These care members could benefit from consultation
by such professionals. Specifically there need to be centres where
depressed mothers can go with their children to build the mother's self-
esteem, to re-establish her relationship with the child and to foster the
child's development, especially in language.

Other facilities include home aids and family befriending programmes.
Health Visitors need more instruction and support to help mothers with
parenting difficulties.

What are the implications for other types of preventive work?

(1) There has been much talk and some action on education for parenthood. Opinion is divided about effectiveness but there can be little
doubt that the outlook for children would be better if potential parents
understood how demanding it is to be a parent, that the task is more
readily done by those beyond their teens, that it works badly to conceive
and use children to solve personal problems, that the best situation for
a child is where parents support each other, that pregnancy and child-
bearing put particular pressures on men and women and it is better to be
prepared, for instance, for the possibility that the mother may not wish
sexual intercourse later in pregnancy. One of our mother's depressive
episode dated from the discovery of her husband having intercourse with
another woman in the bathroom of their flat.

(2) Because many cannot appreciate the nature of parenthood until it is
experienced much education cannot start until the pregnancy has arrived,
in other words until the antenatal period.

(3) Good contraceptive services are an obvious corollary.

What about the clinical setting? There are implications for assessment
and treatment. These implications are perhaps no different from good
current practice but certain features are emphasized.

(1) Don't jump to conclusions. Because a mother has been in care in her
childhood or is depressed it does not necessarily mean she will have
parenting difficulty or a disturbed child. If the child *is* disturbed
then it is important to look particularly at parental sensitivity or
child-centredness. So far the only evidence of a link to depression is
with poorly-tuned parent responsivity and expressive language delay. It
may also be true that there are connections between particular types of

child problems and particular types of parental handling.

(2) In order to understand the detailed character of parent-child interaction direct observation is essential. Difficulties in one aspect of
parenting do not necessarily imply difficulties in others, nor does the
type tell you the cause. The attempt should be made to disentangle poor
competence and poor motivation. Does the mother not know the techniques
or can she not put them into practice?

(3) Assessment of the parental relationship emerges as absolutely
crucial. Fathers or cohabitees need to be seen.

(4) Contrary to much received opinion and some previous findings social
circumstances *are* important. They need to be explored.

(5) The importance of the parents' own history is not new but emphasis
is given to the desirability of discovering the quality of relationships
they have experienced in childhood and later and of their emotional
vulnerability.

When intervening:

(1) Again, don't neglect social circumstances.

(2) Consider the best strategy to assist parenting sensitivity. If the
parents are competent in the sense of understanding children's needs but
can't or don't get themselves to act competently this may point
immediately to work on the marriage and/or mental health of the parents.
Of course they may not be accessible to this and the work may still need
to be via the child's problem initially.

If there are evident deficiencies in competence then be prepared to
instruct. It is hoped that more detailed analysis from the studies we
are undertaking and comparisons between them will reveal more clearly the
possible points for interactions in order to help parents to pick up cues
more appropriately.

Of course deficiencies in both competence and motivation may, and often
do, co-exist.

(3) Don't forget the father. He should have an active part. Always
consider how the strategy adopted is likely to affect the interparental
relationship, since it is the most potent force for good will.

(4) Consider psychotherapeutic work with the parents to help reconcile
past and present experiences, particularly how their own experience of
being parented is influencing current family life.

In summary there are many different points at which it may be possible to
influence whether a potential parent enters a more vulnerable category.
The type of intervention will need to vary according to when and where it
is made. Work on personality development is always relevant, but not
always successful. We need more effective interventions for this purpose
which is most readily achieved by sustaining good family life. Because

there are cyclical inter-generational aspects to parenting no possible
aspect of intervention should be neglected.

PART TWO

Studies of Clinical Groups

CHAPTER 5

Change and Continuity in Behavior Problems from the Pre-school Period Through School Entry: an Analysis of Mothers' Reports

William Garrison and Felton Earls

Washington University School of Medicine, St. Louis, MO 63110, U.S.A.

Abstract

A three year follow-up study of behavior problems in pre-school children is reported. The findings indicate moderate consistency in reports of mothers, but little evidence of consistency between maternal reports in the pre-school period and teacher reports or clinical assessments at follow-up. The study provides epidemiologic support for the premise that rather sharp situational differences exist in children's social adaptation.

Interest in the appearance of behavioral symptomatology during the first few years of the life cycle has been based upon the belief that early identification might lead to more effective prevention of serious psychiatric disturbance at later ages (Chamberlin, 1981; Kupfer, Detre and Noval, 1974). Since the rationale for the study of early indicators of disorder is based on this belief, the degree to which behavioral symptoms appearing during the first few years of life can accurately identify children who will benefit from intervention is a central concern in pediatrics and child psychiatry. The suggestion that certain children can be identified early on as at higher risk for disorder argues for intensive screening efforts and the application of intervention programs within selected groups of children. Indeed, this was in large part the recommendation of the Joint Commission on Mental Health of Children (1969), despite a dearth of empirical support. If, however, early screening can be demonstrated to have little predictive utility then resources might be better spent through implementation of more broadly conceived systems of intervention which are targeted for whole populations of children and parents.

As is true in many situations within the social sciences, empirical evidence in support of both policy orientations toward child mental health exists. Quantitative studies in this area often lend support for one or the other of these policies depending upon the design features or presentation of data. Chamberlin (1981) offers a thoughtful review of relevant studies in this area in which he concludes that there are generally two schools of thought concerning child behavior. One model to describe early child behavior, which he calls the *main effects* model, presumes child and environmental characteristics to be generally consistent over time. Findings from studies with hypotheses couched within this perspective typically rely upon correlational techniques reflecting measurement at the group level. Moderate correlations between measures at two or more points in time would suggest that some continuity exists in a large enough number of cases to allow for early identification of at-risk populations.

A *transactional* model views the child's interaction with the environment as changing constantly, thus the predictability of characteristics across time and settings is assumed to be quite low. Data originating from studies of this sort typically rely upon descriptive statistics which conclude that there is poor predictive utility with pre-school measures for individuals, as opposed to groups. Thus it would appear that while there is some evidence to support a general relationship across time between behavioral indices during the pre-school period and disfunction upon school entry, there is also evidence to argue that individual prediction is decidedly inefficient.

Mothers' reports of behavior problems

By and large, most studies concerned with estimating the prevalence and continuity of child behavior problems have been based upon teacher reports during the school years (Glavin, 1972; Huessy, Marshall and Gendron, 1973; Rubin and Balow, 1978; Werry and Quay, 1971). Reasons for this range from the belief that teacher reports are less biased than those of parents, to an enhanced opportunity to cross-validate these reports by comparison with the school-based observations of researchers. There is some work, however, to suggest that mothers provide reports about their preschool children's behavior problems which agree well with ratings from clinicians (Earls, 1980a; Earls *et al.*, 1982), and much research in this area rests solely on the view that parental reports are comparable to (or better than) other sources of information about the child's behavior (Achenbach, 1979). The fact remains, however, that those studies which have examined the correlations between teacher and parent reports of behavior generally demonstrate poor agreement (Chamberlin, 1981; Rose *et al.*, 1975). This recurrent finding has led some to propose that child behavior, like other human characteristics, should be viewed as situationally-specific across settings (Bem and Allen, 1974; Coleman *et al.*, 1979). It is also possible that the perceptual frameworks for different classes of observers (i.e., parents, teachers, clinicians) are quite distinctive and that agreement may simply be a function of the degree to which a common view of the child's role, and his or her performance in relation to that role, is shared. For example, the fact that teachers report certain types of behavior problems more frequently than parents may reflect how those problems affect school routines and educational tasks. Thus, hyperactivity and aggressivity are examples of behaviors which disrupt the classroom milieu, and may be easily targeted by teachers who provide reports. Similarly, parents probably have generalized expectations regarding a normal or healthy child. Deviations from this ascribed role can lead to parental criticism and perceptions of the child as abnormally problematic. Intertwined with this view is the fact that a good proportion of the data collected from most parents concerning their children probably represents valid observational information.

Just as teacher reports of behavior problems can be viewed as providing insight into the tension and goodness of fit between teacher and student, so too can parental reports inform us about the patterns of child difficulties in the home environment. The recent emphasis upon school-based assessment, while important, has led to a lack of attention to the continuity of behavior problems and their meaning in the home setting. There is a need for more systematic attempts to understand and use parental reports of behavior both to chart behavior over time, and to inform clinical intervention programs with families.

Purposes of this article

Recent findings from an epidemiological survey of young children provide the background for an investigation of the issues discussed above. The aims of this report are to compare prevalence figures of behavior problems at two chronologic points in time, and to evaluate the predictive utility of mothers' reports of behavioral symptoms at three years to behavioral patterns at school entry. While there are clinically-based assumptions that developmental factors operate to transform symptomatology between the pre-school period and middle childhood (Meers, 1977), most empirical studies have chosen to address this question cross-situationally by seeking to draw relationships between behavior in the first five years of life as reported by parents with behavior in school as reported by teachers. Since continuity has not been reliably found in the home-to-school transition, this article will attend primarily to continuity within the home setting (via parental reports).

Sample

Sixty-one children served as subjects for this study (31 girls and 30 boys). This sample is part of a larger epidemiological survey of families of young children which is in progress (Earls). All of the children in this sample were born during a fifteen month period in 1974 and 1975 in an island community off the coast of New England and were included in a survey of 3-year-olds in this same community (Earls, 1980a, 1980b).

A total of 100 three-year-old children were seen in 1978 and of these 83 of their parents agreed to have them participate in the follow-up assessment conducted during the 1981-82 school year. All these children were involved in a school-based data collection strategy that included teacher reports and direct assessments of the children (Garrison et al., 1983; Earls et al., 1983). In addition, data on the children's behavioral symptoms were collected from parents by way of mailed questionnaires. Incomplete responses to this procedure resulted in further sample attrition leaving 61 children and families with complete data sets. This sharp decline in the sample size available for study led us to carefully analyze reasons for non-responses. The results indicate that 15 per cent of the families had moved out of the study population and 24 per cent of the parents refused. These groups were separately evaluated in terms of

critical behavioral and clinical variables collected when the
children were 3 years old since both the groups of out-migrants and
the refusals contained more boys than girls (25 boys and 14 girls in
all). An analysis by sex of child was also carried out. The results
revealed one significant difference between the successfully and
unsuccessfully followed-up groups. Only boys in families that
refused had higher clinical ratings. This rating was an averaged
score on how severely disturbed two independent clinical judges perceived the children to be (Earls, 1980a). In a separate analysis it
was shown that all of the children given high clinical ratings could
also be assigned DSM-III diagnoses based on symptom characteristics
(Earls, 1982). Thus, the follow-up sample was biased by containing a
lesser number of boys with psychiatric disorder when they were 3.

Methods

At 3, each of the children was seen at home for a play session and
parents were separately interviewed concerning the history and current
behavioral status of the child. The methods are described in detail
elsewhere (Earls, 1980b; Earls *et al.*, 1982). Interviews with parents
were based upon a technique developed by Richman and Graham in
Great Britain (Richman and Graham, 1971; Richman *et al.*, 1975) in a
study much like the survey described here. Data taken in the interviews were used to construct scores for the Behavior Screening
Questionnaire (BSQ), a symptom inventory derived from parental
reports of behavior problems which can occur during the pre-school
period. This report is limited to mothers' reports from the BSQ
since earlier studies with this sample indicated greater accuracy for
maternal reports as compared to the reports of fathers when both
these sources were compared to clinical judgments (Earls, 1980a).

The children were again seen at or soon after school entry by an
independent team of researchers. Data were collected from parents,
teachers, and several standardized measures of achievement and apti-
tude were administered. Central to the purposes of this report,
mothers were asked to complete the Child Behavior Checklist (CBC)
(Achenbach, 1979). This instrument offers several advantages over
competing measures of child behavior, the most important of which is
the availability of norm-referenced scores sensitive to both age and
gender differences. The CBC can be used to describe specific
behavioral symptoms in children as well as empirically derived
patterns of behavior. The Child Behavior Profile (CBP), an extension
of data collected on the CBC, provides factor-referenced scores for
the child on several narrow and wide-band behavior factors detected
in large groups of children (Achenbach, 1978; Achenbach and Edelbrook,
1979). For example, summary scores for Internalizing versus Externalizing behavior problems are available, and more specific scores
for behavior factors such as Aggression, Delinquency, Hyperactivity,
and Withdrawal are obtained. Finally, children can be described and
compared to the norming group on several indices of social competence.
Because of these features the CBC and CBP allow direct comparisons
with the BSQ data collected at 3 years of age, as well as an investigation of the relationship between symptoms at 3 and norm-referenced

behavior patterns upon school entry.

In addition, CBC data were collected from the teacher of each child in this sample, and clinical researchers provided ratings of behavior based upon impressions and observations of the child in the school setting. These two sources of report, teacher and clinical ratings, were used to estimate agreement between mothers' reports and school-based assessments of the children.

Results

Agreement across three sources of report

The child's BSQ total score, as reported by mothers during the pre-school period, held no predictive utility for teacher or clinician-generated problem groups at school follow-up. Correlations were found to be negligible and case analyses, using conservative cut-off procedures, revealed no evidence that total BSQ could be used to discriminate those children viewed as maladjusted by teachers or clinicians. There was some evidence that specific symptoms inventoried by the BSQ might be useful in screening pre-schoolers for subsequent maladjustment (e.g. activity levels in boys) but even these results were rather muted.

These findings are consistent with much of the work previously reported in this area (Chamberlin, 1977; Chamberlin, 1981).

Prevalence rates at three and upon school entry
according to mothers' reports

Figure 1 graphically displays the prevalence rates of children with a moderate to high number of behavior problems at 3 and at school entry. Included in this figure is a representation of the overlapping cases across the two points in time.

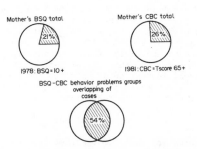

Figure 1.   Prevalence rates and longitudinal
            consistency of behavior problems
            in young children from age 3 to
            6 years

As indicated, prevalence rates are similar across time with a small
increase at follow-up. This may be due to a rise in incidence, differences in measurement characteristics between the BSQ and the CBC, or both.
In each case the cut-off score for inclusion in the Behavior Problems
groups was determined by comparisons to findings from studies with larger
samples (Richman *et al.*, 1975; Richman and Graham, 1971; Rose *et al.*,
1975). The proportion of cases which overlap within these two problem
groups was 54 per cent. This represents 7 of the 61 children or 12 per
cent of the sample as shown in Table 1. It is interesting to note that
of these seven cases, teacher reports and clinicians' observations of the
child indicated strong agreement with parental assessment in three cases,
with low to moderate agreement in the remaining cases.

Table 1. Frequencies of children in behavior problem groups at age 3
and school entry using mothers' reports

	Problem Group At 3 (BSQ = 10+)	Not In Problem Group At 3	
Problem group at school entry (CBC = + 1.5 standard dev)	7 (54%) (44%)	9 (19%) (56%)	16 (26%)
Not in problem group at school entry	6 (46%) (56%)	39 (81%) (44%)	45 (74%)
	13 (21%)	48 (79%)	

N.B. Top set of parentheses are column percentages;
lower set are row percentages

Also depicted in Table 1 is the finding that 9 children in the sample, 19
per cent of those children who were not reported as presenting a high
number of behavior problems at the age of 3, were classified in the
behavior problems group at school entry. If it is assumed that incidence
occurred uniformly over the 3-year follow-up interval this translates to
an expected incidence rate of about 6 per cent of the population each
year. From an epidemiological point of view, the behavior problems
occurring in this developmental period might be characterized as being
high in incidence and relatively short in duration.

Symptom continuity

While prevalence rates are useful for estimating the proportion of
children manifesting behavior problems at each chronologic point in time,
they do not adequately represent the continuity of individual symptoms
during early development. For this reason a correlational analysis of
twelve discriminating symptoms on the BSQ and CBC was completed (see
Table 2).

Table 2. <u>Correlation of individual behavioral symptoms at 3 and 6</u>

BSQ problems	Comparable CBC items	Correlation	Significance
Eating problems	Does not eat well	0.10	
	Overeats	-0.30	< 0.01
Encopresis	Encopresis	0.17	
Activity problems	Can't sit still; active	0.38	< 0.00
Sleeping problems	Sleeps more than most	0.29	< 0.01
	Sleeps less than most	0.03	
	Nightmares	0.04	
Poor concentration	Poor concentration	0.04	
Dependency	Demands attention	0.22	< 0.04
	Clings to adults;		
	dependent	0.03	
Moods	Sudden changes in mood	0.09	
	Stubborn, sullen,		
	irritable	0.27	< 0.01
Worries	Worrying	0.22	< 0.05
	Fears might do		
	something bad	0.35	< 0.00
Fears	Fears animals or places	0.18	
	Fears going to school	0.02	
	Fears might do		
	something bad	0.01	
	Nightmares	0.01	
Relationships with peers	Gets in many fights	0.36	< 0.00
	Gets teased a lot	0.16	
	Not liked by peers	0.00	
	Does not get along		
	with peers	0.17	
Temper tantrums	Temper tantrums		
	hot temper	0.19	
Management problems	Disobedient at home	0.30	< 0.01
	Disobedient at school	0.01	

These particular symptoms from the BSQ were chosen since previous work
had revealed that they have higher discriminative value in population
studies of 3-year-olds (Richman and Graham, 1971). The symptoms on the
BSQ were correlated with comparable items from the CBC. Table 2 shows
that significant correlations ranging from 0.22 to 0.38 were found for
some symptoms. Behavior symptoms with the largest correlations over time
tended to pertain to activity and sleeping problems, worries, moods, poor
peer relationships, and management difficulty. It may be of interest to
note that eating problems at 3 were negatively correlated with overeating
at school entry (-0.30).

Symptom-behavior pattern relationships

The Child Behavior Profile (CBP), a derivation of the CBC for use with
defined age and gender groupings of children, allows analysis of mothers'
reports of behavior problems within a factor-referenced framework. This
feature of the CBC encouraged an investigation of the degree to which
specific symptoms at 3 could be related to the appearance of more generalized behavioral patterns which manifest themselves in populations of
American children. Table 3 presents correlational data from an analysis
of the boys in this sample. It is evident that significant associations
can be made between certain BSQ symptoms at 3 and several behavior patterns at school entry. For example, sleeping problems at 3 are moderately
correlated with the Schizoid factor of the CBP. As another example,
problems regarding peer relationships at 3 were negatively correlated
with the Uncommunicative and Withdrawn factors. There are additional
relationships apparent in this table, but it is of general interest to
note that there were non-significant associations between BSQ Total score
at 3 and the CBP Total & Internalizing T scores. However, BSQ Total
score did correlate moderately well with the Externalizing T score of the
CBP. The BSQ Total correlated negatively with the Social Competence T
score. Interestingly, two single behavioral items from the BSQ had a
negative correlation with the Social Competence T score of the same magnitude as the BSQ total.

Findings from a parallel analysis of girls are presented in Table 4. A
larger number of significant correlations are evident in this table, as
well as higher correlations between BSQ Total and CBP Total and Subtotal
scores as compared to boys. Individual symptom-factor correlations
include a moderately positive relationship between several BSQ items and
the Depressed, Hyperactivity, and Cruelty behavior factors of the CBP.
Particularly strong relationships appear to exist between BSQ Total score
and these three factors, with smaller correlations with the Aggressive,
Delinquent, and Social Withdrawal factors. Generally speaking, eating
and activity problems, encopresis, and fears did not emerge as powerful
as other items on the BSQ instrument.

Multiple regression and discriminant analyses

Using BSQ symptoms as reported by mothers during the pre-school period to
predict behavior problems at school entry is a central concern of this
study. Table 5 presents results from multiple linear regression (MLR)
analyses with all children pooled together. Through a stepwise procedure
summary T scores of the CBP were designated as the criterion variables in

Table 3. Correlations between BSQ items/total and CBP factors/totals*

(Boys Only)

CBP	Eating	Encopresis	Sleeping	Activity	Concentrate	Dependency	Moods	Worries	Fears	Peer Relations	Temper	Manage	Total
										BSQ			
Schizoid			0.47										
Depressed													
Uncommunicative			0.38	0.37		-0.39	0.32			-0.34			
Obsess-Compulsive			0.39	0.37						-0.50			
Somatic Complaints													
Withdrawn													
Hyperactive													
Aggressive		0.57		0.41								0.36	0.46
Delinquent		0.46		0.47									0.36
Total T score		0.42	0.45	0.40									(0.30)+
Intern T score			0.43										(0.15)+
Extern T score		0.49		0.39								0.36	0.40
Social Competence T score							-0.42				-0.42		-0.43

*Correlations with p < 0.02 or better are reported.
+Correlations did not achieve acceptable level of significance and are included for information purposes.

Table 4. Correlations between BSQ items/total and CBP factors/totals*

(Girls Only)

	BSQ												
	Eating	Encopresis	Sleeping	Activity	Concentrate	Dependency	Moods	Worries	Fears	Peer Relations	Temper	Manage	Total
CBC													
Depressed					0.38		0.37	0.34			0.45	0.50	0.58
Social Withdrawal													0.41
Somatic Complaint									0.35		0.38		
Schizoid-Obsessive													
Hyperactive			0.40		0.41		0.36			0.38		0.41	0.56
Sex Problems						0.40							
Delinquent						0.41							0.41
Cruelty							0.38	0.44		0.52	0.36	0.55	0.61
Aggressive					0.36		0.38					0.47	0.48
Total T score					0.37		0.39			0.37	0.41	0.50	0.63
Intern T score			0.38		0.36						0.43	0.39	0.54
Extern T score					0.37		0.38			0.36	0.43	0.56	0.61
Social Competence T score													

*Correlations with p < 0.02 or better are reported.

three MLR analyses.

Table 5. Stepwise Multiple Regression Analyses: CBP summary scores
predicted by BSQ symptoms at three years of age

CBC summary score	BSQ symptom-predictor	R^2	RSQ Change	Adjusted R^2
Behavior Problems Sum*	Sleeping problems	0.144	0.144	
	Management problems	0.255	0.111	
	Worries	0.305	0.049	
	Concentration	0.353	0.047	0.296
Internalizing Problems Sum*	Sleeping	0.156	0.156	
	Concentration	0.215	0.059	
	Eating problems	0.296	0.080	
	Worries	0.329	0.032	
	Dependency	0.368	0.038	0.297
Externalizing Problems Sum*	Management problems	0.214	0.214	
	Worries	0.275	0.061	
	Moods	0.308	0.033	
	Sleeping	0.331	0.023	0.273

*p < 0.02 or better.

Moderate R^2 values were obtained through combinations of from four to
five symptoms. A significant amount of variance within the Total CBP T
score, for example, was explained by the 3 year olds sleeping and management problems and 10 per cent of additional unique variance is accounted
for by worries and concentration problems. Sleeping, eating and concentration difficulties explained 29 per cent of the variance in Internalizing summary scores, and worries and over-dependency contributed an additional 7 per cent. The Externalizing T scores were most powerfully predicted by parental management problems at three; worries, moods and
sleeping problems contributed an additional 12 per cent of the variance.

In an attempt to gauge the predictive utility of the BSQ symptoms for
estimating which children would be placed in the Behavior Problems Group
at school entry, a series of multiple discriminant analyses were completed. A summary of the results from these analyses is presented in
Table 6. The most useful indicator of the predictive power of the BSQ
symptoms inventory for classifying children manifesting a greater number
of behavior problems at school entry is the 'hit rate' which is derived
from Multiple Discriminant Analysis procedures. This term refers to the
percentage of children correctly classified into the Behavior Problems
Group at school follow-up, given that actual membership is known.
Through MDA techniques the predicted membership can be generated using
specified variables as discriminators (in this case BSQ symptoms at 3),
and then compared to known membership. Table 6 shows that overall hit
rates for the Behavior Problems Sum and Internalizing T score of the CBP
were 79 and 77 per cent respectively. These are rates which are well

above that expected by chance suggesting that BSQ symptoms reported by
mothers during the pre-school period have good discriminative utility for
these scores at school entry. MDA analyses of the Externalizing problems
T scores on the CBP, however, revealed an even higher hit rate of 89 per
cent, indicating that only 11 per cent of the cases were incorrectly
classified as false negatives or false positives.

Table 6. Results of discriminant analyses using BSQ symptoms
to classify problem group membership at school entry

CBC summary scores	Prediction Results				Overall Hit Rate
	True Positives	False Positives	True Negatives	False Negatives	
Behavior Problems Sum T Score	73%	27%	81%	19%	79%
Internalizing Problems Sum T Score	71%	29%	79%	21%	77%
Externalizing Problems Sum T Score	88%	12%	89%	11%	89%

Discussion

A preponderance of psychiatric studies concerned with school-aged children
have indicated low to negligible correlations between parent and teacher
reports of child behavior (and this study has essentially replicated
those findings). We view this recurrent lack of agreement as a function
of real cross-situational differences in child behavior, though to some
extent this difference may be sharpened by the particular response
biases of various sources of report. The analyses presented in this
article have been primarily focused on the continuity and change in
behavior as measured through mothers' reports only. Despite competing
views about the validity of parental reports, our findings demonstrate
that consistency in mothers' reports of child behavior over the early
years of the child's life exists and that such information may be clinically useful.

It is important, however, to distinguish between level of symptomatology
in the child and patterns of behavior. The definition of a behavior
problem on which the prevalence figure at both points in time was based
is the number of co-existing symptoms. Children who had more than 5 or 6
symptoms were likely to score above a designated cutoff score and be selected to have a behavior problem. In previous work we found this kind of
quantitative decision to agree well with clinical judgements (Earls *et al.*,

1982), and with currently used diagnostic categories (Earls, 1982). The analysis of prevalence rates at 3 and again at school follow-up indicate only slightly more than half of the children in the behavior problems group at 3 years of age were similarly classified at school entry. Furthermore, among those children selected at both points, less than half were seen as atypical by two or more observers (teachers, parents, and clinical observers). These findings indicate that continuity at the level of defining clinically significant behavior disorders, especially when these decisions are based on different observers, is low. When considered in combination with the finding that an additional 19 per cent of the entire sample developed significant problems by follow-up, the assumption that the presence of early signs of disturbance *necessarily* forecast serious problems during the school years is not warranted.

It is more reasonable to examine general patterns in symptom relationships over time and the specific nature of mothers' consistency in behavioral ratings. Drawing upon the unique aspects of the CBP, interesting relationships among early symptomatology and factor-referenced behavior patterns in the school years were noted. These patterns of association were substantially different with regard to the child's sex. It is important to point out that the BSQ Total score for boys did not correlate strongly with any of the CBP summary scores. Rather, the three cumulative scores from the CBP (Total, Internalizing Subtotal, and Externalizing subtotal) were moderately associated with encopresis, sleeping and activity problems in boys. The BSQ Total, and the individual items of mood and temper tantrums were negatively correlated with the summary Social Competence index of the CBP for boys. In contrast, the girls' summary scores on the CBP were all significantly correlated with BSQ Total score. The Social Competence index, however, did not have a significant relationship with any BSQ item or the total score. Thus, it appears that mothers' reports are generally more consistent for girls than for boys, though less easily interpreted. This may have been due to an artifact created by the selective attrition of a group of boys more disturbed than the norm. Activity problems and encopresis at 3 were significantly associated to mothers' subsequent view of the boys' aggressive and delinquent behavior. In addition, sleeping problems in 3 year old boys were related to mothers' reports of schizoid behavior during the early school years. Girls, as was pointed out, present a less straightforward pattern of relationships. The cruelty behavior of school-aged girls in this sample was associated with several early symptoms, especially parental management difficulties and poor peer and sib relationships. Similarly, girls' depressed behavior at school entry was related to temper and management difficulties in the pre-school period and, to a lesser degree, with concentration problems, negative moods, and many worries.

The value of these results resides in the ways in which clinical intervention techniques can be improved by the knowledge that certain environment/behavior characteristics can be demonstrated to have recognizable continuity for children. We have focused this analysis on mothers' reports of symptoms at 2 points in time and in doing so supported the *main effects* model discussed by Chamberlin (1981). However, the *transactional model* also finds support because we were not able to predict children's behavior across *time* and *setting*. No doubt the level of

prediction will be raised when additional data are added about the
children's environments and about their temperaments. The findings of
this paper are useful, however, in targeting behavioral symptoms in young
children which do persist over a number of years.

Summary

Aside from more difficult questions regarding exactly what parental
reports of child behavior are measuring, the explanatory and predictive
utility of the BSQ was explored and found to be good if limited to the
reports of mothers. Multiple regression analyses revealed a significant
proportion of the variance in CBP summary scores being accounted for by
pre-school symptomatology, most notably sleeping problems and management
difficulties. The practical prediction of CBP scores, especially the
Externalizing Summary T score, was found to be adequate enough to apply
to other samples of pre-school children. This finding indicates that a
high percentage of children who will be perceived as abnormally problematic by their mothers at school entry can be identified using BSQ data
collected at 3. This fact, in light of the finding that only 54 per cent
of the original Behavior Problems group were again classified as such at
follow-up, suggests that the predictive power of the BSQ lies not so much
in the magnitude of behavior problems but in the patterns of those problems.

Acknowledgements

This work was supported by NIMH Grant Number MH-37044.

References

ACHENBACH, T. (1978) The Child Behavior Profile: I. Boys aged 6-11.
    Journal of Consulting and Clinical Psychology, 46, 759-776.
ACHENBACH, T. (1979) The Child Behavior Profile: An empirically-based
    system for assessing children's behavioral problems and competencies.
    International Journal of Mental Health, 7, 24-42.
ACHENBACH, T. and EDELBROCK, C. (1979) The Child Behavior Profile: II.
    Boys aged 12-16 and girls aged 6-11 and 12-16. *Journal of Consulting
    and Clinical Psychology*, 47, 223-233.
BEM, D. and ALLEN, A. (1974) On predicting some of the people some of
    the time. *Psychological Review*, 81, 506-520.
CHAMBERLIN, R. (1977) Can we identify a group of children at age two who
    are at high risk for the development of behavior or emotional prob-
    lems in kindergarten and first grade? *Pediatrics*, 59, 971-981.
CHAMBERLIN, R. (1981) The relationship of pre-school behavior and learn-
    ing patterns to later school functioning. *Advances in Behavioral
    Pediatrics*, 2, 111-127.
COLEMAN, J., WOLKIND, S. and ASHLEY, L. (1977) Symptoms of behavior dis-
    turbance and adjustment to school. *Journal of Child Psychology and
    Psychiatry*, 18, 201-209.
EARLS, F. (1980a) The prevalence of behavior problems in three year old
    children: comparison of the reports of fathers and mothers. *Journal
    of the American Academy of Child Psychiatry*, 19, 439-452.

EARLS, F. (1980b) Prevalence of behavior problems in 3-year-old children: a cross-national replication. *Archives of General Psychiatry*, 37, 1153-1157.
EARLS, F. (1982) An application of DSM-III in an epidemological study of pre-school children. *American Journal of Psychiatry*, 139, 242-243.
EARLS, F. (1983) An epidemiological approach to the study of behavior problems in very young children. In S. Guze, F. Earls and J. Barrett (Eds.), *Child Psychopathology and Development*, pp. 1-15, New York, Raven Press.
EARLS, F., BEARDSLEE, W. and GARRISON, W. (1983) Correlates and predictors of competence in young children. In E. J. Anthony and B. J. Cohler (Eds.), *The Invulnerable Child*, Guildford Press.
EARLS, F., JACOBS, G., GOLDFEIN, D., GILBERT, A., BEARDSLEE, W. and RIVINUS, T. (1982) Concurrent validation of a behavior problems scale to use with 3-year-olds. *Journal of the American Academy of Child Psychiatry*, 21, 47-57.
GARRISON, W., EARLS, F. and KINDLON, D. (1983) An application of the pictorial scale of perceived competence and acceptance within an epidemiological survey. *Journal of Abnormal Child Psychology*, 11, 367-377.
GLAVIN, J. (1972) Persistence of behavior disorders in children. *Exceptional Children*, 38, 367-376.
HUESSY, H., MARSHALL, C. and GENDRON, R. (1973) Five hundred children followed from grade two through grade five for the prevalence of behavior disorder. *Acta Paedopsychiatrica*, 39, 301-309.
JOINT COMMISSION ON MENTAL HEALTH OF CHILDREN (1969) *Crisis in Child Mental Health: Challenge for the 1970's*, New York, Harper and Row.
KUPFER, D., DETRE, I. and NOVAL, J. (1974) Relationship of certain childhood traits to adult psychiatric disorders. *American Journal of Orthopsychiatry*, 45, 74-80.
MEERS, D. (1977) A diagnostic profile of psychopathology in a latency child. In R. S. Eissler, A. Freud, M. Kris and A. Solnit (Eds.), *Psychoanalytic Assessment: The Diagnostic Profile*, pp. 181-223, Clinton, MA, Colonial Press, Inc.
RICHMAN, N. and GRAHAM, P. (1971) A behavior screening questionnaire for use with three year old children: preliminary findings. *Journal of Child Psycholology and Psychiatry*, 12, 5-33.
RICHMAN, N., STEVENSON, J. and GRAHAM, P. (1975) Prevalence of behavior problems in three year old children: an epidemiologic study in a London borough. *Journal of Child Psychology and Psychiatry*, 16, 277-278.
ROSE, S., BLANK, M. and SPALTER, I. (1975) Situational specificity of behavior in young children. *Child Development*, 46, 464-469.
RUBIN, R. and BALOW, B. (1978) Prevalence of teacher-identified behavior problems: a longitudinal study. *Exceptional Child*, 45, 102-111.
WERRY, J. and QUAY, H. (1971) The prevalence of behavior symptoms in younger elementary school children. *American Journal of Orthopsychiatry*, 41, 136-143.

CHAPTER 6

Prevalence and Treatment of Sleep Problems in Young Children

Naomi Richman

Institute of Child Health, Guildford Street, London WC1

So-called 'developmental' problems in young children give rise to much
controversy in paediatrics and psychiatry. Should behaviours like waking
at night or enuresis be considered as part of normal development, as due
to delay in maturation, or as symptoms which merit treatment? Certain
behaviours are extremely common and have a characteristic age distribution. To label these as symptoms could lead to both unnecessary anxiety
in parents and unnecessary treatment.

Epidemiological studies can help to throw light on the significance of
particular behaviours at different ages (Rutter, 1977) and such findings
will be discussed from a population survey of sleep problems in young
children which suggests that although these problems are common, they are
not always trivial or shortlived. Then the results of two evaluation
studies of different ways of treating sleep difficulties will be presented.

The survey was carried out in a London borough. The Waltham Forest
Family Register was used as a sampling frame for drawing a 1 in 4 random
sample of all children aged 1-2 years old living in the borough (Richman
and Tupling, 1974) and a postal questionnaire asking about the child's
sleep pattern was sent to the parents (Richman, 1981). Out of the 1158
questionnaires, 771 (67%) were returned. The prevalence of waking problems is shown in Table 1.

Table 1. Prevalence of sleep disturbances in 1-2 year olds

	Number	Percentage
Frequency of waking per week		
0-1	432	56%
2-4	185	24%
5-7	154	20%
Severe sleep problems	73	10%

56 per cent were waking once a week or less, 24 per cent, 2-4 times a
week, and 20 per cent 5 or more times a week. Ten per cent fell into a
predefined category of severe disturbance, that is in addition to waking
at least 5 nights a week they were also waking 3 or more times a night,
for more than 20 minutes or going to the parents' room. Taking into
account the number of non-responders to the postal questionnaire, the
prevalence of waking problems can be estimated as lying between 13 per
cent and 20 per cent, and of severe problems as from 6 per cent to 10 per
cent of this age group. These figures are similar to those of other
studies and in keeping with these there were no sex differences (Bernal,
1972; Jenkins, Bax and Hart, 1980).

Why do children wake at night? Having identified a community sample,
rather than a clinic sample which is likely to be biased, it was possible
to look for factors associated with sleep difficulties.

Fifty-five children in the community sample with marked sleep problems
were compared with 30 children with the same age and sex distribution
from the same community sample, who were reported as sleeping well. All
the parents were interviewed and the validity of the sleep questionnaire
was confirmed both by the interview and by sleep diaries which the parents
completed (Richman, 1981).

The waking children different from non-wakers in a number of respects
(Table 2).

Table 2. Characteristics of waking and control
children in percentages

	Wakers (55)	Controls (30)	
Difficulty settling at night	62	13	< 0.001
Sleeps with parent	35	7	< 0.01
With other behaviour problems	55	27	< 0.05
Low malleability	62	27	< 0.01
Irritable 0-12 weeks	38	17	< 0.05
Adverse perinatal events	30	16	< 0.05

They were more likely to be only children, or if they had sibs, these
were also more likely to have had sleep difficulties. The wakers more
often showed other behaviour problems, including settling difficulties at
bedtime and sleeping with parents and on a temperamental questionnaire
they were described as less malleable and less rhythmic or consistent in
their behaviours than the controls. In addition they had higher rates of
an adverse perinatal history (using information obtained from obstetrical
records), and early irritability as reported by parents. There were no
differences between the groups in developmental status.

The families of wakers were distinguished by higher rates of social
stress, maternal depression and lack of a confiding relationship between
the spouses (Table 3).

Table 3. Characteristics of waking and control
          children in percentages (N)

	Waking Children (55)	Controls (30)	
Only child	44	17	< 0.05
Sib with sleep problem	56	17	< 0.01
High stress in family	45	13	< 0.01
Mother with psychiatric problem	57	17	< 0.01
Mother confides in father	37	60	< 0.05

As others have found characteristics both within the child and within the
family were associated with night waking (Bernal, 1973; Blurton-Jones *et
al.*, 1980; Carey, 1970). It is not of course possible to deduce causal
relations from a cross sectional survey. However, one could postulate
that some of the identified factors might have contributed to *causing* the
problem (e.g. perinatal factors) and others to *maintaining* it (e.g.
current family tension). It would be of great interest to compare rates
of sleep problems between different societies and to look for specific
cultural factors associated with the possibly higher rates we experience
in the United Kingdom (Caudill and Plath, 1969).

The behaviour difficulties and family stress associated with waking problems prompted me to look at methods of treating them. We know already
that many young children receive sedatives, e.g. a quarter of a sample of
18-month-old children had already done so (Ounstead and Hendrick, 1977),
but there is almost no evidence of their efficacy. I carried out a double
blind trial using Vallergan forte (trimeprazine tartate) and placebo with
a dose of 1-2 teaspoons at night (30-60 mg). Drug and placebo were each
taken for two weeks in a randomized order with an interval of two weeks
between them. Twenty two children, identified in the survey just
described, participated in the trial. Parents kept sleep diaries throughout and these plus parental reports were used to assess the effect of
drug and placebo compared with each other and the baseline (Richman,
1985). One child was sick whilst taking the placebo, otherwise there
were no reported side effects. On parental report sleep was
significantly better on the drug compared with placebo. Mood and
appetite also improved, the latter possibly due to less milk or juice
being taken at night (Table 4). There was no rebound effect from the
drug. However clinically, improvement on the drug was not striking.
Most of the children were still waking at night, even though this was
less often or for shorter periods. Only 5 children were waking less than
three nights a week when receiving the drug (Table 5). On follow-up 6
months later the majority of the children were still waking at night. A
control group whose parents kept sleep diaries and had regular contact
with a research worker did not show significant improvement.

Thus neither drugs nor sympathetic contact appeared very successful in
helping most severe sleep problems. Behavioural techniques appeared to
offer a more rational method of tackling these problems. The hypothesis

underlying the treatment approach is that, whatever had caused the problem initially, it was now being maintained by parental behaviour and the child had become unable to settle to sleep alone, without parental presence. Parents of children aged 1-5 with marked sleep problems were invited to participate in a pilot study of these methods. The behavioural techniques used included:

Extinction - e.g. gradually reducing the amount of attention given on waking by the parents.
Reinforcement - for desired behaviour such as staying in bed using star charts as praise.

Shaping - e.g. gradually making bedtime earlier.

Cueing - e.g. establishing a bedtime routine (Douglas and Richman, 1982).

Table 4. Parental report on effectiveness of drug
          and placebo in percentages

	Drug (22)	Placebo (21)	
Medicine helped	77	19	< 0.01
Falling asleep improved	41	9	< 0.05
Night waking improved	73	29	< 0.05
Appetite improved	43	14	< 0.05

Table 5. Average number of nights waking per week
          when taking drug and placebo

| Average number of nights waking per week | | | | |
	None	1-2	3-4	5+	Total Number
On drug	2	3	10	7	22
On placebo	0	2	4	15	21

Targets for treatment were worked out by parents and therapists together and a contract for a maximum of 6 treatments was made with the parents who were asked to keep the sleep diaries before treatment started to provide a baseline and throughout the treatment period (Richman *et al.*, 1985).

Families were referred mainly from child health clinics and by family doctors. Table 6 shows the select nature of the sample which entered treatment since only half of the referrals were finally treated by behavioural methods. The treated sample differed somewhat from the community sample originally described, and this is probably true of most clinic groups. The community sample tended to have greater family stress, as shown by maternal symptomatology and poorer marital relationships and

were more often working class (Table 7). Also the children showed more
behaviour problems, although the rates of perinatal adversity were not
significantly different.

Table 6. Outcome of referrals for
behavioural treatment

	Number of Children
Never came	8
Already improved	7
Failed after diagnostic	7
Other treatment	7
Total	29
Entered treatment Treatment incomplete	5
Treatment completed	30
Total	35

Table 7. Comparison between the community sample of waking
children and the treated sample

	Community Sample N = 55	Treatment Sample N = 35
Mean age in months	21	22
Problem since birth	46%	76%
Perinatal adversity	30%	32%
Behaviour problem	55%	21%
Social class non-manual	53%	76%
Maternal distress	57%	24%
Confides in husband	37%	79%

Of those who did complete treatment outcome was successful in 90 per cent,
27 out of 20, and was maintained in all but one child at the 4/12 follow-
up.

Although we have not yet examined the efficacy of behavioural methods
using random assignment to treatment and control groups, we have been
impressed by the rapidity with which this treatment can be effective.
The methods are now being used by psychologists, community nurses and
social workers (e.g. Sanger et al., 1981), and with more handicapped
groups such as the blind, autistic and retarded. They also offer a model
of methods which can be tested out in both the treatment and the preven-

tion of behaviour problems in young children.

References

BERNAL, J. (1973)   Night waking in infants during the first 14 months. *Developmental Medicine and Child Neurology*, 14, 362-372.

BLURTON-JONES, N., ROSETTI-FERREIRA, M. C., FARQUAR-BROWN, M. and McDONALD, L. (1978)   The association between perinatal factors and later night-waking. *Developmental Medicine and Child Neurology*, 20, 427-434.

CAREY, W. (1970)   Night-waking and temperament in infancy. *Journal of Paediatrics*, 84, 756-758.

CAUDILL, W. and PLATH, D. W. (1969)   Who sleeps by whom? *Psychiatry*, 32, 12-43.

DOUGLAS, J. and RICHMAN, N. (1982)   *Sleep Management Manual*. Mimeographed. London: Department of Psychological Medicine, Hospital for Sick Children, Great Ormond Street.

JENKINS, S., BAX, M. and HART, H. (1980)   Behaviour problems in pre-school children. *Journal of Child Psychology and Psychiatry*, 21, 5-17.

OUNSTEAD, M. C. and HENDRICK, A. M. (1977)   The first born child: patterns of development. *Developmental Medicine and Child Neurology*, 19, 446-453.

RICHMAN, N. (1981)   A community survey of the characteristics of one to two year olds with sleep disruptions. *Journal of the American Academy of Child Psychiatry*, 20, 281-291.

RICHMAN, N. (1985)   A double blind drug trial of sleep problems in young children. *Journal of Child Psychology and Psychiatry* (in press).

RICHMAN, N., DOUGLAS, J., HUNT, H., LANSDOWN, R. and LEVERE, R. (1985) Behavioural methods in the treatment of sleep disorders - a pilot study. *Journal of Child Psychology and Psychiatry* (in press).

RICHMAN, N. and TUPLING, H. (1974)   A computerised family register of children under five in a London borough. *Health Trends*, 6, 19-22.

RUTTER, M. (1971)   Surveys to answer questions. In P. J. Graham (Ed.), *Epidemiological Approaches in Child Psychiatry*, pp. 1-30. London, Academic Press.

SANGER, S., WEIR, K. and CHURCHILL, E. (1981)   Treatment of sleep problems: the use of behaviour modification techniques by health visitors. *Health Visitor*, 54, 421-423.

CHAPTER 7

The Effect of Residential Setting on Sleep and Behaviour Patterns of Young Visually-handicapped Children

Mary Kitzinger and Heather Hunt

Wolfson Centre, Institute of Child Health, London
and
Department of Psychological Medicine, Hospital for Sick Children, Great Ormond Street, London

Introduction

Many parents accept early residential provision for their young visually handicapped children, not only because of the specialised training offered, but also to obtain relief from the stresses and demands made on the family. Sleep disturbance may be a common source of stress: Jan, Freeman and Scott (1977) reported that 20% of visually handicapped children had difficulty falling asleep compared with 5.9% controls. We know from previous studies that there are predisposing factors associated with sleep disturbance such as temperamental characteristics of low malleability and rhythmicity (Richman, 1981) or adverse perinatal factors (Bernal, 1973; Blurton-Jones, Rosetti-Ferreira, Farquar-Brown and Macdonald, 1978). Anxiety in the infant caused by adverse emotional factors at home (Moore and Ucko, 1957) or maternal over-responsiveness (Bernal, 1973) have been found to be relevant. On the other hand a very low incidence of sleep disturbance in residential settings has also been described: Tizard and Tizard (1971) found only 3.3 per cent of 2 year olds in residential nurseries had sleep disturbance compared with 37 per cent at home, and this was consistent with our own informal impression when talking to child and care staff in residential nurseries for visually handicapped children.

The aim of this investigation was to find out more about the sleeping and behaviour patterns of a group of visually handicapped children, in the home and nursery settings.

Method

There were 23 children (11 boys, 12 girls) aged between 2 and 5 years attending three residential nurseries for visually handicapped children. Twenty children were residential and 3 attended daily. All were congenitally visually handicapped except one who was adventitously blind. Their additional handicaps can be seen in Table 1. Only 5 children had no additional handicaps so the majority were multiply handicapped with intellectual, physical or hearing disabilities.

M. Kitzinger and H. Hunt

Table 1. Handicaps of children in the sample

	Partially sighted	Blind or light/dark perception only	Total
	N = 11	N = 12	N = 23
Moderate mental handicap	8	2	10
Severe mental handicap	2	5	7
Moderate or severe hearing impairment	1	1	2
Physical handicap	6	4	10
No additional handicap	0	5	5
One additional handicap	4	2	6
Two additional handicaps	7	5	12

The sleep questionnaire developed by Richman (1981) was used to obtain information about how the child slept at home and in the nursery. The questionnaire covers five aspects of sleep: going to bed, going to sleep, (i.e. indices of settling problems), waking, sleeping in the parents' bed, and whether the sleeping is stated to be a problem to the caretaker.

It was scored according to the criteria developed by Richman (1981). A child is considered to have a waking problem if the problem had existed for more than 3 months (or since the start of the holidays more than 3 weeks ago)- if the child wakes 5 or more nights a week and if in addition the child had one or more of the following:

  (i)   waking, 3 or more times a night,
  (ii) waking for more than 20 minutes,
  (iii) going into parents' bed.

The other aspects of sleeping problems were scored according to equivalent criteria.

The behaviour screening questionnaire (BSQ) provided information about the prevalence of behaviour difficulties in the child. It covered 12 areas of behaviour initially (Richman et al., 1975; Richman, 1977). Further items were added which were thought to be particularly relevant to visually handicapped children (e.g. the presence of self-damaging behaviour or wariness of using hands) and items giving more information on developmental problems and communication. There was a total of 31 items. On the behaviour questionnaire, the checked answers were assigned a score of 0 (slight or no problem) 1 (moderate problem) 2 (severe problem) and were summed to give a behaviour score.

Parents were asked to complete both questionnaires in July, August
and October, covering both holiday and term-times. The return rate
was 64 per cent, 89 per cent and 61 per cent respectively and school
staff completed them in July and October (the return rate was 22 per
cent and 100 per cent respectively).

Results

Sleep disturbance

Our informal observations that remarkably few sleep problems occur at
school were confirmed (see Figure 1). Out of a sample of 20, only one
child had a severe settling problem and only 2 had a severe waking problem, according to the criteria. Only on one occasion was the sleeping
pattern stated to be a problem to the school staff.

However, looking at the parents' reports (N = 15), a very different picture emerges. Only 2 out of 15 children were reported by parents to have
no sleep disturbance in any of the five aspects covered. In the Richman
study (1981), the most frequently reported aspect of sleeping difficulty
was night-waking (14.3 per cent). However, the sleep questionnaire
returned by parents (August) indicated a different pattern of sleep disturbance; it was more of a problem settling them to sleep (40% of cases)
than it was their waking at night (20% of cases).

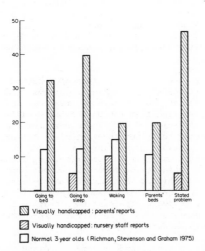

Figure 1.   Prevalence of sleep disturbance in sample of 23
visually and multihandicapped 2-5 year olds

Settling difficulties were more common in the group with a severe visual handicap: 6 out of 7 blind children had settling difficulties compared with 3 out of 9 partially sighted children. There was no clear relation between mental handicap and settling problems. A surprising finding was that there was no association between bed-time sleep disturbance and day-time behaviour problems (Mann Whitney 'U' test was not significant at the 5 per cent level). This is in contrast to Richman's findings (1981).

Thus the prevalence of sleeping problems is higher than in the normal population and there are more problems in settling at night, particularly with the severely visually handicapped. However, the problem is specific to the home situation, as the incidence reported by the schools is much lower even compared with the normal population.

Behaviour patterns

Looking at the frequency with which each item on the behaviour question-naire was rated 2 (i.e. a severe problem) at any one time by the parents it is possible to characterize the behaviour patterns of the sample. One gains a picture of a child still likely to be physically dependent (50 per cent were still wet during the day and approximately half of these were soiling). Characteristically, the child is rather socially with-drawn and almost never shows any clinging behaviour or aggression and relates poorly to other children. If there are any fears or worries these are not communicated and the child's intelligibility and under-standing of simple commands was often very limited. There may well be little interest in playing with toys and rather more interest centred around the child's own body in the form of 'blindisms' or self-damaging behaviour. This is not to suggest that the visually handicapped child typically lacks all demonstrativeness for there were problems reported by parents in controlling their child. Lack of compliance was commonly shown at bed-time.

It is interesting to see how this pattern of behaviour compares with the normal population (see Fig. 2). Taking the items from the Richman, Stevenson and Graham BSQ and the parents' response on the October ques-tionnaire (N = 14) we find that the pattern is broadly similar (Spearman-Rank correlation coefficient 0.6). There were fewer problems with feed-ing, attention-seeking behaviour, overactivity, tempers and control and more problems with wetting and soiling, night-time settling and relating to peers (though not to siblings). The remaining items showed little or no difference. The incidence of severe behaviour problems in the handi-capped sample was much higher than with normal 3-year-olds (36-44% com-pared with 7%). Thus the visually handicapped children though generally more disturbed were on the whole less demonstrative and more compliant than their normal peers and had more difficulty relating to other children. They also needed more physical care.

Comparing behaviour at school and at home on related samples (N = 14) we find that 10 children had more problems reported at home compared with school and only 4 *vice versa* but the difference was not significant (see Table 2). The pattern of problems in the two settings was markedly similar.

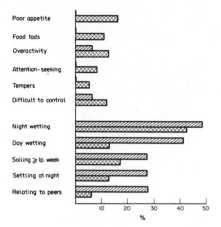

Note: There were little or no observed differences on the
following items: waking ≥ 3/night, sleeping in
parents' bed, concentration, dependency, moods,
worries, fears, relating to sibs.

Figure 2. Percentages of visually handicapped and normal children
rated '2' on behaviour screening questionnaire
(Richman, Stevenson and Graham, 1975)

Table 2. Comparison of behavioural ratings in
home and residential settings.

Setting	Time	N (related samples)	Mean Behaviour Rating	Wilcoxon matched-pairs signed-rank T significance
School	Term (October)	14	13.2	n.s.
Home	Term (October)		16.0	
Home	Term (July)	8	16.9	n.s.
Home	Holiday (August)		17.9	
Home	Holiday (August)	13	20.6	n.s.
Home	Term (October)		18.8	
Home	Term (July)	8	17.0	n.s.
Home	Term (October)		15.75	

Comparing the parents' behaviour ratings for July and October we find no
significant difference. However, there was a non-significant trend for
behaviour problems to be more severe during the holidays. Taking the
total score on the behaviour questionnaire (except the developmental
items) for parents' ratings in August (see Table 3) it appeared that the
more severely visually handicapped children had significantly more
behaviour problems. Similarly the more severely mentally handicapped
group had significantly greater problems than the moderately mentally
handicapped. Those with two additional handicaps had significantly
greater problems than those with one.

Table 3. Behaviour ratings related to degree of handicap

	N	Mean Behaviour Rating	Mann Whitney 'U' significance
Partially sighted	9	13.89*	$p < 0.05$
Blind or L/D only	7	17.43	
Moderate mental handicap	9	12.67	$p < 0.025$
Severe mental handicap	5	20.0	
Physical handicap	7	17.3	n.s.
No physical handicap	9	14.0	
One additional handicap	6	12.17	$p < 0.05$
Two additional handicap	9	17.2	

*Excluding developmental items.

Discussion

The sample is small and heterogeneous so any conclusions are necessarily
tentative. Young visually handicapped children do commonly present at
home with severe sleep and behaviour disturbance. The more profound the
handicap and the greater the number of handicaps, the more severe were
the problems.

As in the Tizard and Tizard (1971) study, remarkably few sleep problems
were found to occur in the residential setting. There were also fewer
behaviour problems. This may reflect the child's greater compliance at
school but our screening questionnaires were not sensitive enough to confirm this. It could also be that parents are more sensitive judges of
their child's behaviour.

It is interesting to note that there are more settling than waking difficulties, which is consistent with the findings of Jan, Freeman and
Scott (1977). There was no evidence that this was associated with
reversals of day-night rhythm as almost no-one slept during the day.
Certainly, the strict routine of the schools defined day and night very
clearly perhaps facilitating settling.

With the high incidence of sleep and behaviour disturbance, many families must be under considerable strain, particularly during the long summer break. Residential nurseries may provide welcome relief and a more even distribution of holiday and term periods might further alleviate the strain.

It is perhaps disappointing that there is no generalization of improved sleeping patterns from school to home. This indicates a great need for more liaison and the school could provide specific management advice on the lines described by Richman, Douglas, Levere and Landsown (1982). An interesting model for blind and mentally handicapped children is outlined by Zeschitz (1981) using parents and siblings and therapists.

The process of developing stable attachments, which is commonly delayed in blind children (Fraiberg, 1977), is likely to be further disturbed by residential placement at a young age. Our finding that blind and multiply handicapped children are often withdrawn, undemonstrative and relate poorly to their peers (though not necessarily to their siblings) must surely have implications for special residential (or even day) provision. Grouping such a child with other children who are similarly isolated is likely to only further their social withdrawal. Though this might make for easier management it is perhaps a price too high to be paid.

Acknowledgment

The authors wish to thank the parents who participated and to acknowledge the co-operation of the Royal National Institute for the Blind.

References

BERNAL, J. (1973) Night waking in infants during the first 14 months. *Developmental Medicine and Child Neurology*, 14, 362-372.
BLURTON-JONES, N., ROSETTI-FERREIRA, M. C., FARQUAR-BROWN, M., and MACDONALD, L. (1978) The association between perinatal factors and later night waking. *Developmental Medicine and Child Neurology*, 20, 427-434.
FRAIBERG, S. (1977) *Insights from the Blind*. London. Souvenir Press.
JAN, J. E., FREEMAN, R. D. and SCOTT, E. P. (1977) *Visual Impairment in Children and Adolescents*, New York, Grune and Stratton.
MOORE, T. and UCKO, L. E. (1957) Night waking in early infancy. *Archives of Disease in Childhood*, 32, 333-342.
RICHMAN, N., STEVENSON, J. E. and GRAHAM, P. J. (1975) Prevalence of behaviour problems in 3-year-olds: an epidemiological study in a London borough. *Journal of Child Psychology and Psychiatry*, 16, 277-287.
RICHMAN, N. (1977) Is a behaviour checklist for preschool children useful? In P. J. Graham (Ed.), *Epidemiological Approaches in Child Psychiatry*, pp. 125-137, London, Academic Press.
RICHMAN, N. (1981) A community survey of characteristics of one to two year-olds with sleep disruptions. *Journal of the American Academy of Child Psychiatry*, 20, 281-291.
RICHMAN, N., DOUGLAS, J., LEVERE, R. and LANDSOWN, R. (1982, July) Methods in the treatment of sleep disorders - a pilot study. Paper

presented at I.A.C.A.P. and A.P. Congress, Dublin.

TIZARD, J. and TIZARD, B. (1971)   The social development of two-year-old children in residential nurseries.   In H. R. Schaffer (Ed.), *The Origins of Human Social Relations*, pp. 147-161, New York, Academic Press.

ZESCHITZ, M. A. (1981)   Model experiment for the early-care of the multiply-handicapped visually damaged child in Germany.   Paper presented at International Symposium of Visually Handicapped Infants and Young Children, Shefayim, Israel.

CHAPTER 8

Disturbed Emotional Development of Severely Asthmatic Pre-school Children

David Mrazek, Irene Anderson and Robert Strunk

National Jewish Hospital and Research Center, Denver,
Colorado, U.S.A.

Childhood asthma begins in early life. Nearly three-quarters of asthmatic children will begin to experience their symptoms before they are 3 years old, with the majority beginning in the first 12 months (Falliers, 1970). Perhaps more importantly, once severe asthmatic symptoms begin in early childhood they are likely to persist at least through adolescence (Mc Nichol *et al.*, 1973), resulting in on-going physical and emotional stresses for both the child and his family.

The American Thoracic Society defines asthma as a disease characterized by 'an increased responsiveness of the trachea and bronchi to various stimuli, and made manifest by difficult breathing due to generalized narrowing of the airways. This narrowing is dynamic and changes in degree, either spontaneously or because of therapy' (Leffert, 1978). There is strong evidence that the illness is a genetically inherited constitutional vulnerability of the airways (Marsh, Meyers and Bias, 1981). A number of external and internal stimuli have been shown to serve as triggers to this reversible obstructive process. Prominent among these triggering stimuli are: (1) allergenic exposure; (2) infections; (3) rapid changes in climatic conditions; (4) irritant exposure; (5) exercise; and (6) intense emotions. It has become increasingly accepted that a given child may have variable sensitivity to each of these triggering mechanisms.

This study examined the behavioral interactions of severely asthmatic pre-school children and their mothers during an inpatient pediatric hospitalization. Since these dyads were by definition evaluated only after the onset of their disease, it was not possible to clearly establish whether stresses experienced in early life may have had a causal role in the genesis of either their physical symptoms or their current emotional difficulties. However, the rationale for expecting that the onset of severe asthma in early childhood would have a potentially negative effect on emotional development was based on the following characteristics of the disease: (1) early onset before development of cognitively sophisticated coping mechanisms; (2) sudden and frightening onset of breathlessness; (3) initial helplessness on the part of both the child and the parent regarding the treatment of an attack; (4) the persistence of recurring episodes with minimal warning; and (5) the either explicit or implicit threat of complete apnea and death. Our primary hypothesis was that if the stresses associated with the illness were of a sufficient intensity and duration, they would have a negative impact on the child's emotional development as demonstrated by overt behavioral difficulties and differences in the parent-child interactional patterns when compared to healthy children.

Methodology

Sample

The study population consisted of 26 children between the ages of 36 and 72 months with the diagnosis of moderate to severe asthma. The diagnosis of asthma was confirmed in each case by documenting the presence of airways obstruction that was reversible with inhaled bronchodilators. This was determined by pulmonary function testing or by detecting wheezing during clinical examination. In addition, diseases other than asthma than can include reversible airways obstruction in their clinical spectrum were excluded by appropriate studies. Specifically excluded were cystic fibrosis, foreign body aspiration, structural abnormalities causing compression of the airways, recurrent aspiration, transient hypogammaglobulinemia of infancy and fungal disease. Using previously defined criteria of the severity of asthma (McNichol *et al.*, 1973) all but one of these children would have been considered to have severe illness. Therefore, to make comparisons based on variability of severity within this sample of seriously ill children, a new system of classification was developed based on each child's response to treatment in our controlled medical setting. Using the degree of persistent respiratory symptoms, dosage of anti-asthmatic medications and corticosteroids, and history of respiratory arrest, these children were divided into sub-groups based on severity of illness (see Table 1). In this sample, the distribution of severity ratings was 46 per cent grade 1, 12 percent grade 2, 15 per cent grade 3, and 27 per cent grade 4. Additionally, 58 per cent of the asthmatic sample had been diagnosed as having eczema at some point in their life, and nearly half of these children still had eczema. Finally, a small number of the asthmatic children had secondary medical difficulties.

The comparison sample consisted of 22 children who were the same age but had no previous serious medical illness and no prolonged past hospitalizations. One of the comparison children had been hospitalized briefly on three occasions for minor cosmetic surgery. Using the Hollingshead system (1975), both samples were predominantly middle-class. Seventy-three per cent of the asthmatic families and 64 per cent of the comparison families were in class II, III, or IV. However, there were eight families in the comparison group who were in class I while only four of the families of the asthmatic sample were in this category. Furthermore, there were three families of the asthmatic sample who were in class V and none in the comparison sample. The parents of the comparison sample had a mean length of formal education of 16 years as compared to 14 years in the sample of

parents of asthmatics. Family income did not vary significantly
between the two groups. Both samples were predominantly Caucasian,
and the sex ratio in both groups was 1.4 boys to 1.0 girl.

Table I. Asthma severity ratings

	Medications		Other Characteristics
Grade 1	Easily controlled on no more than two non-steroid medications. (May not require medication)	AND	Less than 3 wheezing episodes per week
Grade 2	Regular non-steroid medications with steroids given no more frequently than one short course per three month period	OR	More than three wheezing episodes per week despite aggressive treatment
Grade 3	Regular non-steroid medications required with steroids given in courses at a frequence greater than once every three months. May require use of inhaled steroids or low every other day doses of oral steroids on an on-going basis		
Grade 4	Daily steroids or every other day steroid treatment of more than 15 mg of Prednisone	OR	History of documented respiratory failure

Measures

Two primary data collection methodologies were employed. The first
was the Behavioral Screening Questionnaire (BSQ) (Richman and Graham,
1971; Richman, Stevenson and Graham, 1982). This is a semi-structured
parent interview approach that focuses on twelve behavioral areas
frequently seen as problems in pre-school children. The maximum
possible score using this scale is 24. This instrument has been
validated by Earls et al., 1982), who demonstrated that a score above
10 on this scale was an indication of emotional disturbance. Children
who received scores above this cut-off point were found to be
'obviously emotionally disturbed' with definite family disruption
when they were diagnostically assessed by a panel of experienced child
psychiatrists and other child mental health clinicians.

The second assessment strategy used in this study was a direct observational methodology that provided a means of quantifying the interaction of the mother with the child. While parent interviews provide
an important and reliable information base related to the child's

current functioning (Quinton, Rutter and Rowlands, 1976), observational methodologies have been demonstrated to be a more effective
strategy for assessing how interactions proceed and for determining
both the parent's and the child's affective contributions to the
development of an on-going sequential interaction. Consequently, a
method that employs a sequential approach to targeting affectively
charged interactions was used (Mrazek *et al.*, 1982). Specific modi-
fications of that system were made to allow the use of videotaping of
sequences of interaction which then could be analyzed in greater detail
to document the affective contributions of both the mother and child
(Mrazek and Anderson, 1983). Using this system, both mild and severe
oppositionality on the part of the child serve as trigger behaviors
for a control sequence. All subsequent interactions are recorded
sequentially, noting both the context of the dialogue and the affective tone, until resolution of the conflict is determined. Additionally, any expression of overt distress on the part of the child
serves as a triggering behavior for sequential recording of a distress sequence, which continues until there is a resolution of the
child's discomfort.

The use of systematic observational paradigms has been an important
methodological advance in the study of early developmental changes
(Ainsworth and Wittig, 1969; Gaensbauer, Mrazek and Emde, 1979). In
our study, all the children and their mothers were videotaped for 60
minutes in a studio located on the pediatric unit of the hospital.
A standardized observational paradigm was followed that consisted of
three 20-minute segments. The first 20-minute segment was an
unstructured play period during which time the mother was to interact
with her child as she might if she had some free time at home or on
the hospital unit. During the second 20-minute segment the child was
presented with a game called Perfection. The goal of the game is to
place 25 small shapes into a form board, which is attached to a
spring controlled by a timer. At the end of 60 seconds, the form
board pops up and scatters the shapes on the table. Regardless of
how many shapes the child had placed correctly, he would then have to
begin the task again. Prior to this segment, it was explained to the
mother that this is quite a difficult game, but that she should
encourage the child to perform at his peak ability. The third
20-minute segment was designed to examine the response of the child
to the parent's leaving the room for a 5-minute period. The behavior
of the child during the separation and the interaction of the dyad on
reunion was recorded.

All sequences of interaction that were triggered by oppositional
behavior or overt distress on the part of the child were coded by a
rater who was blind to the identity or diagnosis of the children.
Interrater reliability was completed by comparing the rating of the
primary scorer with a second blind rater. The percent agreement was
above 70 per cent for all behavioral categories.

Group comparisons of categorical data were made using a chi-square
analysis, while variables that were continuous in nature were compared using a t-test if they met the requirements of a normal distribution. Correlations were made using a Spearman rank ordered method.

Results

Parental report

The asthmatic group had a mean score of 10.1 on the Behavioral Screening
Questionnaire with 35 per cent of the children scoring in the range
indicative of obvious or severe emotional disturbance. In comparison to
this, the healthy children had a mean score of 6.7 with none of these
children scoring over 11. The difference in the total scale score
between the two groups was significant using the t-test ($p < 0.005$).

In considering the specific items on the BSQ, three characteristics of
the asthmatic children were shown to be significantly different from the
healthy comparison sample using a chi-square analysis. The mothers
described more often that their children were depressed ($p < 0.05$) and
fearful of situations extending beyond their reactions to hospital procedures and personnel ($p < 0.025$). Furthermore, the asthmatic children
had marked sleep disturbances characterized primarily by waking during
the night ($p < 0.005$). As asthmatic symptoms are often worse during
sleep, this characteristic of the illness may in a large part be responsible for this last difference. Results of all 12 of the BSQ variables
are shown in Table 2.

Table 2. Behavioral screening questionnaire items

Item	Significance
(1) Sleep difficulties (waking at night)	< 0.005
(2) Fearfulness	< 0.01
(3) Depressed mood	< 0.05
(4) Worries	Trend
(5) Encopresis	Trend
(6) Eating problems	n.s.
(7) Activity level	n.s.
(8) Temper tantrums	n.s.
(9) Problems in management	n.s.
(10) Problems with independence	n.s.
(11) Peer relationships	n.s.
(12) Concentration span	n.s.

Sequential scoring system

The coding of the interactions demonstrated striking differences between
the two groups. The asthmatic children were more oppositional, providing
greater challenge to their mothers in terms of managing their behavior.
Additionally, they were more likely to become overtly distressed so that

the affective climate of the interaction was much more unpleasant.
Interestingly, the mothers of the asthmatic children were not less affectionate than the mothers of the control group despite the more difficult
behavior exhibited by their children.

One tailed t-test comparisons were computed for the frequency of individual behaviors, the duration of each type of sequence, and the outcomes of
oppositional interactions of the asthmatic versus the healthy children.
Most striking was the difference in overall negative interaction that
took place over the course of the observation. The asthmatic children
and mothers were involved in negative interactions for 23 per cent of the
observational paradigm while the comparison dyads were engaged in such
interactions only 9 per cent of the time (p < 0.005). The nature of
these negative interactions fell both into overt confrontations and
dysphoric periods when the child was overtly distressed. The frequency
of opposition in the asthmatic sample was more than threefold that of the
comparison group (p < 0.01). This was most predominant during the second
segment when there was a high expectation of performance from the child.
Here the frequency of opposition was four times greater in the asthmatic
sample (p < 0.005). However, following the separation in the third segment, the asthmatic children became less oppositional, so that during
this portion of the paradigm there was no difference between the two
groups in frequency of opposition. Interestingly, the oppositional
sequences of the asthmatic children tended to be twice as long, lasting
for an average of 60 seconds. This difference did not reach statistical
significance, however. While the active opposition of the asthmatic
children was most striking, they also were more passively non-compliant.
Over the course of the total paradigm they were more than 2.5 times as
likely to simply ignore their mother's instruction (p < 0.01). Clearly,
the mothers of the asthmatic children were involved in control struggles
of either an active or passive nature for a much greater percentage of
the entire paradigm (p < 0.025).

The outcome of these oppositional interactions was also different between
the two groups. The asthmatic children were persistently non-compliant
during 57 per cent of their oppositional interactions with their mothers
as compared to the comparison children being persistently non-compliant
for only 38 per cent of such interactions. One of the characteristics of
the longer oppositional interactions typical of the asthmatic sample was
that interruptions in the process of resolving the child's oppositional
behavior were more frequent, with the child opposing a second parental
instruction six times more frequently (p < 0.05).

The child's distress was also coded using this sequential approach. The
total duration of distress, when there was no overt or passive non-
compliance, was four times greater for the asthmatic sample (p < 0.01).
The frequency of the child's crying or whining was greatest during the
segment with high performance expectations (p < 0.01), although it was
also higher during the period after the separation (p < 0.05). The mean
duration of these episodes of distress did not differ between the two
groups, but there were many more sequences of overt distress in the
asthmatic group. An additional feature of the distress was that the
asthmatic sample was six times more likely than the comparison group to
have an interaction that began with the child being overtly distressed

subsequently lead to opposition.

Analyzing the frequency of affective expressions displayed by the two samples demonstrated that not only did the asthmatic children display much more frequent negative affect, but their mothers were also more apt to eventually respond to their behavior in a negative manner. Mothers of the asthmatic children regularly displayed angry affect, while this was never seen in the comparison sample. Similarly, in the asthmatic sample, approximately 20 per cent of the oppositional sequences were concluded with the parent resorting to a rejecting or angry response, while such parental behavior occurred in less than 1 per cent of the comparison sample.

One of the striking negative findings was the fact that despite the more confrontational behavior of the asthmatic children and their mothers' more frequent angry responses to these oppositions, the mothers of both groups responded in a positive manner at an equal frequency. Specifically, the total number of approvals and positive reinforcements were similar in both groups of mothers. Furthermore, the number of affectionate touches was the same, as was the frequency of the occurrence of positive affect associated with both verbal and non-verbal expressions used by the mother to either comfort the child in distress sequences or to try to bring about compliance during an oppositional sequence.

Finally, the asthmatic children were more likely to be distressed during separation from their parents. The mean frequency of distress was twice as high in the asthmatic group as in the comparison sample (p < 0.05). Additionally, on examining differences between the 3- and 4-year old sub-samples, a further pattern emerged. While the numbers of children in each subgroup are relatively small, the duration of distress at both 3 and 4 years was approximately twice as great for the asthmatic sample as for the comparison group. Distress was negligible in both 5-year-old sub-samples except for one very distressed asthmatic girl. In summary, these findings were consistent with the observation that short separations were becoming less unsettling for both groups, but the asthmatic children appeared to be slightly slower in making this adaptation.

Discussion

This group of young asthmatic children clearly demonstrated a number of prominent emotional and behavioral difficulties that would have been difficult to anticipate by reviewing the literature. The work of Gauthier *et al.*, at the University of Montreal (1977, 1978) represents the first empirical study of the early emotional development of young children with asthma. While a number of specific difficulties within the mother-child relationship were noted, the most striking finding was that so many of these children and their parents were adapting well following the early onset of this physical illness. This is in contrast to our findings which indicate that during the pre-school years our sample was having considerable difficulty. While the methods used in the two studies were quite different, the most probable reason for the differences in these findings appears to be the selection of the sample of children. The Montreal study included children with less severe illness as measured both by the number of previous hospitalizations and, more specifically, by their required doses of medication. Additional problems in interpreting the data from the Montreal study are presented by the absence of a comparison population of healthy children and the use of unstandardized measures. Nevertheless, their careful observations suggest that children with relatively mild asthma are at less risk for developing psychopathology during the pre-school period.

Comparing our sample of asthmatic children with earlier samples described in the literature, it is clear that by previously established severity ratings all of our children had severe illness. Four other studies divided asthmatic populations based on severity and compared emotional or behavioral characteristics. The first of these was a study by Graham *et al.* (1967). In this study 57 children who were diagnosed as having asthma were divided into two groups, 17 in a more severely affected and 40 in a less severely affected sample. The definition of severely affected included either being prevented from going to school or from engaging in quiet play because of asthma for more than 20 days in the past year, or being restricted in school activities due to asthma. While these are relatively broad criteria for differentiation, all of our children would have been classified as severely affected using this system. Using a methodology that included psychiatric screening questionnaires, parental interviews, and individual psychological testing, it was determined that 42 per cent of the children showed either minor or severe psychiatric disorder. However, when one considered the sub-sample of severe asthmatics, 59 per cent of them were in the psychiatrically disturbed category. However, these group differences did not reach statistical significance.

McNichol *et al.* (1973) did an epidemiological study of 315 asthmatic children in Melbourne, Australia. They classified children into four categories, grades A through D. Grade D was defined as children with a current history of frequent or chronic unremitting asthma. These children either had periods of severe prolonged asthma with remissions of less than one month during the year prior to assessment, or had more than ten attacks in the previous three months. This category represented only 18 per cent of their sample. In contrast, virtually all of the patients in our sample would receive a D rating, with the exception of one child in our grade 1 category who would probably have been coded as grade C using the Australian system.

In a separate report McNichol *et al.* (1973) discussed the behavioral characteristics of the children in each of the four severity grades. Virtually all the positive associations differentiated the grade D children from the more mildly asthmatic children. The primary analyses were done when the children in the cohort were 14 years of age. At that point in their development the most striking finding was that the more severely asthmatic children were more anxious, particularly related to medical visits and interactions with their physicians. Higher anxiety was also noted during contacts with social workers and in the school setting. Additionally, they were seen as more demanding and less socially mature. Both grades C and D were more apt to respond to maternal requests with physical aggression, while those children in the most severe category were significantly more apt to be abusive to their mothers. In

an experimental study, Williams (1975) demonstrated that asthmatic
children with both mild and severe disease had a greater reaction to separation from their mothers and were judged to be more dependent than
either a normal sample or a fibrocystic control group.

Kim, Ferrara and Chess (1980), in a study of asthmatic children between
the ages of 3 and 7, used a three category classification system which they
designated 'mild', 'moderate', and 'severe'. This system utilized four
variables to discriminate these categories: (1) the number of acute
asthmatic episodes; (2) number of school days missed; (3) frequency of
hospitalization; and (4) use of steroid medications. While none of the
children in this report would be classified in Kim's mild category, some
of the more easily controlled children who received a grade 1 classification using our system would have been rated as moderate. However, the
overwhelming majority of our children would have been rated severe by
these criteria. Kim reported that parents of this sample of asthmatic
children described them in such a way that their 'temperament' was best
classified as 'slow to warm up'. These characteristics included lower
rhythmicity, lower adaptability, lower intensity of reaction, lower mood
value, and lower persistence. These findings were contrasted with parent
reports of a sample of healthy children and a sample of children with
chronic allergies but without asthma.

Norrish, Tooley and Godfrey (1977) studied 63 asthmatic outpatients
between 8 and 15 years of age. Judgments were made of severity of illness, quality of control, and psychological 'deviance'. Severity of
asthma was determined by type of medication prescribed over the preceding
six months. Children were rated as 'mild' if they required only bronchodilators, 'moderate' if they required sodium cromoglycate, and 'severe'
if they required steroids. Quality of control of asthmatic symptoms was
estimated on a five point scale based on clinical outpatient notes and
diary records. Psychological 'deviance' was measured by scores on the
Rutter 'A' or 'B' scale. No relationship between severity of asthma and
psychiatric disturbance was found. However, 91 per cent of the 11
children who were rated as having 'poor' quality of control of asthmatic
symptoms were also identified as deviant on the Rutter scales. This
association was statistically significant, and an interactive relationship
between emotional disturbance and clinical control of symptoms was
hypothesized.

Results of the Behavioral Screening Questionnaire interview suggested
that many of the children in our sample were having many behavioral problems. Thirty-five per cent received overall scores that were indicative
of significant emotional disturbance. Fearfulness, depressive mood, and
difficulties with sleep were the predominant characteristics. Additionally, a minority of the mothers of asthmatic children described them as
being very difficult to manage and having persistent temper tantrums,
while this was not a characteristic of any of the maternal reports given
by our comparison group. Increased management problems and frequent
temper tantrums were insufficiently common in the asthmatic sample to
reach statistical significance for the entire group but were highly
associated with each other (p < 0.001). Furthermore, those mothers who
reported behavioral problems were more likely to have their child be
oppositional during the observational paradigm (p < 0.025).

Given the nature of asthma, these findings may be more illness-specific
than typical of all chronic illnesses. Specifically, problems with sleep
may be directly related to increased symptomatology at night. However,
it is also possible that these children's depressive affect may have contributed to sleep difficulties. The fact that their mothers reported
many of these children as depressed was a significant finding. Clearly,
their early histories had often been marked by abrupt and unplanned
hospitalizations, which in some cases had resulted in very difficult
separations from attachment figures for variable periods of time. This,
coupled with their chronic disability, could certainly be a plausible
explanation for early depression. Finally, the fearfulness that these
children displayed was not specifically directed to hospital situations
or medical procedures, but it was associated with a wide variety of
different stimuli. Since severe asthma is often associated with intense
fear when attacks result in extreme breathlessness, this may well lead to
an internalized feeling of apprehension that is generalized to other situations.

The observational findings that these children were both very confrontive
and persistently non-compliant in their interactions with their mothers
was striking. Additionally, during the maternal interview, some of the
mothers of the asthmatic children described these behavioral problems as
being very intense, and many of these mothers were observed to have difficulty with handling their child's frequent oppositional confrontations.
Clearly, the asthmatic children were more likely to be oppositional and
were consequently more of a challenge for their mothers than were the
healthy children. A certain degree of non-compliant behavior is developmentally appropriate at this age, and establishing a normal range of
expected oppositional behavior during the observational paradigm was
essential for interpretation of these interactions. Perhaps the best
reflection of the difference between the two groups was the fact that
while the mothers of the healthy children were faced with oppositional
behavior, albeit at a lower frequency, they were in most cases able to
eventually obtain their child's compliance. The reverse was true with
the asthmatic mothers. In discussing this issue with parents of young
asthmatic children, many of them related incidents involving emotional
conflict that led to an asthmatic attack. Such unfortunate occurrences
seemed central for the development of these patterns of interaction.
Another interesting finding regarding the oppositionality of the asthmatic
children was that it decreased after the separation. Coupled with the
finding that the separations were more difficult for the asthmatic
children, it raises the question of whether the separation distress may
have led the children to reduce their willingness to risk continued confrontation.

Changes in the affective interactions of the mothers and children were
very illuminating. Clearly, there was more overt distress on the part of
the asthmatic children in the form of crying and whining. Not surprisingly, their mothers found this behavior difficult and responded more
frequently in an angry and short-tempered manner. The fact that many of
the crying and whining episodes of the asthmatic children actually led to
a new oppositional sequence gives a good sense of the relatively stressful and difficult atmosphere that evolved over the course of these observational assessments. Given that the asthmatic sample spent nearly

one-quarter of the time during the second and third segments of the paradigm in these difficult interactions, it is clear that the overall quality
of their interactions was neither mutually rewarding nor satisfying.
Quite a surprising finding was that despite the presence of so much
negative affect in the sample of asthmatic children, their mothers displayed as much reinforcing and positively affective behavior as did the
mothers of the healthy children. The interactions of the comparison
sample took place in a relatively easy manner with regular and appropriate
positive reinforcement, while often the interactions of the asthmatic
sample were characterized by periods of intense negative affect inter-
spersed with relatively positive interactions. While the off-again-on-
again quality of the levels of affect did not appear to present either a
very predictable or regular pattern, these shifts in affect were striking.
Currently we are planning to study this characteristic using more sophisticated statistical approaches which will include both conditional proba-
bilities and time series analytic techniques.

The separation reactions of these children were more difficult to inter-
pret. In both the asthmatic and the comparison samples, the younger
children predictably showed more distress on separation than did the
older children. The impression that the group data yielded was that in
both samples the children were slowly mastering their affective response
to a short separation, but in the asthmatic sample this was a delayed
process. One plausible explanation for this apparent delay would be
their previous histories of repeated and abrupt separations. While one
might have predicted that these previous experiences could have provided
an opportunity to develop some mastery over separation distress, this was
not the case. The failure of mastery may have been the result of the
unpredictable nature of these separations which may have made adaptation
difficult.

In considering this systematically collected empirical data within the
context of providing clinical consultations in a hospital setting with a
large inpatient population of pre-school asthmatic patients, we were
struck by some similarities that appear to validate these findings. The
most frequent reason for a psychiatric consultation request was to help
develop a strategy for dealing with confrontational, angry behavior. As
this was also the most striking characteristic of the videotaped paradigms,
the requests provided some concurrent validity to our findings. However,
many mothers had apparently adapted to this rather difficult behavior and
had subsequently modified their threshold of tolerance of confrontations
to a level at which they did not report oppositional behavior as being a
problem for them. The fact that the mothers did report increased
depression was interesting as this had been the second most frequent
request for consultation. It was somewhat surprising that both staff and
parents were sensitive to depressed affect in young children, as it has
previously been observed that medical staff tend to have difficulty identifying depression in young children. One of the reasons that this
characteristic may have been more regularly recognized is that the intensity of the dysphoric affect in these children was characterized by an
overt sadness rather than a subtle withdrawal. Finally, the finding of
increased fearfulness was certainly reminiscent of consultations related
to pre-school children who had panic reactions during both medical procedures and acute episodes of asthma. The question is still an open one

as to whether these findings are specific sequellae to severe asthmatic symptoms, or whether these findings may be generalized to characterize children with other comparably severe chronic illnesses.

The documentation of such overt behavioral difficulties in this severely asthmatic population raises the issue of what are the appropriate early interventions for dealing with these problems. Our approach has been primarily to support parents and work within the family context to provide consistent and firm limits for the children while they are in the hospital setting, as well as to try to understand any environmental precipitants that may have led to depression. Furthermore, we actively encourage parents to be sensitive to their child's affective expressions and provide guidance in appropriate parenting responses. We provide intensive education for families regarding the most effective immediate treatment for acute asthmatic attacks that can result in a more generalized improvement in their sense of themselves as being competent. Finally, we attempt to desensitize the children to medical procedures in a way that decreases their fearful reactions and increases their confidence in their own ability to handle these situations.

In summary, pre-school asthmatic children with severe illness, characterized by the necessity for repeated hospitalization and on-going theophylline and steroid treatment, appear to be at high risk for behavioral difficulties. However, the question of what precipitates either their asthmatic symptoms or behavioral problems is not clear. It is plausible that the intensity of their symptoms, the duration of severe asthmatic attacks, and the abrupt and unpredictable nature of many of the medical interventions for these children may lead to a sense of uncertainty and to difficulties in the interactions between these children and their parents. However, it is difficult to make any causal statement without knowing the quality of the parent-child interaction prior to the onset of the illness. It is clear from clinical experience that for some families the reactive nature of the illness leads to an increased manipulation of the parents because of their fear of possibly precipitating an asthmatic attack. Nonetheless, this does not appear to be a prominent dynamic for all families.

A cross-sectional study can not address the issue of whether severe conflict in young children may lead to an increased exacerbation of symptoms or whether the initial onset of asthma may be related to stressful experiences. However, there are anecdotal reports that suggest that for certain children this may be the case. These questions of causality require a prospective longitudinal approach for clarification. If a group of children at high risk for development of asthma could be followed during infancy and early childhood with an emphasis being placed on careful and sensitive assessment of their emotional development and the quality of family interaction, it would be possible to better understand the relative contribution of psychological factors in the onset of this illness in children who have a strong constitutional vulnerability.

Conclusions

Twenty-six severely asthmatic pre-school children were assessed using parental interviews and direct observational techniques. They were compared to a sample of 22 healthy children. The findings suggest these asthmatic children are at an increased risk for difficult interactions with their mothers. Conversely, many of these families have been able to adapt and interact in a supportive manner. Furthermore, the asthmatic children appear to be at increased risk for depressive and phobic symptomatology and may well benefit from early interventions that focus on helping parents provide more consistent and sensitive support for their child, particularly during times of hospitalization and during severe asthmatic attacks.

Acknowledgments

We would like to acknowledge that this research has been supported in part by funds from the Developmental Psychobiology Research Group of the Department of Psychiatry, University of Colorado School of Medicine.

Additionally, we would like to thank Mrs. Jane Everett for technical help in coding the data and Mrs. Florence Garyet for secretarial help in preparing the manuscript.

References

AINSWORTH, M. D. S. and WITTIG, B. A. (1969) Attachment and exploratory behavior of one-year-olds in a strange situation. In B. Foss (Ed.), *Determinants of Infant Behavior IV*, pp. 111-136. London, Methuen.
EARLS, F., JACOBS, G., GOLDFEIN, D., GILBERT, A., BEARDSLEE, W. and RIVINUS, T. (1982) Concurrent validation of a behavior problems scale to use with 3-year-olds. *Journal of the American Academy of Child Psychiatry*, 21, 47-57.
FALLIERS, C. (1970) Treatment of asthma in a residential center. *Annals of Allergy*, 28, 513-521.
GAENSBAUER, T. J., MRAZEK, D. A. and EMDE, R. N. (1979) Patterning of emotional response in a playroom laboratory situation. *Infant Behavior and Development*, 2, 163-178.
GAUTHIER, Y., FORTIN, C., DRAPEAU, P., BRETON, J. J., GOSSELIN, J., QUINTAL, L., WEISNAGEL, J., TETREAULT, L. and PINARD, G. (1977) The mother-child relationship and the development of autonomy and self-assertion in young (14-30 months) asthmatic children. *Journal of the American Academy of Child Psychiatry*, 16, 109-131.
GAUTHIER, Y., FORTIN, C., DRAPEAU, P., BRETON, J. J., GOSSELIN, J., QUINTAL, L., WEISNAGEL, J. and LAMARRE, A. (1978) Follow-up study of 35 asthmatic pre-school children. *Journal of the American Academy of Child Psychiatry*, 17, 679-694.
GRAHAM, P. J., RUTTER, M., YULE, W. and PLESS, I. B. (1976) Childhood asthma: a psychosomatic disorder? *British Journal of Preventative and Social Medicine*, 21, 78-85.
HOLLINGSHEAD, A. B. (1975) *Four factor index of social status*.

Unpublished manuscript. New Haven, Connecticut, Yale University.
KIM, S. P., FERRARA, A. and CHESS, S. (1980) Temperament of asthmatic
    children. *Journal of Pediatrics*, 97, 483-486.
LEFFERT, F. (1978) Asthma: a modern perspective. *Pediatrics*, 62,
    1061-1069.
MARSH, D. G., MEYERS, D. A. and BIAS, W. B. (1981) The epidemiology and
    genetics of atopic allergy. *New England Journal of Medicine*, 26,
    1551-1559.
McNICHOL, K. N., WILLIAMS, H. E., ALLAN, J. and McANDREW, I. (1973)
    Spectrum of asthma in children. III. *British Medical Journal*, iv,
    16-20.
MRAZEK, D. A., DOWDNEY, L., RUTTER, M. L. and QUINTON, D. L. (1982)
    Mother and pre-school child interaction: a sequential approach.
    Journal of the American Academy of Child Psychiatry, 21, 453-464.
MRAZEK, D. A. and ANDERSON, I. (1983) *An observational methodology for
    analyzing the quality of mother-child interactions*. Paper presented
    at the annual meeting of the American Academy of Child Psychiatry,
    San Francisco, California.
NORRISH, M., TOOLEY, M. and GODFREY, S. (1977) Clinical, physiological,
    and psychological study of asthmatic children attending a hospital
    clinic. *Archives of Diseases of Childhood*, 52, 912-917.
QUINTON, D., RUTTER, M. and ROWLANDS, O. (1976) An evaluation of an
    interview assessment of marriage. *Psychological Medicine*, 6, 577-586.
RICHMAN, N. and GRAHAM, P. (1971) A behavioural screening questionnaire
    for use with 3-year-old children. *Journal of Child Psychology and
    Psychiatry*, 12, 5-33.
RICHMAN, N., STEVENSON, J. and GRAHAM, P. J. (1982) *Pre-school to
    School: A Behavioural Study*. London, Academic Press.

CHAPTER 9

Allergic and Immunologic Factors in Child and Family Psychiatry

Ian C. Menzies

*Young Peoples Psychiatric Department, Royal Infirmary,
Dundee DD1 9ND*

Introduction

'Chronic illness, handicap and psychiatric disorders are now at the centre of paediatric care' (Report of the Committee on Child Health Services, 1976). Behaviourally disturbed and learning disordered children are common (Rutter, Tizard and Whitmore, 1970; Rutter *et al.*, 1975). They make great demands on parental understanding and courage as well as on professional judgment and time.

Many problems of classification in child psychiatry remain unresolved. Although Rutter (e.g. Rutter *et al.*, 1975; Rutter and Hersov, 1977) and others have demonstrated an emotional and a conduct disturbance variable, as well as a hyperkinetic grouping, there is unfortunately considerable overlap between these groupings particularly between the neurotic and conduct groups. As a result a 'mixed' category has had to be included in the derived classification schemes (Wolff, 1971; Rutter, Schaffer and Shepherd, 1975).

The majority of the cases referred to me present as 'mixed' category problems. It seemed therefore that there was merit in looking beyond the psychiatric literature for a description of disturbed and disturbing children capable of embracing the three main groupings - neurotic, conduct and 'mixed', but which would also take account of the hyperkinetic minority.

Review of the literature revealed the work of Speer (1958) on the Allergic-Tension-Fatigue (ATF) syndrome. Speer (1970) and more recently Kittler and Baldwin (1970) and Rapp (1979, 1980) have detailed this syndrome and have stressed the aetiological importance of environmental factors - ingestants, inhalants and contactants.

Speer used the term *Tension* to embrace several different types of overactivity, both motor and sensory. 'Motor overactivity gives rise to restlessness, fidgetiness, clumsiness, coarse tremor, jerkiness and even to stuttering, whereas sensory overactivity is characterized by an oversensitivity to noise, light, pain, scolding and correction and indeed to almost all external stimuli, physical and mental'. The other main component of the syndrome is *Fatigue*, for 'paradoxically, the tension-ridden child is also likely to be subject to fatigue, not benefitted by rest'.

When they are young such children are often irritable, sullen and easily annoyed by trivial incidents. They may lose any desire to play and may respond very negatively to their parents. Later they may exhibit sleep disturbance with restlessness, frequent wakening and disturbing nightmares. Variable mood states, sometimes associated with compulsive behaviour and, at other times with paranoid ideation are also reported. These children may show considerable destructiveness and excitement; surprising cruelty to playmates and attention-demanding behaviour whilst 'some chatter constantly using a high-pitched, strangely different voice'. Parents also report bizarre 'silly' behaviour, emotional liability, mental sluggishness, inability to concentrate or remember details and an incapacity on the part of the child troubled in this way, to carry out instructions.

Vague physical symptoms are also common. These include poor appetite, aching in muscles and joints and excessive sweating, especially at night and over the scalp. There may also be facial pallor, infra- or peri-orbital oedema and a variable bluish-black/purple discolouration of the skin below the eyes (allergic 'shiners'). Headache and vague stomach-ache are also common, as is some degree of constipation, diarrhoea or halitosis. The child may also suffer from rhinitis, urticaria, mouth ulcers or paraesthesiae, and night wetting may be troublesome. In addition, these children may even micturate in strange places at times.

Clinical Findings

I should emphasize that this is not a research study, simply some clinical observations which I hope will encourage others to look more closely at this area.

To my surprise, when I reviewed my own caseload, obtained by non-selective, routine referral, over a recent 12-month period, approximately 40 per cent fell easily into the ATF syndrome category.

Case No. 1

John was typical of a child with an ATF syndrome. Aged 6, he had long presented formidable problems to his parents, especially to his increasingly stressed mother. A cuddly, well behaved infant, his difficulties had began at the age of 18 months shortly after the birth of his brother. He could not be disciplined, had massive temper tantrums when thwarted and was often stubborn and willful. At times mother could only manage to get him to respond by suggesting that he do exactly the opposite of that which she wished. He was overactive, uncoordinated, restless and fidgety. Disinhibited in what he said to people, he could be very hurtful to his parents. He had no age-appropriate sense of danger, cried easily and for little reason, was hypersensitive to smells and inclined to do 'silly things'. He also had a vivid imagination and seemed genuinely unable to separate fact from fantasy, truth from fiction. His mother often

felt there was a barrier between them. His sleep had been disturbed
nightly since the age of 18 months in that he sweated profusely in
bed, wakened early and often had nightmares. 'Allergic' to penicillin, he had had frequent right earache and from time to time developed
headache, looked pale and had 'bloodshot eyes'. At times his mother
had noticed peri-orbital swelling. John's father and brother both
suffered from asthma. His mother presented as a tense, anxious,
phobic lady, whose sleep was often disturbed and who frequently had
feelings of unreality. Treated as a food and chemical sensitivity
problem, John improved dramatically but relapsed when inadvertently
'challenged' with certain additive-containing products. Interestingly, his mother, only 5 st 4 lbs and existing on tea, coffee and
cigarettes when her son's treatment began, decided to remove these
items from her diet. Four months later she too was relaxed, looked
well, and weighed over 7 st.

Allergic-tension-fatigue symptoms played some part in the problems of a
further 20 per cent of my caseload.

Case No. 2

Typical of this group was Robert. The elder of two brothers aged 7½
and 4 he had been referred because of behaviour problems. His
parents' marriage had been shortlived and stormy due to his father's
difficult personality. When seen, however, his mother had the
support and help of a much more supportive and stable man. Robert's
birth was normal. He was bottle fed. As a young child he suffered
from croup and from earache. He also complained frequently of headache and was restless, fidgety, had a short attention span and poor
concentration. At times he had difficulty in expressing himself
clearly, though it was obvious that he understood all that was said
to him. Mother felt that he often seemed a sad boy, easily frustrated, prone to tempers, particularly when unable to say what he
wanted to say or when he was having problems with his homework. At
these times he often became aggressive to his brother and once he had
even taken a knife to his brother's fingers. At times he was withdrawn and emotional, feeling the whole world was against him and
appearing to see everything 'black' or 'white'. He had disturbed
sleep and had even threatened suicide. Robert's mother revealed that
for most of her life she too had had 'upset patches' very like those
experienced by her son. She reluctantly admitted to a fear that she
was going mad. She then reported auditory hallucinations, a poor
memory and said that she kept putting things in strange places to her
subsequent surprise. Moreover, she often experienced 'paraesthesiae',
perspired excessively when in bed and had feelings of depersonalization. She suffered from severe headaches and during these episodes
her whole mood changed. She hated everybody and felt that they hated
her, although deep down she knew that this was not true. When I saw
Robert again he reluctantly told me a story similar to that given by
his mother. When he had a headache he saw ghosts 'like big shadows',
heard noises and insisted that on one occasion he had 'seen pigeons
cracking open my brother's head'. He then went on to speak of his
terrible moods when he felt horrible and angry inside and at that
time he too felt that people were against him.

Robert's electro-encephalogram (EEG) showed a paroxysmal disturbance
whilst his mother's raised the possibility of a left fronto-temporal
dysfunction. However, both mother and child reported substantial
improvement in their headache and in their other symptoms for as long
as their diet was free from milk, cheese and other dairy products;
otherwise they stayed locked in periodic conflict and hate.
Unfortunately, when he was present within the family, Robert's
natural father had frequently taunted his son and had denigrated his
ability, thus adding greatly to the stresses already on the child.

<u>Case No. 3</u>

Mary aged 8 is the smaller of twin girls, middle children in a sib-
ship of six. Born six weeks before her due date, she weighed
1800 g, 40 g less than her twin. She was bottle fed. Her development was slower than that of her twin.

Her only brother, Alexander, now aged 10, had an irritable bowel
syndrome when younger, Her father probably had a viral encephalitis
two years ago, since when he has suffered from a variety of somatic
complaints, chiefly headache and backache. He is 'sensitive' to
certain foods. Her mother, a tense phobic lady, has feelings of
unreality and of depersonalization and is certainly 'sensitive' to
strawberries, shellfish, coffee, soya, eggs and 'bleach'. Mary
herself has a known sensitivity to bee stings.

Although at times warm, pleasant and friendly, she had had frequent,
lengthy spells during which her behaviour became noticeably disturbed.
She was moody and aggressive, especially to her twin. These episodes
either began with bedwetting or with marked morning irritability.
She was 'slow to get going', uncommunicative to the point of appearing mute and often looked angry. During these periods she also
became stubborn, willful and bad tempered at school where her writing
deteriorated and teacher reported that she seemed unable to retain
information.

Although of well below the third centile for height and below the
third centile for weight, she had an excessive appetite, at times
'binged' and also displayed an altered bowel rhythm, chiefly
diarrhoea with large, bulky four smelling stools.

Jejunal biopsy and growth hormone tests were technically unsatisfactory but RAST testing disclosed a 'moderate' specific IgE response to
wheat and egg, and a 'low' response to oats and house dust mite.

In the weeks after her initial assessment her behaviour deteriorated
and the level of tension within her family increased. Mary was
therefore placed on a wheat/oats and egg free diet.

Within a few days the parents noted a considerable improvement in her
behaviour. This was maintained throughout the period she remained on
these exclusions. Her concentration improved as did her school performance. She was less moody, more able to watch television without
fidgeting and more inclined to take the initiative in conversation

and games with others in the family. Her appetite became 'more
normal'. She had less abdominal distention and her bowel rhythm
appeared more satisfactory. She no longer wet the bed and mother
felt that the 'peculiar smell' which she thought emanated from her
daughter from time to time had disappeared.

On 'open challenge' with wheat, Mary's symptoms returned wi*hin a few
days. She became moody, irritable, her behaviour again deteriorated
and the bedwetting reappeared. She slowly improved once wheat was
again removed from her diet.

Stimulated by those and other cases, I decided to look more closely at 25
children for whom the ATF label seemed appropriate. Some interesting
points emerged.

Table 1 illustrates the age, sex, ordinal position and main 'loci' of
problem behaviour in these cases. Children were included in the series
if their symptoms seemed typical of the ATF syndrome. The degree of similarity between the cases in the series is reflected in Table 2. The
clinical pictures exhibited were often dramatic and indicative of severe
disorders as the three cases already described in detail demonstrate.

Table 1.

Case No.	Age	Sex	Position in Family	'Locus' of Problems	
1	2½	F	M5 Pt.	Home	
2	5	F	Pt.	Home	School
3	6	F	Pt. F4	Home	School
4	8	F	Pt. M4	Home	School
5	9	F	F14 M10 F9 Pt. F8 F7	Home	School
6	3½	M	F5 Pt. M18/12	Home	
7	4½	M	Pt. M3	Home	
8	5½	M	M9 Pt.	Home	School
9	6	M	M12 Pt. M6	Home	School
10	6	M	Pt. M4	Home	School
11	6	M	Pt. M2 F1	Home	School
12	7	M	Pt. M5	Home	School
13	8	M	Pt. F5	Home	School
14	8	M	Pt. M1	Home	School
15	9	M	M19 M17 M1(Pt. M10	Home	School
16	9	M	F10 Pt.	Home	School
17	9½	M	Pt.	Home	School
18	10	M	F20 F11 Pt.	Home	School
19	10	M	Pt. M8	Home	School
20	10½	M	F15 M12 Pt.	Home	School
21	10½	M	Pt. F8	Home	School
22	11	M	Pt. F6	Home	School
23	11	M	F13 Pt.	Home	School
24	12	M	Pt. F6	Home	School
25	12	M	M16 M15 Pt. F5	Home	School

Table 2.

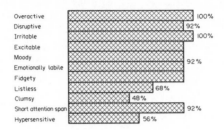

As can be seen from Table 3 other features were also often present in
these children, for example, 'catarrhal' symptoms and 'allergic' features
such as facial pallor and 'allergic shiners'. Six of the mothers complained that on entering their child's bedroom in the morning they were
aware of a 'strange smell' when their child's disturbed behaviour was at
its height. All the children suffered from some degree of sleep disturbance. Eighteen out of 24 were reported to sweat excessively at night,
especially over the scalp and nape of the neck. Alimentary, respiratory
and urinary tract problems were common. It is hypothesized that an
allergic reaction, inducing smooth muscle spasm, forms the basis for most
of these multi-system difficulties.

Table 3.

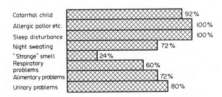

Electro-encephalographic (EEG) investigations were carried out on 21 of
the 25. These disclosed some degree of abnormality, usually non-specific
in all but one case (see Table 4).

As can be seen from Table 5, similar problems seemed almost always to
have been present in one or other, sometimes both natural parents. Where
the proband was a boy, all the mothers had had difficulties whereas the
fathers of four of the five girls in the study had possible allergic/
sensitivity problems. Moreover, the affected parents were often either
obese, or subject to rapid weight change for no obvious reason. Anxiety,
tension, depressive and phobic symptoms were prevalent, as were feelings

of unreality and/or depersonalization and experiences perhaps best
described as hallucinatory.

Table 4.

Case No.	Sex	Age	E.E.G. Results
1	F	2½	Not tested
2	F	5	Minor excess of slow wave activity
3	F	6	Non specific bilateral abnormality. Slow post. rhythmic activity
4	F	8	Excess slow especially over Rt. hemisphere anteriorly
5	F	9	Mild diffuse abnormality. ? Bilateral temp. lobe dysfunction
6	M	3½	Excess slow wave activity in background rhythms
7	M	4½	Slow, poor rhythmic background activity
8	M	5½	Sl. slowing of background – may be maturational
9	M	6	Within normal limits
10	M	6	Sl. asymetrical background activity
11	M	6	Not tested
12	M	7	Runs of slowing especially after hyperventilation espec. Lt. side + yawning → could be paroxysmal
13	M	8	Low amplitude disturbances both temporal areas worse during hyperventilation
14	M	8	Not tested
15	M	9	Excess slow waves especially Rt. occipital. Freq. spikes Rt. parietal and post temp. areas
16	M	9	Minor dysfunction Rt. hemisphere
17	M	9½	Excess of slow waves associated with long duration sharp waves
18	M	10	Slow waves prominent especially over Rt. side on hyper-ventilation – a diffuse abnormality
19	M	10	Bilateral paroxysmal appearance becoming general on hyperventilation
20	M	10½	Bilateral diffuse abnormality with paroxysmal features
21	M	10½	Slow waves. Significant Rt. sided disturbance
22	M	11	Irregular slow waves temp. regions – left hemisphere dysfunction
23	M	11	Bilateral excess of slow waves – Bilateral diffuse dysfunction ? paroxysmal
24	M	12	Not tested
25	M	12	Non specific temporal disturbance

Table 5.

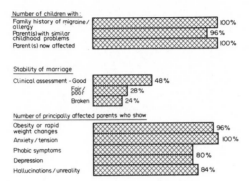

The 'affected' parent's histories suggested that they too had long suffered from food and/or chemical sensitivity problems. This and other aspects of the clinical information they provided lent support for the hypothesis that genetic influences, expressed in allergic/sensitivity disturbances, may have aetiological importance for the longstanding problems they had experienced. A fascinating possibility worthy of further study, given the number of difficulties they displayed and the fact that the stability of the marriage had suffered in over half of these families.

The onset of each child's disorder could usually be related in time to some major stress factor such as infant feeding difficulties, the birth of a sibling, death of a parent or parental separation or even to viral infection. Almost always, therefore, a psychodynamic explanation had been offered for the development of the child's problem. Nevertheless, there was a phasic quality to the child's disturbance and the 'ebb and flow' of the disorder could not readily be equated with change in family psychopathology.

Every child in the series was faddy about food. Each had a most restricted diet which had become increasingly 'skewed' in the direction of 'instant, convenience and junk' foods containing large quantities of chemicals, mostly derived from either coal or oil. Non-affected parents and siblings, on the other hand, often enjoyed far wider and more nutritionally sound food intakes. Interestingly, 13 out of the 25 cases, had had 'allergic' reactions to medicinal drugs, especially penicillin or to baby products (see Table 6).

Table 6.

Number of children with:

Diet skew towards "junk" 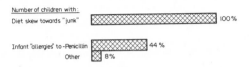 100%

Infant "allergies" to -Penicillin 44 %
Other 8%

Investigation, Treatment and Outcome

Physical examination failed to disclose any significant abnormalities
apart from the signs reported to be associated with the ATF syndrome.

There are, of course, many anecdotal accounts of clinical improvement in
such cases following alteration in diet and of 'impromptu' 'challenges'
resulting in the return of previous symptoms. Such reports *per se* have
little scientific value but, nevertheless, given the inherent safety and
non-invasiveness of the technique, I decided to explore the use of careful but 'uncontrolled' allergic management regimes in the treatment of
some of these cases. Recommendations have included a programme of house
dust mite management combined with carefully supervised elimination diets
involving chemical additives such as flavourings, colourings and preserv-
atives as well as a variety of foods. In addition, some attention has
been paid to other possible 'incitants' such as petrochemical products
and even to the 'out-gassing' from the formaldehyde and phenols contained
in many modern everyday household and school materials.

These treatment strategies have produced several dramatic improvements.
Moreover, relapses, when they have occurred, have always been easily
traced and found to be linked in time to either non-compliance with the
treatment regime or to inadvertent further exposure of the subject to
'incitants'.

Unfortunately, no attempt was made to examine routinely peripheral blood
or to undertake immunopathological investigations in this group of cases.
However, to my surprise, one of the cases was found to have a grossly
abnormal response when an attempt was made to assay his B1 (thiamine)
level. This suggested that he had a severe thiamine deficiency and,
coincidentally, or otherwise, when his diet was supplemented with a substantial daily dose of that vitamin, dramatic improvement in his clinical
state followed within a few days. This chance finding coupled with the
invariable presence of nutritional problems in the 25 children studied
has led me to look at the peripheral blood, immunopathological findings
and at the mineral and vitamin status of similarly affected children.

So far peripheral blood has been examined in ten cases. This has
revealed only a mild eosinophilia in three samples. However, blood was
also taken from these cases for extensive immunopathological screening.
These investigations have included, although not in each case, estimation
of immunoglobulins, of auto-immune antibodies, of C3, C4 aspects of complement cascade, of total immune complexes and IgE specific RAST to house

dust mite and certain foods, as well as Monoclonal antibody studies of
'T' and 'B' lymphocytes.

Although a number of significantly abnormal results have been obtained,
at present these examinations are seen as generally unhelpful in that
they have failed to contribute materially to the understanding of the
clinical situation in any of the children. However, so far, blood samples
for these investigations have been taken whilst the child has been in a
'good' phase. It is quite possible that more useful information would be
obtained from similar investigations carried out on children after
positive 'challenge' or when their disturbances are at their most severe.

Vitamin assays were also carried out on this second group of children,
focussing especially on Vitamins C, B1, B2 and B6. Four out of the ten
children were found to have abnormally low Vitamin C levels - one in
plasma, the others in respect of leucocyte content, whilst there was evidence that at least five out of the ten had some degree of thiamine (B1)
deficiency. Carefully controlled research studies of the vitamin status
of Scottish children are required.

An attempt is also underway to investigate the nutritional status of
these children by examining hair levels of trace elements and of toxic
metals. So far twenty samples of scalp hair, taken from around the nape
of the neck, have been examined by a Commercial Laboratory. Techniques
used are those of atomic absorption spectrometry and computer-assisted
X-ray fluorescence analysis. Abnormal findings have been reported in
every sample studied. However, the significance of these results is far
from clear as it has not yet been possible to compare them with 'matched'
controls. A small research project is now underway.

Discussion

Research by immunologists and clinicians both in the United States and in
the United Kingdom is being increasingly directed towards these and similar problems. The number of single and double blind studies is increasing.
When these have been adequate, clinically as well as scientifically, the
results have been encouragingly supportive of the allergic/sensitivity
hypothesis.

Freed and Carter (1982) has described a 54-year-old male with tachycardia,
'glove and stocking' paraesthesiae, depersonalization, irritability and
depression caused by the ingestion of monosodium glutamate (MSG). Following oral provocation, these symptoms were induced and changes in sensory
nerve conduction were demonstrated together with changes of serum IgA, C3
and C1q complement components. The author felt that the subject's
symptoms were due to an 'allergic' reaction to MSG. This 'flavour
enhancer' is, of course, ubiquitous in the diet of many children.

In other areas of medicine the role of food allergy and of intolerance in
the aetiology of illness is now exciting considerable research interest.
One can point, for example, to the work of Atherton et al., 1978;
Atherton, 1983, on dietary factors in children's eczema and of Minford,
MacDonald and Littlewood, 1982, on food allergy in general paediatrics.

Alun-Jones has made an important contribution to this field with work on
food factors and the irritable bowel syndrome (Alun-Jones *et al.*, 1982).
Hunter *et al.*, (1983) have also recently described a series of 28
patients with Crohn's Disease which, in 20 (71 per cent) of the patients
responded clinically, radiologically and histologically to a diet lacking
certain foods, shown by elimination and challenge procedures, to be
associated with the symptomatology. These patients have remained well
for up to two years. In most, the disease had been severe, some had been
on steroids, nearly a third had had surgical resections and several were
about to undergo operation. This study when published in detail, will
inevitably excite considerable interest in the field of food allergy and
intolerance. Brown *et al.*, (1981) in a double-blind study on food allergy
in polysymptomatic patients produced considerable support for the hypothesis that intolerance to common elements in the diet can be responsible
for the onset of a wide range of symptoms for which objective classification is difficult.

In a careful double-blind study, King (1981) tested the hypothesis that
sublingual exposure to allergens will produce emotional/cognitive symptoms
in allergy patients. The results indicated that allergens may contribute
to psychopathology in some individuals in this way.

McGovern (1980) and McGovern *et al.* (1983) have reported on a study
involving serial immunopharmacologic measurements on 6 patients with food
allergy and chemical sensitivities with associated multi-symptom syndromes
and on normal controls, both prior to and following on, challenge. After
challenge by either the oral or inhalational route with food or chemicals,
there followed a significant, measurable abnormality in some branch of
the immunologic chain associated with meaningful pharmacologic alterations
in the blood. All the patients in the study developed immediate and
delayed symptoms after the provocation challenge.

Levin and colleagues are soon to publish additional support for the
hypothesis that: 'A whole variety of major stress factors, impinging on
an already primed patient, "primed" in the sense of being genetically
predisposed, may give rise to a disease state characterized by a loss or
disorganization of the body's homeostatic mechanisms, a situation created
by the development of immune disregulation'. Moreover, it seems likely
that, at least in some cases, the 'signs and symptoms displayed by these
patients are a result of inflammatory processes occurring in target
organs, including the brain, in response to the presence of either
unacceptably high amounts of immune complexes, or else to delay in the
excretion of such complexes' (A. S. Levin, personal communication,
October 22, 1981).

More than 112 patients have been evaluated, all of whom described the
symptomatology of multiple food and chemical sensitivities. In none of
whom however, had there been evidence of systemic lupus erythematosis,
rheumatoid arthritis, cancer or of severe IgE mediated allergic disorders. These patients have shown significant disturbance of complement
cascade, abnormalities of prostaglandins and significant diminutions in
the absolute numbers of 'T' lymphocyte suppressor cells. Moreover, these
abnormal immunological test parameters have been found to parallel
closely, carefully scored 'clinical' estimations of disease severity.

Removal of harmful antigen influences and other anti-allergy approaches
not only promoted measurable clinical improvement in these cases but was
paralleled by evidence of a return towards normality of the aforesaid
immunological parameters (Levin et al., 1981).

Weiss (1982) reviewed the more important controlled studies of the
Feingold hypothesis which postulates that many children who exhibit disturbed behaviour improve on a diet devoid of several food additives. He
concluded that the hypothesis is in principle correct, adding 'specialists
in child behaviour should be alert to environmental contaminants as one
of the potential contributions to the genesis of disturbed behaviour'.

Tryphonas and Trites (1979) showed a statistically significant association
between the number of allergies and teachers' scores of hyperactivity in
hyperactive children who also had learning disabilities and minimal brain
dysfunction.

Valverde, Vich et al. (1980), investigating 44 patients diagnosed as
suffering from the ATF syndrome, reported on the in vitro response of the
patient's lymphocytes when stimulated by a series of food extracts and
additives. Of the 44 patients studied, 42 produced a positive response.
Moreover, elimination diets prescribed in accordance with the in vitro
results, produced a total remission of the ATF syndrome in 86 per cent of
patients, partial remission in a further 5 per cent and no change in only
9 per cent of the sample.

Finally, there is the exciting work of Egger et al. (1983) on food
allergy and chronic migraine in childhood. They have shown that most of
these children, 66 per cent of whom were atopic, recovered from their
severe migraine when they avoided one or more of a whole variety of
foods. However, not only did they lose their migraine, they also lost
many other associated symptoms including abdominal pain, altered bowel
rhythm and joint pains. A few cases also displayed behaviour difficulties and learning problems and these also improved.

Conclusions

The tragedy of thalidomide, the adverse effects on human sperm of smoking
and the foetal toxicity of alcohol, all point to the importance of
environmental factors. Work on lead intoxication (Bryce-Smith and
Stephens, 1980; Pihl and Parkes, 1977; Needleman et al., 1979) and on
vitamins and neural tube defects (Smithells et al., 1981) are other
examples, as is the recent work on the teratogenic and diabetogenic effect
on future offspring of a diet containing large amounts of smoked food
eaten by prospective parents preconceptually (Helgason and Jonasson,
1981; Helgason et al., 1982). We cannot therefore ignore the role of
environmental factors and the nutritional status of both parents before a
child is conceived and of the mother during pregnancy. Clearly we must
also now look carefully at the effects of environmental factors on the
child himself. Our aim, wherever possible, must be to establish, where
it exists, simple cause and effect.

We have long known that allergic symptoms may be produced or made worse by psychological factors and that allergic symptoms may create an effect upon the psychological state of an allergic individual. It is becoming increasingly clear that allergic exposure *per se* may be directly responsible for both psychological and somatic symptoms, or even for psychological symptoms alone.

Immunosuppression problems are probably much more widespread than we have so far believed. There is growing evidence that cyto-megalo virus infection suppresses certain immune responses in man as well as in animals and other viruses, such as those of measles, influenza, rubella and E.B. mononucleosis virus may also produce immunosuppressive effects in man, and perhaps particularly in children for they after all, are most at risk to the development of these infections. Some drugs may be immunosuppressive in some patients and no-one can deny that children these days live in an increasingly chemically contaminated environment, even as far as the air they breathe, the food they eat and the water they drink, are concerned. However, it is difficult in the United Kingdom to obtain accurate information about the contents of 'instant, convenience and junk foods', especially about the ingredients of sweets, particularly those of the 'penny tray' variety.

We should not therefore ignore the possible role of allergic/immunologic factors in the production of children's emotional, behavioural and cognitive problems. An environmental approach to children with the so-called ATF syndrome is, I believe, likely to be a fruitful area for research.

The science of psycho-neuro-immunology has only just begun (Ader, 1981). I appreciate that the study of allergic and immunologic factors in child and family psychiatry is in its infancy. Nevertheless, I commend this exciting, potentially valuable area as worthy of support and interest. We have, I believe, in this regard begun to open a Pandora's Box.

References

ADER, R. (Ed.) (1981) *Psychoneuroimmunology*. New York, Academic Press.
ALUN-JONES, V., McLAUGHLAN, P., SHORTHOUSE, M., WORKMAN, E. and HUNTER, J. O. (1982) Food intolerance: a major factor in the pathogenesis of the irritable bowel syndrome. *Lancet*, II, 115-117.
ATHERTON, D. J. (1983) Dietary treatment in childhood atopic eczema. In *The Second Fison's Food Allergy Workshop*, pp. 105-108. Oxford, Medicine Publishing Foundation.
ATHERTON, D. J., SEWELL, M., SOOTHILL, J. F., WELLS, R. S. and CHIVERS, C. E. D. (1978) A double-blind cross-over controlled trial of an antigen avoidance diet in atopic eczema. *Lancet*, I, 401-403.
BROWN, M., GIBNEY, M., HUSBAND, P. R. and RADCLIFFE, M. (1981) Food allergy in polysymptomatic patients. *The Practitioner*, 225, 1651-1654.
BRYCE-SMITH, D. and STEPHENS, R. (1980). *Lead or health*. London, Conservation Society.

REPORT OF THE COMMITTEE ON CHILD HEALTH SERVICES (1976) *Fit for the Future* (S. D. M. Court, Chairman). London, H.M.S.O.

EGGER, J., CARTER, C., WILSON, J., TURNER, M. W. and SOOTHILL, J. F. (1983) Controlled trial of diet in migraine. Is migraine food allergy? A double-blind controlled trial of oliogantigenic diet treatment. Paper presented at the Second Fison's Food Allergy Workshop, Harrogate. *Lancet*, 15, 856-869.

FREED, D. K. J. and CARTER, R. (1982) Neuropathy due to monosodium glutamate intolerance. *Annals of Allergy*, 48, 96-97.

HELGASON, T. and JONASSON, M. R. (1981) Evidence for a food additive as a cause of ketosis-prone diabetes. *Lancet*, II, 716-720.

HELGASON, T., EWEN, S. W. B., ROSS, I. S. and STOWERS, J. M. (1982) Diabetes produced in mice by smoked/cured mutton. *Lancet*, II, 1017.

HUNTER, J. O., ALUN-JONES, V., FREEMAN, A. M., SHORTHOUSE, M., WORKMAN, E. and McLAUGHLAN, P. (1983) Food tolerance in gastrointestinal disorders. In *The Second Fison's Food Allergy Workshop*, pp. 69-72. Oxford, Medicine Publishing Foundation.

KING, D. S. (1981) Can allergic exposure provoke psychological symptoms? A double-blind test. *Biological Psychiatry*, 16, 3-19.

KITTLER, F. G. and BALDWIN, D. G. (1970) The role of allergic factors in the child with minimal brain dysfunction. *Annals of Allergy*, 28, 203-206.

LEVIN, A. S., McGOVERN, J. J., MILLER, J. B., LECAM, L. and LAZARONI, J. (1981) Immune complex mediated vascular inflammation in patients with food and chemical allergies (Abstract). *Annals of Allergy*, 47, 138.

McGOVERN, J. J. (Jr.) (1980) Correlation of clinical food allergy symptoms with serial pharmacological and immunological changes in patients plasma. *Annals of Allergy*, 44, 57-58.

McGOVERN, J. J., LAZARONI, J., HICKS, M. F., ADLER, J. C. and CLEARY, P. (1983) Food and chemical sensitivity - clinical and immunologic correlates. *Archives of Otolaryngology*, 109, 292-297.

MINFORD, A. M. B., MACDONALD, A. and LITTLEWOOD, J. M. (1982) Food intolerance and food allergy in children: a review of 68 cases. *Archives of Disease in Childhood*, 57, 742-747.

NEEDLEMAN, H. L., GUNNOE, C., LEVITON, A., REED, R., PERESIE, H., MAHER, C. and BARRETT, P. (1979) Deficit in psychologic and classroom performance of children with elevated dentine lead levels. *New England Journal of Medicine*, 300, 689.

PIHL, R. O. and PARKES, M. (1977) Hair element content in learning disabled children. *Science*, 198, 204.

RAPP, D. J. (1979) *Allergies and the Hyperactive Child*. New York, Sovereign Books.

RAPP, D. J. (1980) Hyperactivity and the tension-fatigue syndrome. In J. W. Gerrard (Ed.), *Food Allergy - New Perspectives*, pp. 186-209). Springfield, Illinois, Charles C. Thomas.

RUTTER, M. and HERSOV, L. (1977) *Child Psychiatry: Modern Approaches*. Oxford, Blackwell Scientific Publications.

RUTTER, M., COX, A., TUPLING, C., BERGER, M. and YULE, W. (1975) Attainment and adjustment in two geographical areas. I. The prevalence of psychiatric disorder. *British Journal of Psychiatry*, 126, 493-509.

RUTTER, M., SHAFFER, D. and SHEPHERD, M. (1975) *A Multi-axial Classification of Child Psychiatric Disorders*. Geneva, World Health Organisation.

RUTTER, M., TIZARD, J. and WHITMORE, K. (Eds.) (1970) *Education, Health and Behaviour*. London, Longmans.

SMITHELLS, R. W., SHEPPARD, S., SCHORAH, C. J., SELLER, M. J., NEVIN, N. C., HARRIS, R., READ, A. P. and FIELDING, D. W. (1981) Apparent prevention of neural tube defects by periconceptual vitamin supplementation. *Archives of Disease in Childhood*, 56, 911-918.

SPEER, F. (1958) The allergic-tension fatigue syndrome in children. *International Archives of Allergy*, 12, 207-214.

SPEER, F. (1970) *Allergy of the Nervous System*. Springfield, Illinois, Charles C. Thomas.

TRYPHONAS, H. and TRITES, R. (1979) Food allergy in children with hyperactivity, learning disabilities and/or minimal brain dysfunction. *Annals of Allergy*, 42, 22-27.

VALVERDE, E., VICH, J. M., GARCIA-CALDERON, J. V. and GARCIA-CALDERON, P. A. (1980) In vitro response of lymphocytes in patients with allergic-tension-fatigue syndrome. *Annals of Allergy*, 45, 185-188.

WEISS, B. (1982) Food additives and environmental chemicals as sources of childhood behaviour disorders. *Journal of the American Academy of Child Psychiatry*, 21, 144-152.

WOLFF, S. (1971) Dimensions and clusters of symptoms in disturbed children. *British Journal of Psychiatry*, 118, 421-427.

CHAPTER 10

Mothers' Perceptions of Handicapped and Normal Children

Carole R. Smith, Laurey J. Selz, Eve Z. Bingham,
Barbara Aschenbrenner, Kendyll Standbury and
P. Herbert Leiderman

*Centre for the Study of Youth Development, Stanford
University, Stanford, U.S.A.*

Under normal conditions the behavioral repertoire of young infants and their parents appear well adapted for the development of harmonious reciprocal interactions (Goldberg, 1977). In contrast, the physically handicapped or preterm infant, who is often less alert and responsive to caregivers and unable to provide clear distress signals, makes demands on the caregiving relationship (Brown and Bakeman, 1979, 1980; Cohen and Beckwith, 1979; DiVitto and Goldberg, 1979; Field, 1979; Kogan and Tyler, 1973). In addition, there may be few positive signs of development (such as social smiles and new motor skills) in the early months; thus parents may need to make many adjustments and may require more time to establish a satisfactory relationship. It is hardly surprising, therefore, that the development of social interactions in this group should follow a different course than that of a normal able-bodied infant.

In fact, the young disabled child may be subjected to a different schedule of socialization pressures (e.g. feeding, toilet-training, language, and cooperation) because he is seen as little more than an infant. As Nancy Busch-Rossnagel (1981) so aptly said, 'Just as society does not expect infants to acquire any social skills, neither does it expect social skills of the handicapped child' (p. 291). If parents do show concern it is in terms of the child's physical well-being, not his cognitive or social development (Richardson, 1976; Shere and Kastenbaum, 1966). Opportunities for exploration and experience with play materials are not likely to be encouraged or recognized as important.

In early studies of development, it was assumed that the problem of a handicapped or preterm infant were confined to the infant alone. More recently, the significance of the caregiving environment as a potent predictor of subsequent development has been explored (Sameroff and Chandler, 1975). Further, since there is little data relating social maldevelopment to deficits in cognitive or social potential, it makes sense to explore the familial environment as a possible source.

Of specific interest is how mothers of handicapped infants differ from mothers of able-bodied infants in their expectations, perceptions, values, and sense of efficacy. Our emphasis on mothers, with the exclusion of

other socializing agents, is defended on the grounds that in the typical
U.S. family, the mother serves as the chief socializer of the infant and
young child, at least through the child's second year. This observation
is even more true for the handicapped child where the mother is usually
the primary caregiver as there are fewer outside resources available.

The specific focus on attitudes, expectations, perceptions, values and
sense of efficacy stems from the notion that what parents think about
their children's capabilities affects the particular childrearing strategies they adopt, which in turn affects their children's developmental
outcomes. The use of parental cognitive processes as a means for interpreting data from complex parent-child interactions has recently been
offered as a more parsimonious method of deriving the meaning of parent-
child exchanges than that of relying solely on direct observation of
behavior (Bell, 1968; Freeberg and Payne, 1967; Hess *et al.*, in preparation; Parke, 1978).

Implied in the work on parental belief systems is the notion of reciprocity - the interplay of mutual influences between parent and child.
Parental belief systems are not closed systems. Parents' own experiences
as children, their cultural heritage, their social and economic status as
well as subsequent experiences as parents, their observations of their
own children and of other children all serve as potential inputs for
beliefs and expectations. The child's own behavior can also provide
feedback in terms of the accuracy of these prior beliefs. As new or dis-
crepant information about the child is acquired and incorporated into the
existing system, the system is modified and becomes more refined.

Often, it is not the child's behavior that shapes parental behavior or
raises parental expectations, but the use of a label. For example, the
descriptive label of 'difficult' has been found to regulate the behavior
of parents such that mothers respond less frequently to the signals of
difficult infants and show less sympathy to their crying than to infants
considered as normal (Donovan, Leavitt, and Balling, 1978; Frodi *et al.*,
1978). Even when initial impressions and labels are shown to be inaccur-
ate, there is a tendency for the impression to persist (Murray and Dolby,
1979). Early perceptions can set into motion a transactional pattern in
which parental expectations evoke or maintain the expected behavior in
the child. This further reinforces the parents' beliefs and justifies
their childrearing behavior. In such instances, the feedback loop does
not allow beliefs to be modified or changed. Instead, parental perceptions of the child become fixed and rigid. The end result is a phenomenon
known as the self-fulfilling prophecy - the child 'becomes' what the
parents expect.

The questions raised in this paper are: (1) Do mothers of physically-
handicapped infants have the same expectations of cognitive, physical and
social growth for their infant as mothers of full-term able-bodied
infants?; (2) Do mothers of physically-handicapped infants differ in
their beliefs about maternal or child-centered control of behavior?; (3)
Do mothers of physically-handicapped infants differ in their sense of
efficacy in helping their child?; (4) Do mothers of handicapped children
have different plans for their child's socialization compared to mothers
of able-bodied children?; (5) Do mothers of handicapped children perceive

the social competence of their children any differently from mothers of able-bodied children?

Method

Sample

To answer these questions we proceeded as follows. Forty-four children between 15 and 21 months of age were recruited from hospital birth records and pediatrician referrals. Twelve were preterm infants of very low birth weight (under 1500 grams), 10 were born with a non-visible physical impairment, 11 were visibly physically impaired at the time of their birth, and 11 were normal full-term controls with no known problems or complications. The non-visible impairments were most commonly respiratory, cardiac, and gastrointestinal problems. The visible disabilities were more diverse with cerebral palsy and various orthopedic problems such as hip dysplasia predominating. Any child who was sensorially impaired or thought to be mentally retarded at the time of admission to the study was not included in the sample.

Upon entry into the study, the children were reclassified into one of five intake groups to more accurately reflect the chronicity and current status of their physical disabilities. Children classified as *multi-handicapped* were visibly impaired and had impairments in all areas of development. Such cases, 7 in all, included children with cerebral palsy, multiple congenital anomalies, and severe heart condition. Children classified as *developmentally delayed* were medically fit but showed considerable delay in areas of psycho-motor and cognitive attentional development. These 6 children were all preterm and had been extremely ill during their first year with related problems. In contrast to the above groups where the deficits were global in nature, the *impaired* group of 7 children included cases with a single disability involving the limbs, such as hip dysplasia or limb deformity. The *repaired* group consisted of children whose disability at birth had been corrected by the time of intake. The 13 children in this category formed a heterogeneous group in terms of initial disability which included pre-maturity, colostomies and cardiac disorders. The fifth group, the *control* group was unchanged from the original birth category.

Twenty-one of the 44 subjects were male. Thirty-one were white, 7 black and 6 either Mexican-American or Asian. Twenty-two were first born. Thirty-five children lived in two parent families which, based on mother's education and father's occupation, were mostly middle class.

Procedures

Forty children and their families of the 44 recruited were followed for one year, though data were not necessarily complete for all 40 cases. The children were visited at home at the beginning, middle and end of the one year study and observed in a laboratory setting

early and late in the study. The home visits included interviews
with mothers regarding their child's past and current health, the
child's developmental progress and accomplishments, and other salient
features of family life that were changed by the birth of their child
or which affected their child in some way. Mother's sense of
efficacy and her future plans for her child also were addressed in
the interviews. In addition to our interviews we used a number of
scales to assess aspects of mother's expectation, perception, values
and childrearing practices.

Results

Mother's expectation of developmental milestones

To assess maternal expectations we drew on the work of Hess *et al*. (1980),
Ambron *et al*. (1977), and a number of researchers in the Department of
Psychiatry at Children's Hospital of Los Angeles (1974). The scale we
constructed was designed to elicit the mother's opinion as to the age she
expected her child and a typical child to accomplish developmental milestones in three domains – cognitive, psychomotor, and social development.
Cognitive items included names objects in a picture book; psychomotor
items included sits without support; and social items included takes
turns. Mothers were asked to record the age they expected their child
and a typical child to achieve the tasks. In order to control for developmental performance, the Denver Developmental Screening Test was given
to independently assess the child's developmental skills in these areas.

Table 1. Maternal expectations of development

Scale (No. of items)	Typical Child (44)	Your Child (44)				
		Control (11)	Repaired (13)	Impaired (7)	Delayed (6)	Multiple (7)
Psycho-motor (7)	1.8 yrs	1.8 yrs	1.7 yrs	1.7 yrs	2.1 yrs	2.8 yrs
Social (9)	2.4	2.2	2.0	2.4	2.6	3.0
Cognitive maturity (10)	3.1	3.1	2.8	3.3	3.7	3.8

Table 1 shows the mean age (in years) of mastery for each of the three
domains that mothers expected of typical and their own children for each
of the five sub-groups. No differences were found for judgments of the

typical child among the sub-groups. With respect to judgments of their
own child, however, there was a clear linear trend over all three developmental domains showing mothers of multi-handicapped and delayed
children to be judged slower in accomplishing developmental milestones
than either the control, repaired or impaired groups. These assessments
were realistic because these groups were found to be behind on the Denver
Developmental Screening Test.

The other interesting finding was the tendency for the mothers of the
repaired handicap group to expect precocious development. This group, as
mentioned above, consisted of children who had physical disabilities or
were preterm at birth, but whose impairments had been corrected by the
time of entry into the study and thus were considered physically normal.
Mothers expected their children to accomplish developmental tasks even
earlier than our group of full-term controls. This anticipation of pre-
cocity cannot be accounted for by the Denver scores as the full-terms
were more developmentally advanced. Nor can it be accounted for by an
increase in home stimulation as the Caldwell HOME inventory shows this
group to score lower than the control group (if these mothers had scored
higher it might indicate that they were more involved in facilitating
precocious development). This suggestive finding is potentially ominous;
unrealistic parental expectations have been implicated in data on child
abuse and neglect, and physically handicapped and premature infants are
over-represented in an abuse/neglect population. If mothers in the
repaired group truly are unrealistic in their expectations of their
children's development then one might well expect to see disharmonious
parent-child relationships.

To assess child rearing attitudes, mothers filled out three developmental
issue scales from the Maternal Attitude Scale (Coher, Weiss and
Grunebaum, 1970) midway through the study. The three scales we selected
dealt with child rearing issues salient to parents of children between
the ages of 12 and 36 months. The issues of interest were self-assertion,
aggression, and independence from mother. The scales assessed the
mother's basis for her child rearing practices - whether this be her own
exercise of control, or the child's developmental needs. Higher scores
indicated mothers favored maternal control, and lower scores, the child's
needs. Table 2 shows the control group to have the lowest scores, indicating that these mothers favored more child-centred practices. The
handicapped group, regardless of the sub-group, had attitudes favoring
maternal control. Differences in maternal education did not account for
these differences. Nor were the differences on the child's verbal or
fine motor behavior sufficient to justify these differences in actual
practice. The implication to be drawn is that mothers of normal children
have a more child-independent orientation compared to mothers of handicapped children. It would appear likely that mothers of handicapped
children are cautious in permitting some independence by their handicapped children. This finding is consistent with those of Kogan and
Tyler (1973) who report greater over-protection by mothers of handicapped
children.

The HOME Inventory (Home Observation for Measurement of the Environment)
(see Elardo, Bradley and Caldwell, 1975) was used to measure the quantity
and quality of support for social, emotional, and cognitive development
within the home. High scores indicated a high degree of home stimulation,
and low scores, little stimulation. Almost half the items could be

C. R. Smith *et al.*

Mother's child-rearing values

Table 2. Home, maternal, and child variables

	Control (10)	Repaired (11)	Impaired (6)	Delayed (7)	Multiple (6)
Maternal control (Cohler scale)	2.6	3.2	3.3	3.3	3.5
Cognitive development (Denver)					
Fine motor (in months)	29.6	26.4	26.9	25.1	9.7
Verbal (in months)	27.5	25.6	22.4	18.1	12.9

answered by simple observation while the remaining half required an
interview probe. The inventory was filled out on the first home visit.

Mothers of handicapped children seem to provide less stimulation to their
children, especially the multi-handicapped and repaired groups as shown
in Table 3. This finding, when combined with possible over-control as

Home stimulation

Table 3. Home, maternal, and child variables

	Control (10)	Repaired (11)	Impaired (6)	Delayed (5)	Multiple (6)
Home stimulation (Caldwell scale)	8.4	7.1	7.7	7.7	7.0

indicated on the Maternal Attitude Scale, suggests that mothers who control their children use less stimulation rather than controlling them
with more stimulation. The net effect of both a more controlled and non-
stimulating home environment would be one of inhibiting a child's cognitive and social development.

Mother's sense of efficacy

Mothers during the interviews were asked as to whether they believed
they could have an impact on their child's cognitive, physical or social
development. The findings in Table 4 indicate the percentage of mothers
who answered these questions affirmatively. Mothers in all sub-groups
thought that they could influence cognitive development more readily
than physical or social development. Mothers in the repaired group

Table 4. Sense of efficacy - from maternal interview

(Percent Responding Affirmatively)

(N)

	Control (10)	Repaired (11)	Impaired (6)	Delayed (5)	Multiple (6)
Cognitive development	100%	73%	83%	83%	86%
Physical development	56%	37%	83%	67%	43%
Social development	100%	60%	83%	67%	43%

thought they could influence their child's cognitive and physical development the least and were exceeded in their pessimism only by the mothers
in the multi-handicapped group for social development. These findings
indicate that mothers place considerable emphasis on the potential for
changing cognitive development, with much less sense of efficacy for
changing the course of physical and social development, two areas surely
capable of being influenced. Apparently mothers of the repaired children
are resigned to the initial label of 'damaged' (presumably on the basis
of an earlier experience with their child) with little modification in
their attitude despite the positive physical outcomes. The reason for
this lack of change is not clear; however it could be due to the lack of
an opportunity to realistically appraise changes when a strong mental set
for disability is created early in the child's development.
The last information on attitudes came from mothers responses to interview
questions regarding what plans they had for their child's future development. Two areas were examined: 1) cognitive and physical skill training;
and 2) peer experience on a formal basis. Seventy-eight percent of the
control mothers indicated that they had plans for their child's cognitive
and physical skill training compared to 18-33 per cent of the mothers of
handicapped children (see Table 5). The question about peer experience
revealed that delayed and multi-handicapped groups were less likely to
plan for these activities than either the control, repaired or impaired
groups. A lack of planfulness suggests a feeling of helplessness or
pessimism about the child, a feeling not necessarily warranted by the
developmental facts or availability of services in the community to aid
in the success of such plans.

The results to this point indicate that mothers of physically-handicapped
children are likely to have attitudes that might restrict the experience
of their children, that the repaired group tends to have unrealistic
expectations for development, that mothers of handicapped children have a
lower sense of efficacy and have fewer plans for physical and cognitive
training or social experiences for their children. We now turn to a set
of findings, perhaps more positive, that deal with a mother's assessment
of her child's social competence.

Mother's plans for future activities

Table 5. Plans for future training and experience

	(Percent Responding Affirmatively)				
	Control (10)	Repaired (11)	Impaired (6)	Delayed (5)	Multiple (6)
Cognitive and physical skills	78%	18%	16%	33%	28%
Peer experience	100%	100%	100%	67%	14%

Mother's perceived social competence

For the purpose of assessing social competence, we developed a scale, drawing on the work of Baumrind (1973), Bronson (1974), White *et al.* (1977), and Wald *et al.* (1983), to measure the social competence of young children. The primary focus of our scale, was to identify children and mothers who might be at greater risk for social maldevelopment, and our chief hope was that it might be utilized by clinicians and researchers to assess social competence of children through the experience of mothers.

This instrument defines social competence as interpersonal resourcefulness, social sensitivity, effectiveness, and normative adherence. Mothers of normal children, prematures and handicapped infants completed this instrument using a five-point scale, from "not at all" to "most of the time." From an initial 64 items, we derived 26 items which have the psychological dimensions of well socialized to adults, social initiation and participation with peers.

We found that the assessment by mothers of full-term and handicapped children were in good agreement with the behavior observations made in the laboratory. The particular laboratory session involved a 15-minute free play session of the study child (handicapped and control) with an able-bodied peer. Observations were coded by independent observers using a 10-second observe/10-second record sequence. Interobserver reliability was judged to be 0.87. These findings suggest that the mothers of handicapped children who participated in our study had the potential for realistic appraisal of their child's social competence, especially when made aware of the child's social behavior through the focus of the research.

The substantive findings which we have obtained with this instrument are also of interest, although we proceed cautiously as our data come from a study with a relatively small sample. As seen in Table 6, mothers of handicapped young children rate the social competency of their children lower than mothers of full-terms, the lowest being the multi-handicapped group. Even though children are quite young (30 months of age), social

deficiencies are judged by mothers and confirmed in the laboratory are
already apparent.

Table 6. <u>Maternal assessment of infant's social competence</u>
<u>when aged 30 months</u>

(Mean Score)

(N)

←——————————— Study Intake Category ———————————→

Control (10)	Repaired (11)	Impaired (6)	Delayed (5)	Multiple (6)
82.0	73.0	72.7	74.2	65.8

The cycle of lowered expectations by some mothers and actual lowered
social competence of the children may in turn lead to a lower sense of
efficacy. Mothers' attempts to cope with a higher degree of control only
serve to exacerbate the negative process. The cycle may well be underway
for even lower social competence. Two case vignettes may serve to illustrate these major points; one is for a repaired case where there is continued concern by mother and the other is a mother of a multi-handicapped
child who is coping well with the child's physical disability.

Case Studies

Case I, Intake category: repaired

'A' is the second child (first daughter) born to a 30-year-old woman
in an intact family where both parents are white, college educated.
Mother works 2 days a week as a health professional. Father has a
professional position. She felt guilty when she left the baby at age
5 months to go back to work but needed to and wanted to work.

The pregnancy was planned and uneventful - the delivery was
'beautiful' and both parents cried with happiness on learning that
the baby was a girl. Shortly after birth the infant was diagnosed as
having possible hip dysplasia. This was treated with triple diapering
and then with a pelvic harness until the baby was one year old - at
that time she was walking and the doctors 'felt everything would grow
in place'.

On learning of the baby's hip problem the mother reported, 'I was
beyond myself ... I felt bad, really felt terrible - at first angry
at myself but then okay except for extreme nervousness ... I worried
that she might not walk or dance ... and do all the things that girls
do ...'. Working as a health professional generated a lot of support
from her co-workers but also caused her to imagine the worst possible
problems for the child.

Except for putting on the harness which soon resulted in a screaming,
kicking battle, mother described 'A' as a very easy, good natured
baby. There were some digestive upsets and sleep disturbances on
account of the harness and the mother was very disappointed not to be
able to dress up the baby in girlish clothes until she was 1-year-old.

Except for the initial hip problem, the child's health was reported
to be excellent. 'A' is observed to be a highly verbal, competent,
very well coordinated little girl. However, throughout the period of
research observation from 19 months until she was 35 months, the
mother expressed concern that residual problems may surface later on,
and she was especially concerned that when she was at work the father
may not have kept the baby in the harness for the required length of
time because it was such a 'fighting battle'. Further concerns were
the many X-rays necessary to assess orthopedic status might cause
later sterility. She admitted that recently she is no longer as concerned about the hip problem but 'is still always in the back of my
mind'.

The father reports the hip dysplasia was a 'hip case' to my wife, but
aside from the temporary harness he regarded everything as normal.
He did express some concern over discipline - namely the child's
extended temper tantrums over routine matters.

At the time of the final interview the little girl was seen as excep-
tionally independent and stubborn with tantrums lasting up to an hour
leaving everyone in the family exhausted and frustrated and inter-
fering with some of the family outings. While the mother feels that
she has been able to influence the child's physical development, she
feels quite ineffectual in the psychosocial area. Her feelings are
aptly expressed in 'when she makes up her mind and she wants to do
it - no reasoning with her - period!'

Case II, Intake category: multi-handicapped

'B' is the third son born to a 31-year-old woman in an intact family
of middle class background. Father has a salaried position. Mother
remains at home taking care of her family.

'B' was born 2½ months prematurely and was separated from his mother
immediately after birth. During the next few days 'M' felt reluctant
to hold or become close to him for fear that he wouldn't live.
Further, she noticed even before touching him that he felt 'wrong and
stiff'. At 10 months 'B' was diagnosed as cerebral palsied.

After 10 weeks of hospitalization 'B' came home. Care was difficult
with feelings of guilt and worry that 'something was wrong'. At one
year, 'B' began to have seizures; nonetheless, in terms of daily
care, he was now easygoing, and 'M' reported, 'I liked having him
with me'.

Partly as a way to cope with her own feelings of uncertainty and
worry, and partly because of her extremely strong belief in the child,
'M' took an active role in 'B's' development and therapy. Almost

immediately after diagnosis she sought information and support
groups. 'B' began to attend a therapeutic pre-school daily, where
'M' volunteered one day a week. Physical and cognitive exercises
continue at home. 'M' expressed gratitude for the small social
strides 'B' made as a result of the group setting.

Over the course of the research, mother focused upon the child's
'curiosity, drive to succeed, *will to live*' as his strongest qualities. She expressed pleasure with his cognitive development, though
her main concern was in the area of communicative/functional skills
such as walking and speech. She felt a deepening emotional relationship with 'B'. 'He doesn't turn to me just for his physical needs
anymore'.

The family was seen as basically close and mutually supportive, even
with the inevitable stresses of 'B's' medical and physical problems.
The middle brother is quite nurturing and protective of 'B'. The
older brother presented several problems at first, with expressed
fears of becoming like 'B', as well as embarrassment around his
friends. But during the year he discovered some new and more satisfying ways of relating to 'B' and has become more understanding of
the families concerns. 'M' feels quite close to all three children,
but wonders if she might be making too many maturity demands on her
older son because of the extra nurturance she must give 'B'.

'B's' father is somewhat less involved with him, though with growing
acceptance of 'B' 'for what he is'. He reported worries about future
problems with his son.

There was considerable progress in 'B' over the course of the research
year. At the first contact he cried insistently and was fairly
oblivious to all except his mother. By the end of the year, he
became progressively more alert, physically and socially responsive
and less fearful.

'M's' philosophy is best described by a poster in 'B's' room: 'To
dream of the person you want to be is to waste the person you are'.
She says she attempts to live this attitude every day, and believes
she can be most helpful to 'B' by 'not spoiling him and not being
sorry for him or ourselves'.

Conclusion

In summary, the following conclusions seem likely to be warranted. They
are offered tentatively, however, because of the small sample size and an
absence of replication on a larger, more diversified sample.

Mothers of physically-handicapped children have a good sense of the
developmental milestones of the typical child and do not differ from
mothers of normal children. Mothers of children who have been repaired
have developmental timetables which exceed those of other handicapped and
full-term normals. Mothers of physically-handicapped children expect
their infants to be behind in all three areas of psychological development

Mothers of physically-handicapped children report more mother-determined child rearing practices compared with more child-determined practices for mothers of full-terms. Also, the mothers of physically-handicapped children provide somewhat less stimulating home environments when compared to the control group mothers.

Mothers of physically-handicapped children reported a relatively high sense of efficacy for cognitive development but lower levels of efficacy for physical and social development. The mothers of the repaired handicapped, once again, differed from the rest of the groups in reporting the lowest sense of efficacy.

The mothers' plans for cognitive and physical help for their children were lower for the handicapped children compared to full-terms, and plans for peer experience were fewer for the delayed and multi-handicapped groups. The latter difference was quite likely due to the effect of stigma associate with these more severe disabilities.

The findings of this study present another interesting observation on how mothers have assimilated facts of child development. The emphasis mothers put on cognitive development and the relative de-emphasis on physical and social development suggests the need for further education for mothers in these areas of child development. (Richardson, and Shere and Kastenbaum made this same point 20 years ago.) This is especially poignant considering the child rearing attitudes espoused by mothers of handicapped children of greater maternal control relative to that of the child. Along with a diminished sense of efficacy and planfulness of the child's development, the potential neglect of social development of these children becomes obvious. Nonetheless, the latent abilities are quite evident in that these mothers can learn to accurately evaluate their children's social competence as judged by the independent observations in the laboratory. Thus, it would appear that educational endeavors which emphasize social development might have some possibility of success.

Finally, the mothers of physically-handicapped children are quite capable after some exposure to researchers or clinicians to make realistic assessments of their child's social competence. Social competence for all handicapped children by mother's assessment is lower than for able-bodied children, with the lowest being assessments for the multi-handicapped child. The fact that physically-handicapped children were noticeably different from able-bodied children in terms of their social skills at 30 months of age suggests that mother's attitudes and child-rearing practices as well as the possible stigmatizing effects of physical handicap may severely restrict the child's social development. It would therefore seem advantageous for mothers and practitioners to attend to social development issues explicitly in the therapy of these young children.

Acknowledgments

This study was aided by Social and Behavioral Science Research Grant No. 12-30 from March of Dimes Birth Defects Foundation, by the Center for the Study of Youth Development, Stanford University, and by a gift from Mr. Norman Stone. We wish especially to thank the parents and children of the Bing Nursery School. We would also like to acknowledge the support of Drs. David Baum, Eugene Bleck, Luigi Luzzatti, and Stephen Shochat along with Ms. Rose Grobstein and Natalie Malachowski of the Surgery and Pediatric Departments, Stanford University Medical Center, Stanford, California, Dr. Hicks Williams of Kaiser-Permanente Medical Center, Santa Clara, California, as well as the cooperation of the Children's Health Council, Palo Alto, California, Palo Alto Medical Clinic, Palo Alto, California, and Santa Clara Valley Medical Center, San Jose, California.

References

AMBRON, S. R., EVERSON, M. and McNICHOLS, J. (1977) Attachment and compliance of two year olds. Paper presented at the Bi-Annual Meeting of the Society for Research in Child Development.

BAUMRIND, D. (1973) The development of instrumental competence through socialization. In A. D. Pick (Ed.), *Minnesota Symposium on Child Psychology* (Vol. 7). Minneapolis, University of Minnesota Press.

BELL, R. Q. (1968) A reinterpretation of the direction of effects in studies of socialization. *Psychological Review*, 75, 81-95.

BRONSON, W. C. (1974) Mother-toddler interaction: A perspective on studying the development of competence. *Merrill-Palmer Quarterly*, 20, 275-301.

BROWN, J. V. and BAKEMAN, R. (1979) Relationships of human mothers with their infants during the first year of life. In R. W. Bell and W. P. Smotherman (Eds.), *Maternal Influences and Early Behavior*. Holliswood, New York, Spectrum.

BUSCH-ROSSNAGEL, N. A. (1981) Where is the handicap in disability?: The contextual impact of physical disability. In R. M. Lerner and N. A. Busch-Rossnagel (Eds.), *Individuals as Producers of their Development: A Life-span Perspective*. New York, Academic Press.

COHEN, S. E. and BECKWITH, L. (1979) Preterm infant interaction with the caregiver in the first year of life and competence at age two. *Child Development*, 50, 767-776.

COHLER, B., WEISS, J. and GRUNEBAUM, H. (1970) Child-care attitudes and emotional disturbance among mothers of young children. *Genetic Psychology Monographs*, 82, 3-47.

DiVITTO, B. and GOLDBERG, S. (1979) The effects of newborn medical status on early parent-infant interaction. In T. Field, A. Sostek, S. Goldberg and H. H. Shuman (Eds.), *Infants Born at Risk*. Jamaica, New York, Spectrum.

DONOVAN, W. L., LEAVITT, L. A. and BALLING, J. D. (1978) Maternal physiological responses to infant signals. *Psychophysiology*, 15, 68-74.

ELARDO, R., BRADLEY, R. and CALDWELL, B. M. (1975) The relationship of infants' home environment to mental test performance from six to thirty-six months: A longitudinal analysis. *Child Development*, 46, 71-76.

FAMILY DEVELOPMENT PROJECT OF CHILDREN'S HOSPITAL OF LOS ANGELES, DEPART-
MENT OF PSYCHIATRY (1974)   Parental expectations questionnaire.
Los Angeles.
FIELD, T. (1979)   Interaction patterns of preterm and term infants. In
T. Field, A. Sostek, S. Goldberg and H. H. Shuman (Eds.), *Infants
Born at Risk*. Jamaica, New York, Spectrum.
FREEBERG, N. E. and PAYNE, D. T. (1967)   Parental influence on cognitive
development in early childhood: A review. *Child Development*, 38,
65-87.
FRODI, A. M., LAMB, M. E., LEAVITT, L. A. and DONOVAN, W. L. (1978)
Fathers' and mothers' responses to infant smiles and cries. *Infant
Behavior*, 1, 187-198.
GOLDBERG, S. (1977)   Social competence in infancy: A model of parent-
infant interaction. *Merrill-Palmer Quarterly*, 23, 163-177.
HESS, R. D., KASHIWAGI, K., AZUMA, H., PRICE, G. G. and DICKSON, W. P.
(in preparation)   Maternal expectations for early mastery of develop-
mental tasks and cognitive and social competence of pre-school
children in Japan and the United States.
KOGAN, K. L. and TYLER, N. (1973)   Mother-child interaction in young
physically-handicapped children. *American Journal of Mental
Deficiency*, 77, 492-497.
MURRAY, A. D. and DOLBY, R. M. (1979, August)   Effects of obstetric medi-
cation on the newborn. Paper presented at the annual meeting of the
Australian Psychological Society, Hobart, Tasmania.
PARKE, R. D. (1978)   Parent-infant interaction: Progress, paradigms, and
problems. In G. P. Sackett (Ed.), *Observing Behavior: Theory and
Applications in Mental Retardation* (Vol. 1, pp. 67-93). Baltimore,
Maryland, University Park Press.
RICHARDSON, S. A. (1976)   Attitudes and behavior toward the physically-
handicapped. *Birth Defects*, 12, 15-34.
SAMEROFF, A. J. and CHANDLER, M. J. (1975)   Reproductive risk and the
continuum of caretaking causality. In F. D. Horowitz (Ed.), *Review of
Child Development Research* (Vol. 4, pp. 52-98). Chicago, University
of Chicago Press.
SHERE, E. and KASTENBAUM, R. (1966)   Mother-child interaction in cerebral
palsy: Environmental and psychological obstacles to cognitive develop-
ment. *Genetic Psychology Monographs*, 73, 255-335.
WALD, M. S., CARLSMITH, J. M., LEIDERMAN, P. H. and SMITH, C. R. (1983)
Intervention to protect abused and neglected children. In A. D. Pick
(Ed.), *Minnesota Symposium on Child Psychology*. Minneapolis, Univer-
sity of Minnesota Press.
WHITE, B., KABAN, B., SHAPERO, B. and ATTNEUCCI, J. (1977)   Competence
and experience. In F. C. Uzgiris and E. F. Weitzman (Eds.), *The
Structuring of Experience*. New York, Plenum Press.

CHAPTER 11

The Diagnosis and Treatment of Depressive Sub-types in Children

Brian McConville and Quentin Rae-Grant

Department of Psychiatry, Queen's University, Kingston,
Canada
and
Department of Psychiatry, University of Toronto, Toronto,
Canada

The frequency both of depressive symptoms, and of full depressive illnesses in childhood is now fairly clearly established. Kashani (Kashani, 1982; Kashani et al., 1981a) has suggested a prevalence of 1.9 per cent depressive illnesses in a randomly selected group of children in the general population, and similar figures are suggested in a longitudinal study of children followed in New Zealand (J. Kashani and S. Clarkson, personal communication, 1982). Albert and Beck (1975) reported 33 per cent depressive symptoms in 63 children in the classroom setting. Children studied under conditions of greater stress had a higher rate of depression. Petti (1978) found 59 per cent of children showing depression in a psychiatric inpatient group, while McConville, Boag and Purohit (1973) found 53 per cent of a similar group as showing severe depressive symptoms; of these 6 per cent warranted a full diagnosis of depression. In a combined group of psychiatric outpatients and inpatients, Carlson and Cantwell (1979) made the diagnosis of affective disorder in 27 per cent of 102 cases, and Kashani, Venzke and Millar (1981) found that 23 per cent of children admitted to a hospital for orthopaedic procedures had evidence of depression, as diagnosed by DSM-III criteria.

At this time, the criteria for diagnosing depressive illnesses are also more firmly established. Earlier studies (Carlson and Cantwell, 1982; Kashani, Barbero and Bolander, 1981; Kashani et al., 1981b; Petti, 1978; Weinberg et al., 1973) used a wide variety of methods for establishing depression in children, but more recently, at least in North America, there has been increasing use of the DSM-III criteria, using the same phenomena for childhood depression as for adults. Some authors (Poznanski et al., 1982; Robbins et al., 1982) have used the R.D.C. criteria for depression (Spitzer, Endicott and Robins, 1977), which strongly resemble those used in the DSM-III (American Psychiatric Association, 1980). There is still some use of the Weinberg criteria (Carlson and Cantwell, 1982; Petti, 1978), although this classification is less restrictive than the DSM-III or R.D.C. criteria. Quantification of change in depressive symptoms is possible by the use of such instruments as the Kiddie-Sads-P (Piug-Antich et al., 1980), the Children's Depression Rating Scale as designed by Poznanski (Poznanski, Cook and Carroll, 1979) or the M.S.L. questionnaire designed from the DSM-III criteria for melancholia, major depressive episode and dysthymic disorders (McConville, Swanson and Levine, 1982).

There is also great interest in biological markers, at least for the more severe childhood depressive disorders. Puig-Antich (1982) has recently reviewed such newer endocrine correlates as growth hormone hyporespons-ivity to insulin-induced hypoglycemia, and cortisol hypersecretion in prepubertal depression. Poznanski et al. (1982) have reported on the usefulness of the Dexamethasone Suppression Test to help diagnose children showing symptoms consistent with endogenous depression, using the R.D.C. criteria. Polysomnographic correlates have so far been negative, as Puig-Antich (1980) has indicated, and we have recently con-firmed (Young et al., 1982).

Another area of research is the response of depressed children to anti-depressant medication. Here Puig-Antich and his co-workers (Puig-Antich et al., 1978; Puig-Antich et al., 1979) have shown that imipramine admin-istered in doses of up to 5.0 mg/kg/day with current safety features does not show a response better than that found by placebo. However, when the group receiving placebo is divided into those with plasma levels above and below 155 ng/ml, the response with the high plasma level is 100 per cent, while in the low level sub-group it is only 33 per cent. There is a six-fold interindividual difference in plasma levels between children receiving comparable doses of imipramine, as Weller et al. have recently shown (Weller et al., 1982). Hence determination of plasma levels of imipramine is crucial in determining the likelihood of drug effects.

Although this recent work has greatly clarified aspects of childhood depression, it tends to assume that depressive illness in childhood is a fixed clinical entity, and focuses on the more severe forms of childhood depression, tending to disregard the more prevalent dysthymic disorders, or adjustment disorders with depressive mood. But there are clear reasons for considering childhood depression in a spectrum of severity, and also from a developmental perspective. Philips and Friedlander (1982) have recently reviewed some of the conceptual differences implied in regarding childhood depression from a developmental viewpoint rather than from the assumption of similarity to the adult model. Poznanski (1982a, b) in two recent papers has also stressed the differences in some of the phenomenology of childhood versus adult depressions. For example, depressed affect can be inferred from a child's unhappy facies, with downcast eyes and sagging lips evident, and with fleeting smiles dis-appearing rapidly. However, the child's ability to perceive his own depression is often limited. In contrast, anhedonia in a child is often striking, since having fun is so much of the child's life. Morbid ideation is often present, and does not necessarily co-exist with suicidal thoughts. Poznanski points out that the idea of suicide is well known to children, so that questions about this can be asked even with young children.

Low self-esteem is particularly important, and guilt is often present but needs to be asked for specifically, and often from other informants. Social withdrawal is frequent, and poor peer relationships occur in many conditions. Impairment of school work, hypoactivity and complaints of fatigue are also frequently seen, and contrary to the original observations of Cytryn and McKnew (1974) fantasy material is frequently reduced. On the other hand, sleep disturbance is usually related to initial phases, and less commonly found in middle or terminal phases of sleep than in adults. Weight loss is quite common, and needs to be asked for carefully.

These observations suggest some similarities with the adult phenomena shown in the more severe depressions, but there are also clear differences in the nature and expressivity of symptoms in children, which make uncritical cross-comparisons with adult depression unwise. There is a clear need for careful clinical studies of depressed children of varying ages to establish the alterations in phenomenology for different groups of children. For example, Glasberg and Aboud (1982) found that younger children denied sad experiences more than older children, and were less likely to see sadness as part of their emotional disposition. We have found similar differences in a group of children after a common severe loss (McConville, Boag and Purohit, 1972); younger children showed more egocentric comments, regression, denial, animistic fantasies about the persons who had died, and simple restitutive fantasies. Older children showed more concern for others, as part of a more complex view of the world. These results strongly suggest age and stage changes in depressive response in children, and both Bemporad (1982) and Kazdin (1981) in reviewing childhood depression, suggest the need for study from a developmental perspective.

Bemporad remarks on clear differences between the phenomenology of depression as seen in infancy and early childhood, compared to those seen in middle and late childhood, which in turn are different from symptoms seen in adolescence. His view of the symptoms and causes of depression at various stages of development are as shown in Table 1, which is reproduced from his recent paper. (Bemporad, 1982).

Essentially, infants show a sequence of withdrawal after crying and protest, due to loss of stimulation and security, and with consequent deprivation. In early childhood, children show inhibition and clinging behaviour following disapproval by parents, with inhibition of the emerging sense of will. By middle childhood, sadness automatically follows rejection by parents and loss of gratifying activities, and the unsustained crying is directly related to frustrating or depriving situations. In contrast, late childhood depression is accompanied by low self esteem arising from a cognitive component or negative deductions about circumstances. By adolescence there is an exaggerated urgency about depressive symptoms; symptoms are accentuated by cognitive distortions about the finality of events, with guilt about consequences, and with inability to meet long-term goals and ideals. These observations are consistent with our findings in 75 inpatient children showing severe depressive symptoms in a psychiatric unit (McConville *et al.*, 1973). Fifteen verbally expressed depressive themes were observed most frequently, and these fell into three groups. Five items related to expressed sadness, helplessness, loneliness, loss and a general feeling of being bad; these were the affectual depression sub-group (D-1) (see Table 2). The second group of five items related to negative self-esteem, (D-2) with expressed concerns of being no-good or punk, of being unable to help or do things for others, and of being unliked, along with long-term expectations of being used or exploited, and an estimate that the situation would not change (see Table 3).

Table 2. Affectual depression

1. 'I feel sad/I cry'. (sadness, crying).

2. 'Someone must help me/take care of me or no one will'. (helplessness-hopelessness).

3. 'I feel lonely/empty inside'. (withdrawal, inner loss).

4. 'I have lost people/others whom I need to care for me/look after me'. (separation, nurturance concerns).

5. 'I must have been bad in some (unspecified) way/it must have been something I did'. (non-specific, unfocused guilt).

Table 3. Negative self-esteem depression

6. 'I feel that I am no good inside/I never will be any good (to myself)/I am mean, stupid, punk'. (self estimate).

7. 'I am no help to others/can't do things for others/have nothing to give others'. (estimate of worth to others).

8. 'No one likes/wants to like me for myself'. (assumption regarding others' estimate).

9. 'People will use me/take advantage of me/and be unfair to me'. (assumption regarding others' actions).

10. 'I will (probably) always be treated this way, I should accept it/things will always be this way'. (assumption of continuity).

A third group included feelings of being wicked, hated and justly punished, with wishes to kill oneself, or to be dead, associated with restitutive fantasies. These constituted the guilt depression sub-type (D-3) (see Table 4).

Table 4. Guilt depression

11. 'I am a bad (sinful) wicked person/others hate/must hate me'. (explicit guilt).

12. 'I justly deserve to be treated this way'. (punitive self estimate).

13. 'I should be/wish to be dead. (passive self destruction).

14. 'I should/wish to kill myself. (active self destruction).

15. 'I want to be with the dead person/make up to him by hurting myself'. (restitution).

Table 1. Symptoms and causes of depression at various stages of development

Developmental Stage	Symptoms	Major Psychodynamics	Type of Dysphoria	Loevinger Ego Developmental Stages*
Infancy	Withdrawal after crying and protest	Loss of stimulation, security, and well-being supplied by the mother	Deprivation of needed stimulation	Presocial, symbiotic
Early childhood	Inhibition, clinging behaviour	Disapproval by parents	Inhibition of gratification of emerging sense of will	Impulsive, self-protective fear of being caught, externalizing blame, opportunistic
Middle childhood	Sadness as automatically responsive to the immediate situation	Rejection by parents, loss of gratifying activities (i.e. chronic illness)	Sadness, unsustained crying directly related to frustrating or depriving situation	Conformist: conformity to external rules; shame and guilt for breaking rules; superficial niceness
Late childhood	Depression with low self-esteem	Unable to meet parental ideal, unable to sustain threat to parental relationship	Depression with a cognitive component, affect resulting from deduction about circumstances	Conscientious: conformist; differentiation of norms and goals; awareness of self in relation to group; helping
Adolescence	Depression with exaggerated urgency, time distortion, and impulsivity	Unable to fulfill internalized parental ideal, inability to separate from family	Accentuation of depression by cognitive distortions about the finality of events	Conscientious: self-evaluated standards; guilt for consequences; long-term goals and ideals

*Adapted from Loevinger (1976)

Each item was noted in terms of frequency and intensity of reference in the first six weeks of the assessment period, and two child psychiatrists also rated the child on a structured interview, with adequate reliability in two independent settings. It was found that affectual (D-1) items were significantly more common than negative self-esteem items in younger (age 6-8) children, while negative self-esteem items became more common than affectual at age 8-12 and became steadily more common with increasing age. The guilt (D-3) items began from age 10 and always followed extreme traumatic events such as the loss of one's brother by sudden death. The three sub-groups were combined to give a total depression score, which also increased with age. Hence the different sub-types were not independent of each other, but represent the interplay of affectual and cognitive factors in children at different ages.

Recent traumatic loss preceded the guilt depressions but were uncommon in the group overall, suggesting that acute losses were usually well handled. In a further study of this group, 73 inpatients with moderate to severe depression scores were identified. Boys were more common than girls, but the ratio was similar to that seen for other disorders within the unit. Seventy per cent of the children had significant bereavement or loss of parents or siblings, and usually such losses had occurred cumulatively over time. Fifty-one per cent of the group had suffered significant rejection by their parents or parent figures over the previous three years, and significant parental depression had occurred in 63 per cent of parents, with the majority occurring in mothers (McConville, 1982).

The overall multidisciplinary therapy approaches for this group were complex, but resemble those described by Petti *et al.* (1980) in their evaluation and multimodality treatment of a depressed pre-pubertal girl.

Individual psychotherapy showed differences between the clinical sub-types, largely because of the way in which the child related to the therapist. In younger children with predominantly affectual depressions, the initial relationship was intense and based on an early parent/child model stressing body contact, 'being with' and structured nurturance. Initially the child's expressed sadness and wishes to die decreased, and he became more spontaneously affectionate. But in the middle phase of therapy themes of being harmed or killed by the therapist or by frightening fantasy figures often emerged. In a final phase the child was able to accept affection, with increased self-esteem and decreased demandingness.

In contrast, older children with predominantly negative self-esteem often had a basic mistrust of the therapist, and goals had to be set concretely in terms of what it was worth to the child to form relationships. Long-term arrangements for nurturance needed to be spelled out clearly and the child began slowly to trust, with frequent periods of angry rejection where he maintained that he did not need or wish for help. Later more clinging behaviour often occurred, with some internalization of other's standards and associated guilt for rejecting behaviour.

The uncommon predominantly guilt depressions had a high risk of suicide, often with related auditory hallucinations. The therapist was initially supportive but also limit setting towards the self-destructive impulses, and with later reality oriented planning. Those with mixed affectual and negative self-esteem depressions showed combinations of the first two responses to therapy.

In pharmacotherapy for the depressed children, the guilt depression sub-type responded promptly to use of tricyclic antidepressants, but the other sub-types responded less clearly. It would seem that responses to antidepressants may vary with severity and sub-type of the depressive disorder, consistent with the studies of Lucas, Locket and Grimm (1965), Weinberg *et al.* (1973), Puig-Antich *et al.* (1978) and Petti *et al.* (1980) on children with pre-pubertal major depressive disorders.

The overall results in our study were that the guilt depressions responded best to drug and psychotherapy treatment, judged by changes in the total depression scores at discharge and follow-up, and by time spent in treatment. Affectual depressions and the mixed D-1 and D-2 sub-type depressions responded less well, and the negative self-esteem depressions responded worst on the above criteria. All differences were significant.

Current studies are underway to indicate how these depressive items fit into more general classifications of depression while retaining questions regarding differences in age, sex and prior experience as criteria to be investigated in childhood depression.

In summary, our studies have suggested that there may be a progression of responses, especially in younger children, from early affectual responses involving sadness, grief and a need for nurturing persons into a colder and non-accepting pattern of depressive responses characterized by self-hatred, and by change in the child's cognitive perception. These observations are consistent with those postulated by Bemporad (1982), Kazdin (1981) and others, and suggest the presence of depressive sub-types whose diagnosis is made by presence or absence of particular items, and where the predominance of a sub-type or sub-types has serious implications both for treatment and for prognosis. In particular, long-term negative self-esteem depressions seem to have a poor outcome, and Lewis and Lewis (1979) recently suggested, following Mandell (1976), that sustained monoamine transmitter depletion in children might follow chronic deprivation experiences. Perhaps these ideas could inter-relate with our observations.

Children have considerable plasticity to stress, especially in the context of a supportive family and social matrix. But prolonged deprivation and loss in a non-caring environment, and especially where parenting figures are diffuse, negative or unknown, seems to provide for long-term deleterious effects. Those with frank major affective disorders may respond well to pharmacotherapy. But many depressed children do not clearly fit into this category, and may have rather debilitating and long-term depressive symptoms or minor affective disorders. Especially for children with chronic negative self-esteem, the results of either drug therapy or psychotherapy often seem to be poor, and the possibility of uncared for children being unable to care for others in due course is high. There is therefore a strong need for early intervention in children showing depressive symptoms, with caring therapists allowing for mourning and restructuring before more permanent changes occur.

References

ALBERT, N. and BECK, A. (1975) Incidence of depression in early adolescence: a preliminary study. *Journal of Youth and Adolescence*, 4, 301-307.

AMERICAN PSYCHIATRIC ASSOCIATION (1980) *Diagnostic and Statistical Manual of Mental Disorders*. (3rd edition). Washington, D.C., A.P.A.

BEMPORAD, J. (1982) Childhood depression from a developmental perspective. In L. Grinspoon (Ed.), *Psychiatry 1982, Annual Review* (pp. 272-281). Washington, D.C., American Psychiatric Press.

CARLSON, G. and CANTWELL, D. (1979) A survey of depressive symptoms in a child and adolescent psychiatric population. *Journal of the American Academy of Child Psychiatry*, 18, 587-599.

CARLSON, G. and CANTWELL, D. (1982) Diagnosis of childhood depression: a comparison of the Weinberg and DSM.III criteria. *Journal of the American Academy of Child Psychiatry*, 21, 247-250.

CYTRYN, L. and McKNEW, D. (1974) Factors influencing the changing clinical impression of the depressive process in children. *American Journal of Psychiatry*, 131, 879-881.

GLASBERG, R. and ABOUD, F. (1982) Keeping one's distance from sadness: children's self-report of emotional experience. *Developmental Psychology*, 18, 287-293.

KASHANI, J. (1982) Epidemiology of childhood depression. In L. Grinspoon (Ed.), *Psychiatry 1982, Annual Review* (pp. 281-288). Washington, D.C., American Psychiatric Press.

KASHANI, J., BARBERA, G. and BOLANDER, F. (1981a) Depression in hospitalized paediatric patients. *Journal of the American Academy of Child Psychiatry*, 20, 123-134.

KASHANI, J., HUSAIN, A., SHEKINS, W., HODGES, K., CYTRYN, L. and McKNEW, D. (1981b) Current perspectives on childhood depression: an overview. *American Journal of Psychiatry*, 138, 143-153.

KASHANI, J., VENZKE, R. and MILLAR, E. (1981) Depression in children admitted to hospital for orthopaedic procedures. *British Journal of Psychiatry*, 138, 21-25.

KAZDIN, E. (1981) Assessment techniques for child depression. *Journal of the American Academy of Child Psychiatry*, 20, 358-375.

LEWIS, M and LEWIS, D. (1979) A psychobiological view of childhood depression. In A. French and I. Berlin (Eds.), *Depression in children and adolescents* (pp. 29-45). New York, Human Sciences Press.

LOEVINGER, J. (1976) *Ego development*. San Francisco, Jossey-Bass.

LUCAS, A., LOCKET, H. and GRIMM, F. (1965) Amitriptyline in childhood depressions. *Diseases of the Nervous System*, 26, 105-110.

MANDELL, A. (1976) Neurobiological mechanism of adaptation in relation to models of psychobiological development. In E. Schopler and R. Reichler (Eds.), *Psychopathology and child development* (pp. 21-22). New York, Plenum Press.

McCONVILLE, B. (1982) The causes and treatment of depression in young children. *Journal of Children in Contemporary Society*, 15, 61-68.

McCONVILLE, B., BOAG, L. and PUROHIT, A. (1972) Mourning depressive responses of children in residence following sudden death of parent figures. *Journal of the American Academy of Child Psychiatry*, 11, 341-364.

McCONVILLE, B., BOAG, L. and PUROHIT, A. (1973) Three types of childhood depression. *Canadian Psychiatric Association Journal*, 18, 133-138.

McCONVILLE, B., SWANSON, J. and LEVINE, J. (1982) *The M.S.L. question-naire for depression.* (unpublished manuscript).
PETTI, T. (1978) Depression in hospitalized child psychiatry patients. *Journal of the American Academy of Child Psychiatry*, 17, 49-58.
PETTI, T., BORNSTEIN, M., DELAMARE, A. and CONNEIS, C. (1980) Evaluation and multimodality treatment of a depressed prepubertal girl. *Journal of the American Academy of Child Psychiatry*, 19, 690-702.
PHILIPS, I. and FRIEDLANDER, S. (1982) Conceptual problems in the study of depression in childhood. In L. Grinspoon (Ed.), *Psychiatry 1982, Annual Review*, pp. 265-272. Washington, D.C., American Psychiatric Press.
POZNANSKI, E. (1982a) The clinical characteristics of childhood depression. In L. Grinspoon (Ed.), *Psychiatry 1982: Annual Review*, pp. 296-307. Washington, D.C., American Psychiatric Association.
POZNANSKI, E. (1982b) The clinical phenomenology of childhood depression. *American Journal of Orthopsychiatry*, 52, 308-313.
POZNANSKI, E., CARROLL, B., BANEGAS, M., COOK, S. and GROSSMAN, J. (1982) The dexamethasone suppression test in prepubertal depressed children. *American Journal of Psychiatry*, 139, 321-324.
POZNANSKI, E., COOK, S. and CARROLL, B. (1979) A depression rating scale for children. *Pediatrics*, 64, 442-450.
PUIG-ANTICH, J. (1980) Affective disorders in childhood - a review and perspective. *Psychiatric Clinics of North America*, 3, 403-424.
PUIG-ANTICH, J. (1982) Psychobiological correlates of major depressive disorder in children and adolescents. In L. Grinspoon (Ed.), *Psychiatry 1982, Annual Review*, pp. 288-296. Washington, D.C., American Psychiatric Press.
PUIG-ANTICH, J., BLAU, S., MARX, N., GREENHILL, L.L. and CHAMBERS, W. (1978) Prepubertal major depressive disorder: pilot study. *Journal of the American Academy of Child Psychiatry*, 17, 695-707.
PUIG-ANTICH, J., PEREL, J., LUPATKIN, W., CHAMBERS, W. J., SHEA, C., TABRIZI, M. A. and STILLER, R. L. (1979) Plasma levels of imipramine (IMI) and desmethylimipramine (DMI) on clinical response to prepubertal major depressive disorder. *Journal of the American Academy of Child Psychiatry*, 18, 616-627.
PUIG-ANTICH, J., ORVASCHEL, H., TABRIZI, M. and CHAMBERS, W. (1980) *Schedule for affective disorders and schizophrenia for school-age children* (Kiddie-SADS). New York, N.Y. State Psychiatric Institute.
ROBBINS, D., ALESSI, N., COOK, S., POZNANSKI, E. and YANCHYSHYN, G. (1982) The use of the research diagnostic criteria (R.D.C.) for a depression in adolescent psychiatric inpatients. *Journal of the American Academy of Child Psychiatry*, 21, 251-255.
SPITZER, R., ENDICOTT, J. and ROBINS, E. (1977) Research diagnostic criteria (R.D.C.) for a selected group of functional disorders. Third Edition. New York, N.Y. State Psychiatric Institute.
WEINBERG, W., RUTMAN, J., SULLIVAN, L., PENICK, E. and DIETZ, S. (1973) Depression in children referred to an educational diagnostic centre: diagnosis and treatment. *Journal of Pediatrics*, 83, 1065-1072.
WELLER, E., WELLER, R., PRESKORN, S. and GLOTZBACH, R. (1982) Steady-state imipramine levels in prepubertal depressed children. *American Journal of Psychiatry*, 139, 506-508.
YOUNG, W., KNOWLES, J., MacLEAN, A., BOAG, L. and McCONVILLE, B. (1982) The sleep of childhood depressives: comparison with age-matched controls. *Biological Psychiatry*, 17, 1163-1168.

PART THREE

Evaluation of Intervention

CHAPTER 12

The Leeds Truancy Project

Ian Berg, Alison Goodwin and Roy Hullin

Department of Psychiatry, University of Leeds, Leeds

Juvenile court magistrates in Leeds, a city in the north of England, have
been playing an active part in the investigation and management of
truancy during the last few years.

Children up to the age of 16 in Britain are required by law to attend
school and they risk being taken to juvenile court under care proceedings
if they stay off without sufficient reason. Truants are usually investigated by Educational Welfare Officers who can institute legal proceedings
if absence from school is sufficiently severe and persistent.

When this happens, a court procedure often used in Britain is the supervision order. As a consequence a social worker supervises the child and
there is no necessity for any further contact with the court. However,
about ten years ago juvenile court magistrates in Leeds were becoming
more and more dissatisfied with the supervision order as a way of dealing
with truancy since many children subjected to this procedure appeared to
continue to stay away from school. Increasingly, magistrates were preferring not to make supervision orders or indeed any kind of court order.
They merely adjourned the court proceedings and brought the child to
court, often repeatedly, so they could monitor progress in school attendance themselves. Some children returned 20 or 30 times. When improvement did not occur the child might be sent to a residential assessment
centre for three weeks on an interim care order. If subsequent adjournments still failed to improve matters a full care order was often made.
This enabled social workers to put the child into residential care if
this seemed appropriate.

A survey was carried out (Berg *et al.*, 1977) and it showed that children
were currently being dealt with by both supervision orders and the adjournment procedure. Age, sex, social background and criminal beahviour were
similar in the children subjected to the two procedures and it wasn't
clear why one was chosen rather than the other in most instances. The
children were mainly in their early teens. They had been absent from
school about two-third of the time on average before coming to court.
The research confirmed what the magistrates had suspected, that school
attendance improved more in those adjourned than those supervised despite
few obvious differences in the features of the two groups of children at

the outset.

Circumstances were such in Leeds at that time that it was possible to
evaluate the two court procedures in the only really satisfactory way.
A randomly controlled trial was set up (Berg *et al.*, 1978). A sheet of
lined paper in each court contained the names of children due to appear
for failure to attend school. A series of 'A's for adjournment and 'S's
for supervision had been written opposite the names in random order and
were obscured by sticky labels. Once the case against the child was
proved the label opposite the name was removed and the indicated procedure was carried out. Any child under this system of allocation had an
equal chance of being managed by supervision or adjournment. Three courts
were involved and dozens of magistrates. Forty five children received
adjournment and 51 supervision orders. Results were clear-cut. Children
brought back to court repeatedly under the adjournment procedure improved
significantly in their school attendance more than those put on supervision. Improvement was maintained for at least a year. There was also
some evidence that adjourned children committed less criminal offences
than supervised individuals.

No differences were apparent when children allocated to the two procedures
were compared on a whole variety of features. This helped to confirm
that the process of random selection had been successfully carried out.
The demonstrable differences in outcome concerning attendance at school
and criminal offences thus appeared to be due to the court procedures
employed. No evidence emerged from the study that any particular group
of children would have done better under supervision. Questionnaires completed by teachers showed that children taken to juvenile court for failure to attend school were essentially a psychiatrically disturbed group
showing both antisocial and emotional disorders. Boys and girls were
equally represented.

Following the successful completion of the study Leeds juvenile court
magistrates virtually abandoned the supervision order for truancy. A
survey carried out subsequently showed that adjournment gave similarly
good results to those obtained during the trial. It was found that a
system of flexible adjournment was often used, so that when a child was
improving in school attendance court appearances occurred after one week,
then two weeks, then three weeks and finally monthly. Failure to
improve resulted in more frequent appearances and interim care orders.
However, some magistrates considered that monthly adjournments were
sufficient irrespective of progress. There was also a system of letters
excusing actual appearance in court if school attendance became satisfactory.

Another trial was set up (Berg *et al.*, 1983) using random allocation to
compare the two varieties of adjournment and to evaluate the letters procedure.

One hundred and sixty eight children, with about equal numbers of boys
and girls were included in the study and 83 were randomly allocated to
flexible and 85 to inflexible adjournments. Letters were allocated
randomly to 42 of the children dealt with by flexible and 46 of those
managed with inflexible adjournment. As before, no significant differ-

ences in the features of children assigned to the four 'treatment' groups
were found and any subsequent differences could confidently be attributed
to the procedures used. Although the flexible adjournment group came
back to court roughly a couple of times more in the ten week period after
first coming to court and children on 'letters' appeared in court two
occasions on average less often than those not on letters, there was no
significant difference in outcome between the groups. It was concluded
that inflexible monthly adjournments and letters to excuse actual appearance in court once school attendance became satisfactory is the procedure
of choice. No particular group of children would have responded significantly better to any one of the procedures.

A surprising discovery during the trial was that in the intervening
period between this study and the two previous ones the attendance of
children taken to court for truancy had substantially improved from 25
per cent to nearer 55 per cent on average. A criterion of 70 per cent
attendance had been used in the second trial so that any child falling
below this level of school attendance had one interim care order. If the
criterion was not met a second time the child was considered a failure of
the system. Only 11 children in each group failed the system over 30
school weeks. Attendance in the remainder showed no significant difference between the two groups. It was also found that about a third less
children were being taken to court for failure to attend school suggesting a considerable improvement in severe school attendance problems in
Leeds. This was later confirmed by a review of 10 schools from various
parts of the city.

In this trial, controls from the same class at school attended between 85
per cent and 90 per cent of the time. School attendance in the whole
group of children taken to court improved from 45 per cent before to 65
per cent during the five week period before first appearance in court
indicating an anticipatory effect once they knew they were going to be
brought to court. It improved dramatically after starting court appearances to about 80 per cent in those who continued to attend court over 30
weeks after first coming to court.

Criminal offences averaged one per child before court and fell to 0.3 per
child in the 6 months after court appearances began. Again there were no
significant differences between the groups. Changes in offences were
similar to those found in the previous trial. However in the sample as a
whole and in line with children dealt with by adjournment in the first
prospective trial, the number of children committing offences for the
first time and the number committing more than one offence fell significantly in the year after starting adjournment.

What you may ask is the relevance of all this to psychiatry. Well,
children who show antisocial behaviour including truancy are dealt with
by a variety of medical, social and legal agencies somewhat indiscrimin-
ately. Truancy has been identified both in the USA and in Britain as an
important forerunner of antisocial behaviour in adult life (Berg, 1980).
It is thus important for psychiatrists to concern themselves with school
attendance problems however they are dealt with. In the medical field
the controlled clinical trial which exemplifies the experimental method
in medicine has become the acceptable way of evaluating treatment. This

is by no means the situation in legal circles. The Leeds Truancy Project
has hopefully made a start in this direction.

Acknowledgment

We would like to thank the Home Office who provided a grant.

References

BERG, I., HULLIN, R., McGUIRE, R. and TYRER, S. (1977) Truancy and the
courts: research note. *Journal of Child Psychology and Psychiatry*,
18, 359-365.
BERG, I., CONSTERDINE, M., HULLIN, R., McGUIRE, R. and TRYER, S. (1978)
The effect of two randomly allocated court procedures on truancy.
British Journal of Criminology, 18, 232-244.
BERG, I., GOODWIN, A., HULLIN, R. and McGUIRE, R. (1983) The effect of
two varieties of the adjournment procedure on truancy: a randomly
controlled trial. *British Journal of Criminology*, 23, 150-158.
BERG, I. (1980) Absence from school and the law. In L. Hersov and
I. Berg (Eds.), *Out of School*, pp. 137-148. London, John Wiley.

CHAPTER 13

The Effect of Different Routines in a
Special Care Baby Unit on the
Mother-Infant Relationship

Joanna Hawthorne Amick

*Child Care and Development Group, University of Cambridge,
Cambridge**

Several studies have attempted to improve the conditions in hospital for
parents separated from their babies in special and intensive care units.
(In this paper the term 'special care' includes 'intensive care'). There
are suggestions that distortions in the mother-child relationship could
follow from early separations. Klaus and Kennell (1976) suggest that
these distortions are brought about by a disruption in the single process
called bonding which occurs at birth if the mother and baby are together.
However, I believe it is the interruption of several processes that may
influence the mother and not only one process like bonding.

Richards (1978), Ross (1980) and Rutter (1981) describe the processes
that are affected by the separation of mother and baby from the point of
view of the mother's psychology. A disruption in maternal feelings is
brought about by the separation which violates expectations of contact
with the infant. The mother's self-confidence may disappear since the
staff seem so much more capable of looking after her baby. She must also
cope with the emotional crisis of a pre-term birth. She may experience a
sense of failure, guilt or loss of self-esteem if her baby is born prematurely, since she not only failed to carry the baby to term, but may
find that the baby differs from the one she had anticipated (Kaplan and
Mason, 1960). The baby's physical characteristics and behaviour will
also influence the mother-infant relationship, as pre-term or ill new-
borns can vary in their responsivity which can result in frustrating
interactions (DiVitto and Goldberg, 1979). A mother's behaviour after a
separation from her baby will also be determined by the emotional and
medical support she receives after delivery.

She must also cope with the inhibiting effect of hospital routines on
spontaneous interactions with her baby. A mother may feel that the
hospital has denied her contact with her baby, or the staff may convey to
her that there is something special about her infant and this may
influence her behaviour with the infant. In the hospital setting, mothers

---

*Present address: Department of Child Psychiatry, University of Chicago,
Chicago, Illinois, U.S.A.

can feel inadequate and confused as they lack a clear role among the many
people dealing with the baby. Their maternal feelings can be thwarted by
routines imposed upon them in the special care unit. Staff are often
resistant to parental involvement, feeling that parents get in the way of
their work. It is only when the staff find they have a role in advising
the mother that the barriers may be removed.

Factors in the hospital environment which impose restrictions on the
developing mother-infant relationship can be altered once they are identified. Studies have shown that parental rates of visiting to babies in
special care units are low (Barnett *et al.*, 1970; Klaus and Kennell, 1976;
Hawthorne, Richards and Callon, 1978; Rosenfield, 1980). Some mothers
need more support than others in order to make them feel autonomous in a
situation that deprives them of their infant.

With this in mind, I set up the first intervention study done in England
in the special care baby unit at Mill Road Maternity Hospital in Cambridge
from 1976 to 1978. The hospital is the regional centre in East Anglia
for mothers at risk for obstetrical problems and in 1976 delivered 3,300
women, 7 per cent of which were premature deliveries. The special care
unit has 24 cots, including 4 for intensive care, and a ratio of one
nurse to three babies. My aim was to provide more contact between
parents and baby, more information and more support for parents and
follow-up in the first year. In my pilot study, I had interviewed 10
mothers to find out their needs during the separation. Two groups of
mothers and low-birthweight babies were followed-up for one year (control
group N = 14, intervention group N = 11). The intervention group
received the following treatment:

1. Increased encouragement to visit.

2. Increased encouragement to touch, cuddle, change (nappies, clothes,
   sheets), tube, bottle and breast feed and bath baby. Babies were
   transferred to cots at a lower weight (at 1500 grams).

3. An explanatory booklet 'A Guide for Parents of Babies in the Special
   Care Baby Unit' (written by myself and available from the Sister,
   S.C.B.U., The Rosie Maternity Hospital, Rosie, Cambridge).

4. Polaroid photograph of baby.

5. Two discussions with paediatrician on baby's admission and discharge
   from S.C.B.U.

6. Mothers were asked to stay in mother and baby room with baby for two
   nights before the baby went home.

7. Health Visitors were asked to visit:

   (a) Once a week before baby comes home

   (b) Every day for first 5 days baby is home

   (c) Once a week for the next month.

The control group's treatment differed in several respects. Mothers did
not change their babies until they were in a cot, did not tube feed or
bath. There was no photograph or booklet, some may never have talked to
a doctor and may only have stayed in the mother and baby room for one
night or not at all. The Health Visitor usually did not visit as much.

Data consisted of the Brazelton Neonatal Behavioural Assessment Scale
(Brazelton, 1973) performed at the baby's discharge from hospital when
both groups had a mean age of 38 weeks gestation; the Prechtl neurological
examination (Prechtl and Beintema, 1964) done at discharge and at 8 weeks
conceptual age; the Denver Development Screening Test at 7 months and 12
months post-natal age; medical information, visiting and contact rates;
7 extensive interviews with the mother (three before the baby went home,
then at 8 weeks conceptual age, and at 6 months, 9 months and 12 months
post-natal age); observations of the mother's affectionate behaviour at
the baby clinic (Klaus and Kennell, 1976) at 8 weeks conceptual age, 7
months and 12 months post-natal age; Schaffer and Emerson's (1964) brief
separation index at 6 months, 9 months and 12 months; Health Visitors'
reports (Hawthorne *et al.*, 1978); and 48-hour diaries given to the mother
to record the baby's behaviour at 5 different time periods during the
first year. These diaries were similar to those used by Richards and
Bernal (1971).

The groups were collected one after the other with the control group
being collected from November to May and the intervention group from June
to December. This avoided any contamination in treatments, but may have
created other problems.

The sample characteristics are seen in Table 1.

It can be seen that birthweight, gestational age, the number of boys and
girls and their length of stay in the special care unit were similar in
both groups. Although there tended to be a few more very ill babies in
the control group, this was not a statistically significant difference.
No babies with serious handicap or congenital malformations were recruited
for the study.

If we now look at the mothers in the sample, we see that there were similar characteristics between the two groups, with no statistically significant differences (Table 2).

It was hypothesized that the intervention group mothers would feel closer
to their babies and more confident in their ability to cope at home. I
thought that the mothers would feel less inhibited with the special care
unit staff and report fewer negative recollections of the time their baby
was in the special care unit. Finally, I thought the intervention group
mothers would report fewer difficulties at home with their babies over
crying, feeding and sleeping.

Results showed that it was more difficult to influence visiting patterns
than it was to increase the number of caretaking activities the mother
took part in. However, visiting rates were high in the unit with all
mothers visiting at least once a day on average in both groups. Mothers
first changed their babies sooner and more mothers tube-fed their babies

in the intervention group. It can be seen that intervention group
mothers spent longer on their visits during the second week, presumably
since they had more to do for the baby.

Table 1.   Characteristics of babies in the sample

	Control	Intervention
	N = 14	N = 11
Birthweight in grams – mean	1555	1545
– range	1110–1840	910–1940
Gestational age in weeks – mean	33	33
– range	28–38	27–37
Sex (Boys:Girls)	8:6	7:4
First born	9	6
Length of stay in SCBU in days – mean	35	33
– range	21–64	19–63
Severity of illness*		
– not very ill	4(28%)	6(54%)
– moderately ill	5(36%)	3(27%)
– very ill	5(36%)	2(18%)

*Not very ill – no oxygen, or oxygen for less than 3 days.   No umbilical
arterial or venous catheter.

Moderately ill – oxygen therapy for more than 3 days, UAC or UVC in
use.

Very ill – oxygen therapy at 60 per cent or more for more than 3 days,
intermittent positive pressure ventilation or continuous positive
airways pressure in SCBU.

The intervention was successful in changing both the attitudes of staff
and mothers.   None of the intervention group mothers felt shy, self-
conscious or in the way in the special care unit.   The intervention group
mothers tended to show more concern about the way the staff handled their
baby and tended to feel more confident about coping at home.

There were many subtle differences between the two groups which could have
been influenced by the intervention and it is clear from the findings
that parents with babies in special care units experience varying degrees
of anxiety and problems.   The intervention group mothers reported feeling
better informed due to the fact that they had received the booklet, the
photograph and had more discussions with the doctors.   The booklet made
the parents better able to understand their baby's problem and therefore
feel more confident when talking to the staff.   The photograph gave the

Table 2. Characteristics of mothers in the sample

	Control	Intervention
	N = 14	N = 11
Mothers age in years — mean	26	28
— range	18-34	21-37
Marital status — married	13	11
Delivery		
— normal	4(28%)	5(45%)
— elective caesarean section	1(7%)	3(27%)
— emergency caesarean section	9(64%)	3(27%)
Age completed education in years	16	16
Social class of husbands occupation		
— I, II	4(28%)	6(54%)
— III non-manual	2(14%)	0(0%)
— III manual, IV	8(57%)	5(45%)
Length of stay in hospital in days — mean	8.2	8.0
— range	2-13	2-12
Length of separation of mother and baby in days — mean	27	25
— range	8-57	10-54
Distance between home and hospital in miles — mean	13.0	10.4
— range	1-27	1-22

mothers a tangible reminder of their baby who was not beside them in the post-natal ward. Mothers were able to show it around to staff and other people who were not able to visit the baby in the unit, and when they were at home the photograph could reassure them of the baby's appearance so that they would not have to imagine the worst from a distance. It seemed that the introduction of the booklet and the photograph helped to change the style of interaction in the special care unit, which resulted not only in an increase of information for the parents, but also possibly in the realization that the staff were taking an interest in their emotional needs. It is worth speculating that the staff also reacted to the intervention by becoming more aware that the baby belongs to the parents, since they were including the parents in the baby's care more than usual.

Table 3. Significant differences between the intervention and control groups

Mother-infant contact:	Control N = 14	Intervention N = 11	Significance
day mother first changed baby - mean	23.3	8.1	$p < 0.0003$*
number of mothers who tube fed	1(14%)	8(73%)	$p < 0.005$†
length of visits in minutes (8-14 day) - mean	353.5	400.0	$p < 0.06$*
Mothers felt shy/in the way/self conscious in the SCBU	6(43%)	0(0%)	$p < 0.02$†
Babies weight in grams - mean at 2 months	4051.0	4798.0	$p < 0.01$‡
- mean at 7 months	6003.0	6956.0	$p < 0.02$‡
Mothers affectionate behaviours at baby clinic (frequency)	2.2	3.6	$p < 0.03$‡
Baby protests at 9 months:			
in cot at night - yes	1(7%)	7(64%)	
- sometimes	7(50%)	1(9%)	$p < 0.04$‡
- no	6(43%)	3(27%)	
when left alone in room - yes	4(29%)	8(57%)	
- sometimes	7(50%)	0(0%)	$p < 0.02$‡
- no	3(21%)	3(27%)	
Mother has had routine since baby came home (asked at 9 months)	2(14%)	7(64%)	$p < 0.02$†
Baby fussy with food at 1 year	1(7%)	7(64%)	$p < 0.004$†
Baby has sleeping problems at 1 year	7(50%)	1(9%)	$p < 0.04$†
Lack of closeness	5(36%)	0(0%)	$p < 0.04$†
Overprotective, possessive	2(14%)	6(54%)	$p < 0.04$†

*Mann-Whitney U test, one tail.
†Fisher Exact Probability Test.
‡Mann-Whitney U test, two tail.

There are other results presented in Table 3 to suggest that the intervention group mothers and babies were different. The intervention group
babies weighed significantly more at 2 and 7 months, the mothers showed
more affectionate behaviour at the 2 month baby clinic, more babies
always protested at two brief separations at 9 months, and the mothers
felt they had a routine at home sooner when asked at 9 months. More control group babies had sleeping problems at one year, but more intervention group mothers reported that their babies were fussy with food. The
intervention group mothers tended to breastfeed for longer (a mean of 9
months compared to 5 months in the control group). Another trend,
although non-significant, was that 6 babies (42%) in the control group
were readmitted to hospital within the first year, while only 2 babies
(18%) in the intervention group were readmitted. Three of the 6 control
group babies were admitted for feeding and management problems, while
none of the intervention group babies was admitted for this problem.
Another study reports a 30 per cent readmission rate of special care
babies during the first year (Hack et $al.$, 1981).

Although conclusions drawn from these findings must be tentative due to
the small sample size and some background differences between the two
groups, it seems that the intervention group mothers tended to be more
anxious and their babies were fussier. Other studies have shown that
maternal anxiety is heightened by having early contact with an ill baby
and the consequent parental nervousness may result in overprotectiveness
(Douglas and Gear, 1976; Harper et $al.$, 1976). However, Harper et $al.$
were unable to determine whether it was the contact that produced the
parents' anxiety, or the anxiety which caused an increase in the parents'
contact with their baby, which was high in their unit.

The Brazelton scale was used to compare the two groups of babies before
they left hospital. It was performed only once, or twice if the situation
was not optimal, and one score was taken. The scale was performed without the mother present, although its value as an intervention should not
be underestimated. If the scale is done with the mother she can learn
about the baby's abilities. However, in this study the scale was used to
assess the babies' characteristics in order to determine whether or not
one group might have been more rewarding to the mother and therefore give
her a more positive feeling about her baby.

When the scale was used in 1976 and 1977, it was not yet developed for
pre-term babies, but the full-term scale had been used satisfactorily for
pre-terms who had reached 37 weeks gestational age. Scores on each of
the items were compared between the two groups. I also wanted to use the
scale to make my own assessment of the baby's behaviour so that I was
familiar with the baby's repertoire and could better understand the
mother's reports about her baby at home.

Comparison between the scores of the two groups was analysed by a two-
tailed Mann-Whitney U test. There was one statistically significant
difference between the two groups on the variable 'pull-to-sit'
($p < 0.05$), where the control group babies were floppier. Of a possible
score between 1-9 the control group babies scored 3.7 and the intervention group babies scored 5.0. No further analysis could be carried
out, but this finding along with others pointing in the same direction

suggests that the control group babies behaved differently from the intervention group babies.

While the numerical differences were not large between the two groups, it was evident from comments made in the mothers' interviews, and the changes that took place in the special care unit, that a change in staff attitude towards the inclusion of parents did take place. An outsider may go into a special care unit and through a gradual process of discussions with the head nurses and information to the staff, change routines so that the parents' needs can be better met. I think that the success of the intervention lay in the fact that I entered the hospital as a participant-observer and carried out the study in this manner (see Gans, 1968; Becker, 1970).

It took a year of my presence in the unit and discussions with the staff before the changes were accepted by the hospital and special care unit staff. It is clear that change must be gradual. However, it is also clear from this study that the emotional needs of many of the mothers were not met. Mothers in both groups felt that the separation had affected them or their baby in some way. How this continued perception may affect their relationship with their baby could have important consequences.

Many of the mothers in this study would have benefitted from some form of counselling or support group in order to overcome some of their anxiety and better understand their feelings. The intervention group mothers reacted positively to the increased number of visits they received from the Health Visitors who visited them at home, both before and after the baby came home. However, it is also evident that each mother will react differently to the situation. Each mother's needs must be understood individually. Some mothers may not like certain forms of intervention. For example, two mothers in the sample did not want to tube-feed their baby but rather preferred to caress him or hold his hand while the nurse tube-fed him. It would probably be detrimental to require all parents to perform a particular activity. Instead, the communication and understanding between staff and parents must be such that each mother's preferences are understood and acted upon, and parents must be given the choice in doing certain things for their baby.

Another finding was that the special care unit retained the intervention approach towards the inclusion of parents and now use the polaroid photograph, they print and distribute the booklet and allow grandparents and siblings into the special care unit. The unit is more cheerfully decorated with pictures and toys and parents are seen looking after their babies. The head nurse is considering starting a discussion group for parents and the new maternity hospital opened in 1983 includes six mother and baby rooms, a kitchen and sitting room and possibly the services of a counsellor.

In summary, these findings from this English study are similar to those of some American and Canadian studies that have reported reactions of parents and ways of supporting parents of special and intensive care babies (Harper *et al.*, 1976; Brown *et al.*, 1980; Minde, 1980). I think it would be profitable to continue to explore parents' reactions so that

we can thoroughly understand their needs, and of course, follow-up the
sample for as long as possible in order to determine the effects of some
of the interventions that researchers are introducing.

Acknowledgments

This study was carried out for a Ph.D. degree at the Maternity Hospital,
Mill Road, Cambridge with the kind permission of Dr. N. R. C. Roberton
and the staff, and under the supervision of Dr. M. P. M. Richards at the
Child Care and Development Group, University of Cambridge. The research
was supported by a studentship from the Medical Research Council and
funding from the Health Education Council.

References

BARNETT, C. R., LEIDERMAN, P. H., GROBSTEIN, R. and KLAUS, M. H. (1970)
    Neonatal separation: the maternal side of interactional deprivation.
    Pediatrics, 45, 197-205.
BECKER, H. S. (1970) *Sociological Work: Method and Substance*, Chicago,
    Aldine Publishing Co.
BRAZELTON, T. B. (1973) *Neonatal Behavioral Assessment Scale*, Clinics in
    Developmental Medicine No. 50. London, Spastics International Medical
    Publications/Heinemann Medical Books.
BROWN, J. V., La ROSSA, M. M., AYLWARD, G. P., DAVIS, D. J.,
    RUTHERFORD, P. K. and BAKEMAN, R. (1980) Nursery-based intervention
    with prematurely born babies and their mothers: Are there effects?
    Journal of Pediatrics, 97, 487-491.
DiVITTO, B. and GOLDBERG, S. (1979) The effects of newborn medical
    status on early parent-infant interaction. In T. M. Field,
    A. M. Sostek, S. Goldberg and H. H. Shuman (Eds.), *Infants Born at
    Risk*, pp. 311-332. New York, S. P. Medical and Scientific Books.
DOUGLAS, J. W. B. and GEAR, R. (1976) Children of low birthweight in the
    1946 national cohort. *Archives of Disease in Childhood*, 51, 820-827.
GANS, H. J. (1968) The participant-observer as a human being: observ-
    ations on the personal aspects of field work. In H. S. Becker *et al.*
    (Eds.), *Institutions and the person*, pp. 300-317). Chicago: Aldine.
HACK, M., DeMONTERICE, D., MERKATZ, I. R., JONES, P. and FANAROFF, A. A.
    (1981) Rehospitalization of the very-low-birthweight infant.
    American Journal of Disease in Childhood, 135, 263-266.
HARPER, R. G., SIA, C., SOKAL, S. and SOKAL, M. (1976) Observations on
    unrestricted parental contact with infants in the neonatal intensive
    care unit. *Journal of Pediatrics*, 89, 441-445.
HAWTHORNE, J. T., RICHARDS, M. P. M. and CALLON, M. (1978) A study of
    parental visiting of babies in a special care unit. In
    F. S. W. Brimblecombe, M. P. M. Richards and N. R. C. Roberton (Eds.),
    Separation and Special Care Baby Units, pp. 33-54. London, SIMP/
    Heinemann Medical Books.
KAPLAN, D. and MASON, E. (1960) Maternal reactions to premature birth
    viewed as an acute emotional disorder. *American Journal of Ortho-
    psychiatry*, 30, 539-547.
KLAUS, M. H. and KENNELL, J. H. (1976) *Maternal-infant bonding*.
    St. Louis, C. V. Mosby Co.

MINDE, K. K. (1980) Bonding of parents to premature infants: theory and
    practice. In P. M. Taylor (Ed.), *Parent-infant Relationships*, pp.
    291-313. New York, Grune and Stratton Inc.
PRECHTL, H. and BEINTEMA, D. (1964) *The neurological examination of the
    full-term newborn infant*. Little Club Clinics in Developmental
    Medicine No. 12. London, SIMP/Heinmann Medical Books.
RICHARDS, M. P. M. (1978) Possible effects of early separation on later
    development in children. In. F. S. W. Brimblecombe, M. P. M. Richards
    and N. R. C. Roberton (Eds.), *Separation and Special Care Baby
    Units*, Clinics in Developmental Medicine, pp. 12-32. London,
    SIMP/Heinemann Medical Books.
RICHARDS, M. P. M. and BERNAL, J. (1971) Social interaction in the first
    days of life. In H. R. Schaffer (Ed.), *The Origin of Human Social
    Relations*, pp. 3-13. London, Academic Press.
ROSENFIELD, A. G. (1980) Visiting in the intensive care nursery. *Child
    Development*, 51, 939-941.
ROSS, G. S. (1980) Parental responses to infants in intensive care: the
    separation issue re-evaluated. *Clinics in Perinatology*, 7, 47-61.
RUTTER, M. (1981) *Maternal Deprivation Reassessed*, second edition.
    London, Penguin Books.
SCHAFFER, H. R. and EMERSON, P. E. (1964) The development of social
    attachments in infancy. *Monographs of Society for Research in Child
    Development*, 29, Serial No. 94.

CHAPTER 14

An Evaluation of Focussed Casework in Improving Interaction in Abusive Families

Rory Nicol, Christopher Mearns, David Hall, Barbara Kay, Barbara Williams and Jane Akister

Nuffield Psychology and Psychiatry Unit, Fleming Memorial Hospital, Newcastle-on-Tyne

Several investigators have recently looked at the interactions of abusive parents and their children. A common strategy has been the stranger technique (Ainsworth *et al.*, 1978). Hyman (1980) compared twelve abused infants 6-24 months with controls from deprived families. The abused infants showed more discomfort, less looking at a stranger and were less likely to look at or play with toys than the controls. They showed more distress and less play at reunion but where this did occur, it contained an angry and aggressive component. Lewis and Shaffer (1979) observed reunions between abused and neglected infants and their mothers in a day care centre in which controls were also present. They found that the abused and neglected children were less likely to approach their mothers and more likely to avoid proximity.

Two themes seem to emerge from these findings. First, the theme of anxious attachment and detachment described by Ainsworth and second, excessive anger and its expression by physical aggression. Since samples are small and heterogeneous, it is not surprising that the findings of different studies are inconsistent. Burgess and Conger (1978) used three tasks designed to stimulate family interaction in their comparison of abusive and neglectful families with a control group drawn from the same poor rural settings. As one might expect, both groups showed fewer positive and more negative interaction than controls. Less expected was that it was the neglect group that was in most respects the more deviant.

Apart from the small scale of the studies, there are more general reasons why it is not surprising that only rather general relationships have been found between measures of family interaction and family pathologies such as child abuse and neglect. Hinde (1979) has eloquently described the difficulties of developing a science of human relationships. Relationships are critically determined by characteristics of the individuals involved and yet the relationship itself has qualities that are more than the sum of the parts. In the case of child abuse this is well shown by the many 'risk' factors that have been isolated - parents' childhood experience, current stresses, births status, temperament and even sex of the child. Each of these is associated with a raised probability of abuse yet together they give us no idea of how the breakdown in the relationship occurs. Dubanoski, Evans and Hignell (1978) are no doubt

correct in drawing attention to a range of factors which may be implicated such as lack of parenting skills, negative attitudes towards the
child, a pre-disposition to impulsive aggression and a primitive style of
discipline.

A fertile body of theorizing about difficulties in parent-child relationships in the behavioural approach of the Patterson group. In a series of
studies, Patterson *et al.* have investigated the control of aggression in
natural settings and the effects of interaction. Patterson (1976)
reviews evidence from their studies concerning the origins and at the
same time the effects of aggressive and 'aversive' behaviour in children.
The child's environment is characterized by plenty of models of such
negative behaviour - particularly in aggressive families. A second problem arises if the parents are inconsistent in their response to the
child's aversive behaviour so that a proportion of them are followed by a
reward instead of by an appropriate punishment. These randomly scattered
rewards serve to accelerate the 'aversive' behaviour. Equally, ineffective punishment encourages the child to higher levels of
aversive behaviour until eventually the parent stands off. Inherent in
the parents 'stand off' is further reward for the child's deviance. The
student of child abuse may be tempted to view the problem from the opposite angle i.e. to examine the way the child's responses reinforce
chaotic but 'aversive' responses from the parent. In reality, as
Patterson explains, both parent and child are locked into a mutual interaction in which each is drawn into attempts to 'coerce' desired behaviours
from the other rather than gain such behaviour by a process of mutual
reinforcement. While the relevance of this formulation to child abuse
problems is obvious *a priori* there is still the empirical problem of how
often it is actually applicable in child abuse families with their mani-
fold background problems.

The strength of the Patterson *et al.* work lies in their development of a
system for coding relevant family behaviour (see below). This has
allowed them to make comparisons of the families of normal and aggressive
children and to measure the results of treatment. Although the system
has most commonly been used in connection with problem behaviour in
children it is, in fact, equally applicable to monitor behaviour deviance
and behaviour change in any member of the family including adults.

Sandler, Van Der Car and Milhoan (1978) reported the treatment of two
families where child abuse had occurred. He used the Patterson coding
system to monitor behaviour over baseline, treatment and follow-up phase.
Treatment consisted of encouraging the mother to increase her rate of
positive reinforcement to the child. To achieve this a standard treatment package was used. The results indicate considerable success, in
both cases, in modifying aspects of the parents behaviour. Little is
reported concerning the family problems or child's problems apart from
the fact that child abuse had occurred. For one of the cases there was,
apparently, a high correlation between mother's rate of 'positive command' and child's rate of 'compliance' but there is no information as to
whether 'compliance' was a problem in the first place. In a later paper
(De Nicola and Sandler, 1980) a further two cases were reported. The
authors recognize that child abuse is a complex problem and they sought
to compare a treatment aimed at correlating simple ignorance of the

skills of child rearing with a treatment which aimed to help the parent control impulsive anger and frustration. Again, there was a rapid decrease in aversive behaviours and an increase in positive reinforcement in both families with the commencement of treatment although there was little to distinguish the separate effects of the different interventions.

In their wide clinical experience of families with child abuse, the present authors have been impressed by the fact that these families often have complex problems which extend well beyond the simple fact of the abuse itself. There seemed much to be gained by developing interventions that were 'tailor made' to the problems of the individual families we were seeing. Clearly, there was a basic range of strategies that could be used such as problem definition, enhancement of a therapeutic relationship and treatment alliance, empathy, confrontation, reinforcement, modeling etc., but their development should be determined by a problem identification and analysis. Because of limited resources and also because the family problems were so complex and unique we employed a single case approach. This paper reports the results for seven cases on the load of a local agency where the regime was put into effect.

Method

The service agency

The N.S.P.C.C. Special Units in Britain have been set up to provide a lead in identification, management, treatment and research into child abuse. The Unit involved in the present study opened in 1975. It had as one of its functions the long-term intensive support of families where child abuse is a problem. The support includes visits up to several times per week and a 24 hour telephone crisis service. There was also a weekly mothers group. Families are included in the Unit's treatment programme if there is a vacancy and if it seems likely that they will benefit from the treatment offered.

The sample

The sample was drawn from the Unit's current caseload. It consisted of those families which contained an index child between the ages of 2 and 6. By index child is meant a child who has been physically abused or who has otherwise been a centre of the family problems. Relevant characteristics of the treated families are shown in Table 1. In all but one there had been physical abuse and in this one, the index child was judged so dangerously at risk that there had been repeated admissions to a paediatric ward at times of crisis (Family No. 4).

In all, 7 families were considered for treatment. Of the two who were not treated, one was assessed but the family interaction was considered normal and the risk of further abuse minimal. The other family was so unstable at the time of research that family members were continually splitting up and living in different places. It was not possible to obtain even a stable series of observations under

these circumstances. By the time the situation had calmed down, the
study was over.

The evaluation

The evaluation consisted of a series of single case studies in which
family interaction was compared before, during and after treatment in
a continuous time series of observations for each family. Family
interaction was measured by direct observation using the Family
Interaction Coding System (F.I.C.S.) of G. R. Patterson and his
colleagues (Reid, 1978). This consists of 29 clearly defined behavioural categories giving prominence to clearly pro-social and agres-
sive behaviours. After piloting and careful definition we added one
additional aversive behaviour category which was 'threat'. The procedure is that the behaviour of a 'target' individual is noted every
6 seconds together with a note of the response of the individual with
whom he or she is interacting at the time. The different members of
the family, with the exception of babies, are each the 'target' in
turn for a consecutive series of observations lasting 5 minutes. In
each total observation session, each family member may be the 'target'
for one or two 5 minute observation session. For each family there
were at least 7 pre-treatment, 7 during treatment and 6 post-treatment
observation sessions. These were carried out as far as possible in a
continuous time series of 2 to 3 observation sessions per week.

Extensive piloting and training with the F.I.C.S. was undertaken
before the project started. Training was continued until there was
more than 75 per cent agreement on each of the categories between two
interviewers coding the same interaction. Re-checks of reliability
were made at intervals between two raters throughout the study using
videotapes of family interactions. Of particular importance in
Patterson's theorizing (see Patterson, 1976) is a compound category
called Total Aversive Behaviour (T.A.B.). This consisted of Command
Negative; Cry; Disapproval; Dependency; Destructiveness; High Rate
(of activity); Humiliate; Non Compliance; Negativism; Physical Negative; Teaze; Whine; Yell; Ignore and, in addition, Threat. T.A.B. is
applicable to all family members, not just the children. In the main
studies all observations were made by one observer (C.M.) who was
kept as ignorant as possible of the treatment plan.

The design

Preliminary observations suggested to us that each patient's problems
were highly individual and this led us, as mentioned above, to adopt
a single case study approach to evaluation. As there were 5 repli-
cations (cases) we were able to compare measures before and after
treatment for the 5 cases as a group as well as inspecting individual
trends in the measures across the 3 phases before, during and after
treatment.

The treatment approach

This may be summarized as follows:

1. A sometimes protracted supportive casework phase during which a trusting relationship with the family was developed (see Table 1.)

2. Each family was the subject of discussion of a multidisciplinary team meeting. The families were looked at from two points of view - first their problems as seen from the point of view of the agencies involved and secondly the problems as seen by the family themselves. In undertaking this analysis the team used the personal knowledge gained by the caseworker, case records and the pre-treatment observations from the Family Interaction Code Schedule. From this analysis a dynamic hypothesis was developed concerning the interlocking family problems.

3. At the same meeting, strategies were developed for decreasing undesirable parenting and increasing desirable parenting in accordance with the dynamic hypothesis. The strategies consisted of instruction, reinforcement of the parent by the therapist, confrontation and problem analysis and on some occasions participant modeling all in the context of an empathic therapeutic relationship. There was an emphasis on including all family members in the treatment (with the exception of case 4 where the father was excluded because the problems mainly occurred while he was at work).

4. The conclusions of the analysis were fed back to the family with due respect for the fact that they had their own view of what their problems were which often failed to coincide with that of the professionals. It was found that recognition and respect for the families view made it possible to negotiate a treatment contract with the family where their view could be extended and integrated with the professional view.

5. The treatment was carried out over 3 to 4 weeks in home visits 2 to 3 times per week.

6. There was follow-up with supportive casework, although the specific focussed casework was discontinued.

Results

The results will be presented as an overview. Following this, one case will be reported in detail to illustrate the approach. Two other cases will be reported to illustrate clinically significant points not shown in this first case.

In Table 1 some demographic characteristics of the sample are presented. It can be seen that 3 of the 5 families were unemployed. This meant that the fathers were around for a lot of the time but also that the families were under real financial stress. Family No. 4 was the only one where father was left out of both observation and treatment

Table 1. Characteristics of the 5 families in the study

Family No.	Age		Father Occupation	Children				Time in Treatment (Supportive Casework)
	Father	Mother		No.	Oldest Age	Youngest Age	Index Age	
1	25	24	Unemployed	3	6–1	2– 6	2–6	1 year 3 months
2	32	27	Unemployed	2	3–1	0–10	3–1	1 year 1 month
3	29	29	Unemployed	3	9–4	6	9–4	5 years 7 months
4	37	33	Department manager	2	6–1	1– 5	1–5	1 month
5	24	24	Security guard	3	7–6	2	6–3	2 years 2 months

Table 2. Mean readings in pre-, during and post-treatment phases for the five cases in the study of 'total aversive behaviour' (mean observations per minute)

Family No.	Index Child			Father			Mother		
	Pre-	During	Post-	Pre-	During	Post-	Pre-	During	Post-
1	1.1	1.0	0.2	0.15	0.31	0.03	0.66	0.26	0.66
2	1.8	0.4	0.4	1.04	0.28	0.23	0.67	0.25	0.30
3	2.4	0.5	0.7	0.87	0.44	0.10	1.40	0.48	2.00
4	1.1	0.8	0.5	Not included			0.40	0.15	0.17
5	0	0	0	1.32	0.86	0.75	1.04	0.46	0.93

Repeated measures ANOVA

Index child	$F = 6.0$ d.f. 2,8 $p < 0.05$	Linear Trend	$F = 17.6$ d.f. 1,8 $p < 0.005$	
Father	$F = 7.6$ d.f. 2,6 $p < 0.05$	Linear Trend	$F = 19.5$ d.f. 1,6 $p < 0.005$	
Mother	$F = 4.4$ d.f. 2,8 $p < 0.05$	Quadratic Trend	$F = 14.6$ d.f. 1,8 $p < 0.005$	

Table 2 compares measures to total aversive behaviours before, during and after treatment. It can be seen that there is a steady fall in T.A.B. across the treatment phases in the index children and the fathers but that in the mothers there is a sharp fall of T.A.B. during treatment but an equally sharp relapse once treatment has finished. These trends are highly significant statistically.

Behaviours which reflected affectionate behaviour (Approval, Physical positive and Laugh) were also analysed for the two parents across the three treatment phases. In this case there was no significant changes.

A single family will now be presented to illustrate the treatment process.

Family No. 2

In this family, both the family and the therapist thought the treatment had been very successful. The problem identified by the family was the older child's poor sleep pattern. The background was that the older daughter Susan had been seriously non-accidentally injured by her father two years before and was in foster care when the involvement of the Special Unit began. A care order was granted and Susan was eventually placed at home with her parents. Early intervention was along traditional social work lines. Both parents had had disrupted childhoods and displayed characteristics typically found in abusive parents. Intervention was aimed at giving support and insight. Susan attended nursery school. There was no focus on the parent-child interactions as such. This support had continued for many months.

Summary of pre-treatment observations

There was a high level of 'total aversive behaviour' from Susan. Analysis identified one sub-category as drawing most extreme type of aversive responses from the parents. This was 'high rate' and occurred three times as often as any of the other sub-categories. The parents used most often those responses that were least effective (e.g. 'yell') and used least often those responses that were most effective (e.g. 'disapproval"). Although father was physically present, he was very passive and his most common response to the child's 'high rate' was to 'ignore'. Mother on the other hand was both more active and with a broader range of responses. She sometimes distracted, or re-channelled the T.A.B. but more common used extreme but ineffectual responses such as 'yell'.

Plan developed

1. Feedback of pre-treatment observations to parents.

2. Agreed tasks about bedtime routine.

    (a) Settling her on sofa at agreed time each evening prior to moving upstairs to bed.

(b) Immediate return to bed without anger if she gets up at night.

(c) Instruction to father about occupying and distracting Susan.

3. Recording of bedtime, number of times she came down and when she settled.

4. Rewarding of good behaviour by increased attention.

5. Distraction from high rate behaviour.

6. Caseworker lavishly rewarded signs of progress.

7. Caseworker modelled alternative methods of handling Susan's behaviour.

Expected changes

Improved bedtime routine.

Reduction in general anxiety and improvement of constructive control techniques - these should lead to drop in 'high rate' and 'T.A.B.' behaviour.

The plan in action

During the observation period there was a crisis in the family due to Susan's escalating aversive behaviour. Treatment was therefore started somewhat earlier than planned.

The family complained about the poor sleep and could not see that structuring bedtime routine would help. They consulted their G.P. for a night sedative so this was given by the team psychiatrist for a short course and was included in a modified design.

Results

1. Response to bedtime. This was completely successful.

Even before night sedation was started there was an improvement in regularity of bedtime and rapid reduction in number of times Susan had to be returned to bed after first settling. This led to the impression that the night sedation was irrelevant; it certainly had not worked on previous occasions.

Susan's behaviour There was a reduction in total aversive behaviour especially 'high rate' as shown in Table 3.

Parents' behaviour The total negative exchanges initiated by parents showed only modest change. The biggest change caused in father's behaviour was that he became more active, particularly in his use of commands. Mother showed a fall in rate of overall activity.

Most important, the *effectiveness* of parental intervention changed
dramatically in that mother became less effective, even for those
interventions she did use, whereas father not only increased his
interventions but a higher proportion of them were effective. This
is shown in Table 4.

Table 3.   Family No. 2
Index child's high rate behaviour

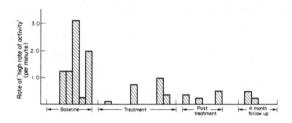

Table 4.   Family No. 2
Parental differences in
obtaining compliance

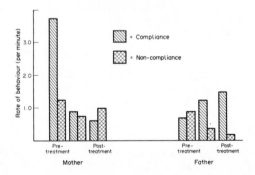

This raises the question of what interventions are effective in terminating the deviant behaviour of the child. Analysis revealed that
there were big differences in how often different control techniques
were associated with terminating deviant behaviour. This is shown in
Table 5 for both parents combined.

'Physical negative' and 'disapprove' are the most consistently effective parental interventions. Clearly 'physical negative' is the less
desirable of the two and it is encouraging to note that for the much
reduced deviant behaviour of the treatment and post treatment phases
the 'physical negative' exchange has disappeared.

Table 5.   Family No. 2
           Effectiveness of parents control
           of child's aversive behaviour

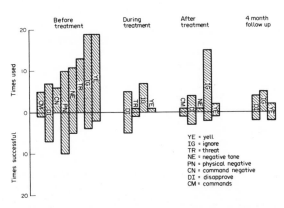

In conclusion, it was possible in this family to pinpoint just where
the improvements occurred.   However it was not so easy to see exactly
how the intervention led to the particular changes that were observed.

Family No. 4

This family also showed clear positive changes with treatment.
Mother, at home alone with her 18 month old, Michael, complained of
his wingeing and crying constantly and aroused such concern by her
negative attitude that she was repeatedly admitted to a paediatric
ward.   As soon as help was offered the family turned it down and the
problem continued.   However, since referral to the Special Unit with
the intensive programme of home visiting, co-operation had improved.

Summary of pre-treatment observations

Whining and crying were very high but 'total aversive behaviour' was
no more than developmentally appropriate behaviour, but unlike some
of the other families there were no negative threats, yelling or
defeatism.   There was rapid approval of the frequent compliant
behaviour.   We identified a 'distancing strategy' in mother's
behaviour.   This consisted of mother giving neutral physical contact
when the child seemed to want physical affection (e.g. holding his
arms out to be lifted).   In other instances the child's demands for
physical affection were passively received or repelled.   When either
of these were accompanied by the child's distress, this was called
'distancing strategy'.

Plan developed

1. Implementation of star chart for good behaviour. Each time a
    star was awarded mother was to give Michael a cuddle and it was
    role-played with mother since she tended to hold the child at
    arms length thereby increasing his frustration.

2. At the fourth treatment session it was agreed to continue 1, and
    that, when Michael was naughty he would be put in his room for 5
    minutes.

Expected changes

Increase in warmth of mother's interaction.

Decrease in winging and crying by baby.

Plan in action

Mother implemented star chart and also gave her daughter (6 years)
stars. Michael quickly learnt that when he earned a star he also
received a cuddle and would put up his arms for one. Mother found
physical contact with Michael, when he was not crying, rewarding and
this enabled her to move onto 2.

Up to this time mother had only cuddled Michael to console him which
she had not found pleasurable.

Mother became more confident in handling Michael over the treatment
period and this combined with finding him more pleasurable gave her
motivation to comply with the treatment.

Results

There was little change in 'total aversive behaviour', there was a
very low baseline rate of parental total negative exchange. The most
striking parental maladaptive behaviour was the 'distancing strategy'
described above. This was shown to decrease across the study
(see Table 6).

Mother's reinforcing of good behaviour showed a positive change as
shown in Table 7 with an increase in responses of physical affection,
approval and laughter.

In conclusion, this family clearly shows the potential for this
flexible intervention to encourage positive interaction from parents
as well as inhibiting negative interaction as shown more clearly in
Family No. 2. It may be that the positive elements of intervention
are more subtle than the negative ones and hence didn't show up so
clearly over the group of results as did the reduction in T.A.B.

Table 6. Family No. 4
          Rates of 'distancing strategy'
          (i.e. neutral response to
          child's demand for affection)

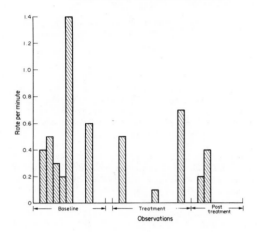

Table 7. Family No. 4
          Mothers positive responses to
          child's pro-social behaviour

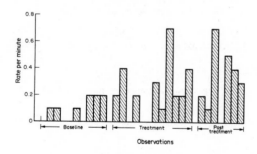

Family No. 5

In this family, the therapist thought that little significant progress had been made in treatment, although objectively there was a
trend towards improvement (see Table 2).

The problems identified by the family were various trivial medical
symptoms in the children.

The parents had been cohabiting for 2-3 years. The two older
children were mother's from a previous liaison. Two years before the
start of the study, the two older children sustained cuts and bruises
on their faces and head by father. A Care Order was obtained and the
children were away from home for 6 months.

There was constant relationship difficulties with the neighbours.

Summary of pre-treatment observation

The rate of 'total aversive behaviour' was virtually nil among the
two older children, the only bad behaviour coming from the youngest.
Both parents show very high rates of 'total negative exchanges' to
the older children despite the fact that they showed no misbehaviour.
Table 8 shows the positive and negative interactions initiated by
parents towards each child. This demonstrates the marked favouritism
towards the youngest child, Debbie.

This family showed to a unique degree the so called 'frozen watchful-
ness' of the abused child. This was shown in the frequency of the
code of 'attentiveness' in the three children. This code was seldom
used with other families. In the same way 'work' is hardly used in
other families. The eldest girl, Donna, emerged as a watchful and
constantly humiliated drudge in the family. The index child, Gary,
was more passive but still continuously humiliated. The observer
gained the impression that these interactions were, if anything,
exaggerated for his benefit.

Plan developed

There was feedback of the results.

Father to be encouraged to improve relationships in the neighbourhood.

The family to be encouraged to reduce the negative interaction.

Expected changes

Reduction of total negative exchange by parents to the two older
children.

Decrease in special treatment and favouritism of the youngest child.

The plan in action

During the period of treatment there were so many crisis that the
coherence of the plan was severely curtailed. For example:

    Attacks of neighbours on the house.
    Attacks on children going to school.
    Panic visits to hospital about minor physical symptoms.
    Mother's broken arm.

These problems severely restricted the number of settled casework
sessions where problems could be focussed on in a systematic manner.

Results

Superficial observation of results did show some promising changes –
there seemed to be a reduction in T.A.B. and some increase in affectionate behaviour from the parents. The true picture emerged,
however, when the target of the improved behaviour was taken into
account. This is shown in Table 8.

Table 8. Family No. 5
Parents' positive and negative
behaviours towards children

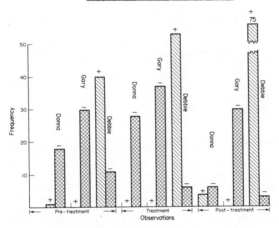

It can be seen in Table 8 that all the increased positive behaviour
is directed towards Debbie who was grossly spoilt and indulged while
the plight of the two elder children remained substantially unchanged
apart from minor changes in degree.

Discussion

There has been an increasing popularity in recent years for planned,
active and focussed psychotherapy and casework. This has at least partly
been due to a very healthy trend in hard headed evaluation which has
shown such approaches to be as or even more effective than longer term
interventions (e.g. Reid and Shyne, 1969). Ideas derived from social
learning theory and from behaviour modification have achieved general
acceptance – hopefully without becoming too diluted in the process.
Several authors have reported the adaption of this approach to the treatment of child abuse (Hutchings, 1980; Reavley and Gilbert, 1976).

The present study carries the application to child abuse a stage further
in its attempt to build in an evaluation of the technique used. Attempts
at evaluation give rise to many problems for the therapist. In order to
generate reproducible and valid the results, the therapeutic approach and
the problems tackled have to be controlled or standardized in some ways,
but in doing so, it is important not to render the therapist totally
impotent or the therapy unrecognizable. There seems little point, also,
in treating totally unrepresentative subjects such as college students.
If we compare our procedure with what appears to be the only other
successful attempt at evaluation, that of Sandler and his colleagues
(Sandler *et al.*, 1978; De Nicola and Sandler, 1980) there appear to be
some important differences in the approaches. Sandler, like the present
authors, used the Patterson coding system as the main measure for pre-
treatment assessment and change.

What is not clear from the published accounts is whether the Sandler
group took into account the clients' perception of their problems and,
indeed, whether the clients perceived themselves as having any problems
at all. This, in our experience is a major problem with the child abuse
family and one which, as shown in the above account of Family No. 2, we
had to give a lot of thought to. In general, we found the best approach
was to start 'where the client was' and accept their definition of the
problem. It was then often possible to develop and extend their perception once some initial success had been achieved and one could reflect
with them on how the changes had been brought about.

While we used the baseline observations in our formulation of the family
problem, it appears that we did this less specifically than Sandler *et
al.* (1978). The treatment of those authors in the two cases described
was directed specifically at correcting deficits in the parents' behaviour
as revealed in the Patterson baseline measures. In the current project
the baseline measures were used with other data to develop a more general
picture. It may be that the greater specificity of Sandler's approach
was partly responsible for his success in promoting positive parenting.
In the present study, we obtained a very striking and significant reduction in aversive behaviour in all family members but this was not matched
by a consistent measurable increase in positive behaviour. However, as
shown in Family No. 4, closer scrutiny reveals large changes in positive
interaction as well. One might expect that relapse would be likely under
these circumstances. It is reassuring that in the one family where a 6
month follow-up was possible, the favourable changes had persisted
(Family No. 2), even when positive interaction is not significantly
increased.

However, as shown in Family No. 4, closer scrutiny reveals large changes
in positive interaction as well.

The main contribution of the present study is that although it is small
scale, it is large enough to give some confirmation of the effectiveness
of a focussed casework approach to child abuse families. How much confidence can we have in these positive findings? Basically we used two
designs: a simple before and after group design and a series of single
case studies.

The before and after comparison is a relatively weak design. In the present case the main alternative explanations for the positive results are twofold. First, the results may be due to non-specific factors such as the general enthusiasm and expectancy that accompanies any research programme. While the force of this criticism is undeniable, an attempt was made to minimize such placebo effects by continuing supportive treatment both before and after the specific programme. The second problem is likely to be due to statistical regression. The likelihood of regression seems minimal when we consider that the sample was not selected on their high scores on any of the Patterson measures or, indeed, or any criteria apart from their attendance at the N.S.P.C.C. Special Unit.

Clearly, however, the findings of this study require confirmation in a larger scale study with an appropriate control group.

There has been considerable discussion in the recent psychotherapy literature (e.g. Hersen and Barlow, 1976) on single case methodology. It has been suggested that in some way group designs are not the most appropriate methodology for psychotherapy research. The present study was originally envisaged as a series of single case A-B-A designs in which the effectiveness of treatment is assessed by a reversion of treatment measures to the baseline level once the specific intervention is discontinued.

In the present study, there was a trend in this direction among the mothers. However this formulation, while appropriate in the case of some drug treatments for example, does not allow of the alternative possibility that the effects of treatment are enduring. Even if the results did conform to an A-B-A format the result would be inconclusive. The main value of single case analysis seems to us to be hypothesis generating rather than hypothesis testing and as such it is an essential adjunct to practical therapy.

The three case studies reported above illustrate the value of quantitative analysis of the single case. In Family No. 2, for example, we were able to pinpoint which of the management techniques employed by the parents were effective and to compare the effectiveness of the parents before and after treatment.

This brings us on to the difference in the results for mothers when compared with the fathers and children. The mothers seemed to quickly revert to their coercive child management once treatment had finished whereas the improvements in fathers and index children persisted. A possible explanation is that the mother is the family member who traditionally carries the most responsibility in the household. It is perhaps not surprising given the stressful circumstances of these families, that the mother reverts to her well tried, if inefficient practices.

Finally, a word about the relevance of the F.I.C.S. to the problems of abusive families. In the 5 families in this study so called 'coercive' behaviour was clearly a problem and one that was closely linked with the problems of abuse. Patterson (1976) describes 'bursts' of mutually coercive behaviour. In our data, there were clear occasions when there were very high rates of T.A.B. This can be seen in the series of observations for Family No. 2 shown in Table 3.

Throughout the series of observations, there are occasions when 'high rate' behaviour was absent and others when rates were high. On inspection of the different phases of the programme for Family No. 2 it seems that two processes were at work. First, once treatment had started, there were fewer occasions when *any* 'high rate' was recorded. This would suggest that there were fewer 'bursts' of deviant behaviour associated with mutual attempts at coercion between parents and children. In addition to this, when there is a significant record of 'high rate' in any session, the score is not as high in during and post-treatment records as it is on pre-treatment occasions. As mentioned in the introduction, the applicability of Patterson's theorizing to child abuse is an empirical matter. There will be a need in future studies to combine a detailed investigation of the effect of treatment on family interaction with other outcome measures including monitoring the rate of recurrence of abuse itself. The likelihood of recurrence of child abuse has been estimated at between 7 per cent and 39 per cent according to circumstances in the area where the present study took place (Speight, Brideson and Cooper, 1979). This proportion is consistent with international estimates. Clearly, larger-scale treatment studies are needed to confirm and extend the present study and investigate wider outcomes measures.

References

AINSWORTH, M. D. S., BLEHAR, M. C., WATERS, E. and WALL, S. (1978) *Patterns of Attachment: a Psychological Study of the Stranger Situation*. Hillsdale, N. J., Lawrence Erlbaum Associates.

BURGESS, R. L. and CONGER, R. D. (1978) Family interaction in abusive, neglectful and normal families. *Child Development*, 49, 1163-1173.

De NICOLA, J. and SANDLER, J. (1980) Training abusive parents in child management and self-control skills. *Behaviour Therapy*, 11, 263-270.

DUBANOSKI, R. A., EVANS, I. M. and HIGNELL, A. A. (1978) Analysis and treatment of child abuse: a set of behavioural propositions. *Child Abuse and Neglect*, 2, 153-172.

HERSEN, M. and BARLOW, D. H. (1976) *Single Case Experimental Designs*. New York, Pergamon Press.

HINDE, R. A. (1979) *Towards Understanding Relationships*. London, Academic Press.

HUTCHINGS, J. (1980) The behavioural approach to child abuse. In N. Frude, (Ed.), *Psychological Approaches to Child Abuse*, pp. 181-191. London, Batsford.

HYMAN, C. (1980) Families who injure their children. In N. Frude (Ed.), *Psychological Approaches to Child Abuse*, pp. 100-110. London, Batsford.

LEWIS, M. and SHAFFER, S. (1979) Peer behaviour and mother-infant interaction in maltreated children. In M. Lewis and C. Rosenblum (Eds.), *The Uncommon Child: The Genesis of Behaviour Volume III*, pp. 193-223. New York, Plenum.

PATTERSON, G. R. (1976) The aggressive child: victim and architect of a coercive system. In E. Marsh, L. Hamerlynch and L. Handy (Eds.), *Behaviour Modification and Families*, pp. 267-316. New York, Brunner/ Mazel.

REAVLEY, W. and GILBERT, M. J. (1976) The behavioural treatment of potential child abuse. *Social Work Today*, 7, 166-168.

REID, J. B. (Ed.) (1978) *A Social Learning Approach to Family Interventions. Vol. 2 Observation in Home Settings.* Eugene, Oregon, Castalia.
REID, W. J. and SHYNE, A. W. (1969) *Brief and Extended Casework.* New York, Columbia University Press.
SANDLER, J., VAN DER CAR, C. and MILHOAN, M. (1978) Training child abusers in the use of positive reinforcement techniques. *Behaviour Research and Therapy*, 16, 169-175.
SPEIGHT, A. N. P., BRIDSON, J. M. and COOPER, C. E. (1979) Follow-up survey of cases of child abuse seen at Newcastle General Hospital 1974-75. *Child Abuse and Neglect*, 3, 555-563.

CHAPTER 15

Supporting Bereaved Parents after Perinatal Death

Gillian Forrest and Elizabeth Standish

Park Hospital for Children, Headington, Oxford

In the United Kingdom, about 1 in 70 babies dies at or around the time of birth (Office of Population Census and Surveys, 1980). Despite the relative frequency of this event, it is only in the last 10 years or so that the family's reactions to the loss of the baby, and the management of their emotional needs, have received the attention of obstetricians, paediatricians and psychiatrists. In particular, the difficulties of mourning a stillbirth have been emphasized by Lewis and Page (1978), Klaus and Kennell (1976) and others. Two different approaches have been developed to try and improve the care of these families, and thereby prevent atypical grief reactions or prolonged emotional disturbance that may follow perinatal bereavement. The first approach consists of recommendations for the practical management of the stillbirth or neonatal death, such as those ones contained in the leaflet produced by the British National Stillbirth Study Group in 1978. These include encouraging parents to see and name the baby, hold a funeral, make opportunities for discussions with the medical staff and obtain obstetric and genetic counselling (Health Education Council, 1978).

The second approach is to provide families with some form of bereavement counselling, either by professionals or by self-help groups such as the Society of Compassionate Friends, or the Stillbirth and Perinatal Death Association.

The present study was designed to evaluate a combination of supportive care and bereavement counselling for parents who had lost a baby in the perinatal period. The study was carried out in the John Radcliffe Maternity Unit, Oxford, with the collaboration of the departments of obstetrics and paediatrics.

Hypothesis

The hypothesis to be tested was that psychological recovery from stillbirth or early neonatal death (death of the baby within the first 7 days after birth) is enhanced by a planned programme of support and counselling.

Method

The study was a randomized controlled trial, and was carried out in the
John Radcliffe Maternity Hospital in Oxford.

Fifty unselected mothers of babies over 28 weeks gestation were recruited;
25 were mothers of stillborn infants and 25 mothers of babies who died in
the newborn period. Mothers of babies or foetuses of 28 weeks gestation
or more were chosen because of the changes in administrative procedures
for dealing with the body after this point, and not because it was felt
that parents of babies under that gestation suffer any differently.
Immediately after the death or stillbirth of their baby, the mothers were
randomly allocated either to a group which received planned support and
counselling; or to a contrast group which received routine hospital care.

The supported group (S) was guaranteed the comprehensive application of
the recommended proposals for 'ideal' care. They were all encouraged to
see, hold and name their dead baby; a photograph of the baby was taken
and kept; the mother was given the choice, wherever possible, of returning to her own ward or to the isolation floor; and discharge was not
hurried, to allow time for contact with the medical staff, social workers,
community midwife and general practitioner. Bereavement counselling was
offered to both parents between 24 and 48 hours after the baby's death.
The follow-up arrangements were planned to ensure that parents received
obstetric counselling from their obstetrician, genetic counselling if
necessary, and an opportunity to discuss the post mortem results with a
paediatrician.

The contrast group (C) had a wide variation of care, which depended on a
number of factors including the attitude of individual staff members and
the parents' own reactions to their loss. The minimum care (which
applied in very few cases) consisted of no opportunity to see the baby;
automatic placement in a single room on the isolation floor; discharge
home within 24 hours and no hospital follow-up.

Inevitably, it proved difficult to maintain this comparison as the study
proceeded, and staff attitudes changed.

Evaluation

Both the supported group and the contrast group were assessed 6 and 14
months after the baby's death. The families' general practitioners were
first asked for permission to proceed; then a letter was sent to the
parents asking for their cooperation with the study. The evaluation took
place in the parents' home and was carried out by a trained interviewer
who did not know to which group the family had been allocated. A semi-
structured interview was used, based on the work of Parkes (1964). In
addition, the parents were asked to complete two standardized self-rating
scales to measure psychiatric disorder: the General Health Questionnaire
(Goldberg, 1972) to give a general assessment of the presence of psychiatric disorder; and the Leeds Scales (Snaith, Bridge and Hamilton,
1976) to give more specific information about the presence of depression
and anxiety.

Counselling

The first interview was offered to both parents in the supported group
before they left hospital – usually between 24 and 48 hours after the
baby's death. If one of the medical social workers already knew the
family, she offered this counselling. Otherwise, one of the midwives
would offer the parents an interview with a family psychiatrist (GCF).
(20 parents (80 per cent) accepted this offer; and the fathers seemed
pleased to be included). For most families this was their first
experience of bereavement and they welcomed help with the mourning process. The aims of the first interview were to establish rapport with the
parents; assess their personal resources for coping with their loss;
define their supportive network at home; help create real memories of the
baby; and facilitate the expression of emotion. It was found that a
thorough knowledge of the registration procedures and funeral arrangements was helpful in establishing rapport (see Forrest, Claridge and
Baum, 1981). Afterwards a home visit was always offered for additional
counselling and 12 parents accepted this. Further counselling was
offered until it was felt that the parents were well established in their
mourning and well supported in their neighbourhood. For most couples
this took 2-6 weeks; for 4, it required longer – up to 3 sessions spanning
4 months (Fig. 1). In 2 of these cases, it was felt that normal mourning
was never successfully achieved.

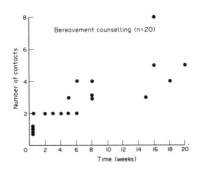

Figure 1. Bereavement counselling

Results of the Assessments

Thirty five women were interviewed at 6 months (16 of the supported group
and 19 of the contrast group; compliance rate 70 per cent. Ten women
declined to take part; the general practitioners of another 4 did not
wish their patients to be contacted 'for fear of upsetting them'; and one
couple had left the country. Some information relating to these 14 women
was collected from their general practitioners. The interviews took
between 1 and 2 hours, and although husbands were invited, only 6 attended. However, 26 husbands completed the self-rating scales and posted

them a few days later.

All the mothers interviewed had experienced typical bereavement symptoms; initial shock and numbness. 'We looked at her in our arms. I thought: Why doesn't she wake up now?' This was followed by tearfulness, sadness, lethargy, insomnia, physical manifestations of anxiety such as palpitations, guilt and irritability - all these symptoms tending to intensify in bouts, the 'pangs' of grief. They had all searched for a cause of their baby's death, and most had experienced angry feelings in the first month or so. They recalled with great clarity any unhelpful remarks like the obstetrician who asked one mother how she wanted her baby 'disposed of', or another who said 'there's a lot of wastage all along the line'.

Results of Self-Rating Scales

The standard cut-off point for psychiatric disorder with the 60 item General Health Questionnaire (GHQ) is a score of 12+. At 6 months, 2 of the 16 supported mothers versus 10 of the 19 contrast mothers were scoring 12+ on the GHQ indicating a lower rate of psychiatric disorder in the supported group ($p < 0.01$ - Fisher's Exact Test). When the scaled version of the GHQ was examined (Goldberg and Hillier, 1979) anxiety, somatic symptoms and impairment of social functioning were as common as depressive symptoms in the high scorers.

Three particular symptoms were experienced by the high scorers: a preoccupation with thoughts of the dead baby; frequent feelings of numbness; and difficulty accepting that the baby was dead. There was no statistically significant difference in incidence of high scores after stillbirth compared with neonatal death.

At 14 months 4 women declined to be interviewed a second time, stating that they felt nothing had changed. One woman had moved abroad, and could not be traced. A total of 30 women were interviewed. The results of the GHQ at this time showed no statistically significant difference between the supported and contrast group. Half of the women in both groups who had had scores of 12+ at 6 months were now scoring below 11: one of the 12 supported women versus 4 of the 18 contrast women remained ill (n.s.): and there were 2 new 'cases' in the supported group and one in the control group (2 of these associated with the birth of another baby))Fig. 2).

We concluded that support and counselling had significantly shortened the length of the bereavement reactions.

Pregnancies

One mother put it like this:

'All you want after an experience like that is to have another baby. There is such a gap, it has to be filled'.

By 6 months, 16 (32%) of the 49 women in the study had become pregnant again (including 3 who miscarried later). By 14 months, this figure had risen to 28 (56%). During the study, 11 women delivered live babies.

The incidence of pregnancies in the supported group and the contrast
group was similar at both 6 and 14 months in spite of the fact that the
women in the supported group had been advised to wait until they felt
they had recovered from the loss of the baby. However, there appeared to
be a difference in the association between psychiatric disorder and pregnancy in the 2 groups. At 6 months, of the 35 women interviewed, 11 were
pregnant - 3 of the 16 supported group and 8 of the 19 contrast group.
None of the 3 pregnant women in the supported group was showing psychiatric disorder (as measured by the GHQ); by contrast 6 of the 8 pregnant women in the contrast group were showing psychiatric disorder (p =
0.06, Fisher's Exact Test). At 14 months, 7 of the interviewed group
were pregnant. This time, only one of the 5 pregnant contrast group
women was showing psychiatric disorder compared with one of the 2 supported women.

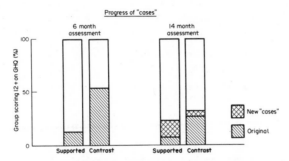

Figure 2.   Progress of 'cases'

We concluded that the unsupported women were not ready by 6 months to
cope with the stress of another pregnancy. By 14 months however, they
had recovered sufficiently with or without support and counselling to
cope with a pregnancy.

'At Risk' Factors

In an attempt to identify 'at risk' factors in the women in this study, a
number of factors were studied retrospectively in the contrast group and
their association with high scores in the GHQ at 6 months assessed
(Table 1). The mother was rated as socially isolated if she could not
name anyone among her family or acquaintances whom she perceived as supportive. The marital relationship was rated low in intimacy if the mother
reported an inability to share or discuss emotionally-charged topics with
her husband.

The only statistically significant associations with a high score were
social isolation (p = < 0.04) and poor relationship (low intimacy) with
husband (p = < 0.02). It is of course unsatisfactory to rate these factors retrospectively but our results were remarkably similar to Raphael's

findings that widows who lacked a (perceived) supportive network were most
at risk for atypical bereavement reactions (Raphael, 1977). More research,
i.e. a prospective study, is needed to clarify these possible risk factors.

Table 1. 'At risk' factors for high GHQ
scores in the contrast group

Infertility	n.s.
Low social class	n.s.
F.H. psych. illness	n.s.
Previous psych. illness	n.s.
Children under 14 at home	n.s.
Caesarian section	n.s.
Stillbirth	n.s.
No previous bereavement	n.s.
Social isolation	p = 0.04
Poor relationship with husband	p = 0.02

Mothers' Comments on Their Care

At the end of the interviews, the mothers were asked to comment on the
care they had received, in hospital or at home (Table 2). Only one woman
stated that she would not go back to the same unit to have another baby.
Nearly half, however, felt that their care could have been improved.
Most comments concerned communications with medical staff. The vast
majority of the mothers did not blame their doctors for their baby's
death, nor did they expect their doctors to say something to make them
feel better. They wanted them to explain in clear, simple language what
had gone wrong, and then to listen and accept their distress. Some had
found lack of sympathy or understanding of their predicament among the
staff very upsetting; e.g. the technician who prevented one father accom-
panying his wife while she had a scan to confirm the intra-uterine death
of their baby, saying, 'It's not a peep show, you know'.

Lack of communication between staff was another source of distress for
the mothers; e.g. the day after one woman's baby boy died, a midwife came
in and inquired when they were going to deliver her; 2 weeks after her
discharge home the Health Visitor arrived 'to check on the baby', and
finally, after sending a small sum of money to the Special Care Baby Unit
they received a note thanking them for their donation and sending 'best
wishes to your little boy'.

Where mothers had felt that their care had been good, it appeared that
'flexibility' had been an important part of this; e.g. mothers who had
been able to choose where they wanted to go afterwards (to a single room,

or back to the ward and 'friends'); those parents who had been encouraged
to choose the kind of funeral they wanted for their baby, and had been
allowed to make special arrangements for the service, like adding their
own prayers or readings. The photographs of the dead babies that had
been taken for the supported group proved to be of value mainly to those
parents who had declined to see their baby at delivery, and regretted
this later. They were then very glad to be able to have the photograph.

Table 2. Mothers' comments on care

N = 32	
Poor communication with doctors	18
Poor management of pregnancy/delivery	12
Poor management of postnatal care	6
Inadequate follow up	4
Difficulties with friends	3
Registration difficulties	2

Conclusions

The results of this study showed that support and counselling significantly shortened the length of the bereavement reaction after a perinatal
death. They also suggested that women were not ready to cope with
another pregnancy before 6 months, unless they have been so supported.

We concluded from this study that child psychiatrists, psychologists and
psychiatric social workers can play a vital part in the care of bereaved
parents in the following ways:

1. Stimulating maternity unit staff to take an interest and become
   actively involved in the psychological aspects of the care of
   parents whose baby dies. This should include developing a famil-
   iarity with the local procedures for registration and burial as
   well as paying attention to the practical management of the death,
   follow up arrangements, etc.

2. Providing counselling for the small proportion of parents who will
   require this in addition to general supportive care. It is clearly
   important to try and identify those women most 'at risk' of prolonged or abnormal bereavement reactions. Further research is
   needed, but socially isolated women appear to be particularly vulnerable.

3. Teaching the emotional aspects of death and bereavement to student
   midwives, paediatricians and obstetricians.

4. Being available for consultation by the hospital staff, e.g. social

workers and the self-help organizations such as the Stillbirth and
Perinatal Death Association.

References

FORREST, G. C., CLARIDGE, R. and BAUM, J. D. (1981) The practical manage-
    ment of perinatal death. *British Medical Journal*, 282, 31-32.
GOLDBERG, D. P. (1972) *The Detection of Psychiatric Illness by Question-
    naire.* London, Oxford University Press.
GOLDBERG, D. P. and HILLIER, V. F. (1979) A scaled version of the
    General Health Questionnaire. *Psychological Medicine*, 9, 139-145.
KLAUS, M. H. and KENNELL, J. H. (1976) *Maternal-infant Bonding.* London,
    H. Kimpton.
LEWIS, E. and PAGE, A. (1978) Failure to mourn a stillbirth - an over-
    looked catastrophe. *British Journal of Medical Psychology*, 51, 237-
    241.
HEALTH EDUCATION COUNCIL (1978) *The Loss of your Baby.* London, Health
    Education Council.
OFFICE OF POPULATION CENSUS AND SURVEYS (1980) *Monitor DH3 81/3.* London,
    H.M.S.O.
PARKES, C. M. (1964) The effects of bereavement on physical and mental
    health. *British Medical Journal*, 2, 274.
RAPHAEL, B. (1977) Prevention intervention with the recently bereaved.
    Archives of General Psychiatry, 34, 1450-1454.
SNAITH, R. P., BRIDGE, G. W. and HAMILTON, A. (1976) The Leeds Scales
    for the self-assessment of anxiety and depression. *British Journal of
    Psychiatry*, 128, 156-165.

CHAPTER 16

Bereaved Children — Family Intervention

Dora Black and Marie Anne Urbanowicz

*Department of Child Psychiatry, Edgware General Hospital,
Edgware, Middlesex*

In 1963 Bowlby suggested that pathological forms of grief were more
common in children. Research studies at the time and subsequently showed
a small but significantly increased risk of children whose parent dies
developing psychiatric disorders later in childhood or in adult life.
(Rutter, 1966; Birtchnell, 1970, 1972; Hill, 1969; Brown, Harris and
Copeland, 1977). What is the cause of the association between childhood
bereavement and later psychiatric disorder? And is it possible for us to
devise preventative programmes for bereaved children?

For women bereaved of a spouse, numerous research studies have demonstrated
that certain situations predispose to pathological outcomes - for
example, widows with poor networks of support, who have experienced
other recent bereavements, where the prior relationship was ambivalent
and where the spouse contributed in some way to his death. (Summarized
in Parkes, 1972.) Intervention studies in adults (Parkes, 1977; Raphael
and Maddison, 1976) have shown that, especially with widows at high risk,
intervention at the time of bereavement can significantly improve short-
term outcome.

There have as yet been no research studies with unselected groups of
children, trying to link outcome with experiences before and at the time
of bereavement. The problems of such research are of course immense, not
least of which is the ethical one. If pathology is high in bereaved
children, then can we justify studying them without offering help? And
if we intervene then we may alter outcome. The widowed are very protective of their young - and rightly so - and where they may accept an
interview for themselves with no promise of benefit, risking anew the
arousal of painful grief, they will not permit it for their children.

Bowlby and others have suggested that the pathological outcome in
bereaved children may be related to difficulties in the expression of
grief, and that this may be due to a development incapacity to mourn, to
difficulties that the surviving adults have in permitting children to
mourn and to difficulties in sharing their own grief with their offspring. (See Bowlby, 1969, 1972, 1980 for review.) If this is the case,
then we hoped that by promoting communication within the family about the
dead parent, and stimulating grief reactions by techniques familiar to

family therapists (Black, 1981) we might increase healthy mourning and
reduce pathology.

The Study

The present study attempted to overcome some of the ethical and
practical problems in studying bereaved children by including the
surviving parent in the intervention. We therefore identified 100
unselected families where a parent had just died and where there was
a child or children of 16 or under. Recruitment to the study required
the co-operation of records clerks in 4 hospitals and receptionists
in 12 general practices, over a three-year-period (1977-1980). The
general practitioners of all patients between the ages of 20 and 65
who died in hospital were contacted. If the family contained
children, permission was obtained to include them in the study.

The families were randomly allocated to two groups and in one group
(treatment) contact was made with the surviving parent within two
months of bereavement. An offer was made by a specially trained
social worker under the aegis of Cruse - a national charity for the
widowed and their dependents, to meet the whole family at their home
for six sessions in order to help with problems arising from the
death.

The control families were not contacted at this time. We felt it
would have been unethical to do so without being prepared to offer
help if it were needed.

Both groups of parents were interviewed at home at one year after the
death and again at two years. On both occasions a structured interview lasting $3\frac{1}{2}$ to 4 hours, was administered by a psychologist or
social worker trained and experienced in interviewing techniques who
had not taken part in the treatment.

Of the 100 families identified, 80 were approached, 46 in the treatment group and 34 controls. The other 20 were not part of the
study - 6 were discarded after piloting the interviews, 7 lived too
far away or were recruited too late, one 'dead' parent was still
alive, in 4 the general practitioner refused permission to contact
and 2 were already in treatment with one of us (D.B.). Of the 46
offered treatment, 22 (48%) completed 3-6 sessions and 21 accepted
the first follow-up interview. Of the 34 controls, 24 (70%) accepted
interview, at one year post-bereavement.

Although to have lost 50% of the families who were offered treatment
may seem at first an unacceptably high rate of attrition; to have
engaged about half the families approached in an intervention programme they did not seek, which involved their children, within two
months of bereavement, is reasonably satisfactory. Raphael and
Maddison's paper (1976) does not mention the attrition rate and no
similar study with children is known to us. There were no age or
sex differences between the treatment refusers and the treatment
acceptors.

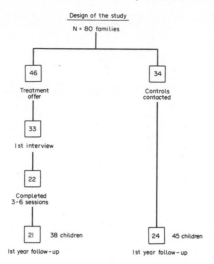

Figure 1.

The Intervention

Six family counselling sessions were offered starting about two
months after the death, at about 2-3 week intervals. The aims of the
therapist were to explore and try to help with emotional and practical problems arising from bereavement, to facilitate communication
about the dead parent between family members, and to help with the
expression, communication and resolution of grief. Toys and drawing
materials were taken to each interview as appropriate and towards the
end of the contract, the therapist tried to help the family to anticipate the grief reaction, albeit of a minor kind, her departure would
evoke, and to help them deal with it.

Results

We report on some of the data from the 1st year follow-up only. The
follow-up interviews were the same for both groups, apart from questions
evaluating treatment. Measures of parent's health and mood (Parkes,
1975), and children's mood, behaviour and health (Richman, Stevenson and
Graham, 1975; Rutter, Tizard and Whitmore, 1970), and school behaviour
and attainment (Rutter, Tizard and Whitmore, 1970) were used. Scales
measuring child sleep, home behaviour and parental mood were developed.
Other measures used will not be reported here.

D. Black and M. A. Urbanowicz

Table 1. Characteristics of the treatment and
control groups (children)

		T = 38	C = 45	
Sex	M	17	25	
	F	21	20	n.s.
Age at	0- 5	4	10	
bereavement	6-11	13	19	n.s.
	12+	20	15	
Family	1	14	13	
position	2	15	15	n.s.
	3	7	7	
	4+	2	10	

The total sample consisted of 83 children and 45 surviving parents.
Since the control group were not contacted until one year post-
bereavement, it was not possible to match them at the time with the
treatment group. Tables 2 and 3 show that in spite of this, the groups
were surprisingly well matched and although there were more younger
children and surviving mothers in the control group, the differences did
not reach significance.

Table 2. Characteristics of the treatment and
control groups (surviving parents)

		T = 21	C = 24	
Sex of	M	12	7	
surviving				n.s.
parent	F	9	17	
	30	1	2	
	40	6	7	n.s.
	50	11	5	
	65	3	5	
Number of	1	8	9	
children	2	8	9	n.s.
under 17	3	5	4	
	>3	0	2	

Outcome of Treatment

The outcome of treatment will be reported in detail elsewhere (Black and
Urbanowicz, 1983). The treatment group were significantly better on a
number of measures and these differences were maintained even when

corrections were made to allow for children's age and parental sex differences between the two groups. The treatment/control differences are summarized in Tables 3 and 4.

Table 3. Summary of major differences between treatment and controls

---

Treated children at 1st year follow-up

---

1. Had fewer and more transient behaviour
   problems at home and at school
   [C = 41% *vs* T = 21%]   p = 0.05

2. Had fewer post-bereavement sleep
   problems (children over 5 years)   p = 0.05

3. Had better health   p = 0.08

4. Cried more about the dead parent   n.s. but trend

5. Had parents who were less depressed   n.s. but trend

6. More often talked about the dead parents   p = 0.04

7. Were less restless and had less nail-   p = 0.09 and 0.02
   biting (Rutter A)

8. Had fewer learning problems   p = 0.09

Table 4. Summary of major differences between treatment and controls

---

Treated parents at 1st year follow-up

---

1. Mood less depressed   p = 0.05

2. Sought less help from professional
   agencies [C = 25%, T = 0%]

3. Had better physical health   p = 0.09

In addition to the results which reached or approached significance nearly all other results tended to be in the predicted direction - for example the Rutter A (Parents' questionnaire) scores were all higher in control children than treatment children, 33 per cent of control children having scores higher than 9 compared with 10 per cent of the treatment children (p = 0.06).

This paper looks particularly at the characteristics of the total group
of bereaved parents and children. On the whole the bereaved women seemed
to fare worse on measures of physical and mental health than the men.
The men in our group were able to continue their work but even working
women were more depressed than working men. However women earn less, so
finances could have caused this difference. More children of surviving
fathers acquired some kind of substitute parent than of mothers. None of
the parents gave their children up to children's homes or other families,
a solution used more often in the past. More of the men had remarried (4
men compared with one woman) by the first anniversary of the death.
Children of surviving mothers less often talked about the dead parent
than children with surviving fathers. Parental mood – a measure of
present grief, worry, depression, and suicidal thoughts – was a sensitive
measure, and on this measure more women than men were depressed.
Children who had a depressed parent talked less frequently about the dead
parent and had more behaviour problems, at follow-up. Their behaviour
changes following bereavement were more likely to persist. The closer
the family the better the parent's mood. There seems to be a tendency
for children to protect an ill parent – be it physical or emotional illness. If a parent was in poor physical health the children were less
likely to talk about the dead parent and less likely to do well at
school. This reluctance of the child to stress an ill parent was very
obvious in our treatment sessions: one 9-year-old child whispering when
mother was out of the room 'no child should have to bear what I have to'.

About half the children had behavioural changes after the bereavement and
there were few age or sex differences (see Table 5). By one year the
incidence of behaviour problems was about one-third (26/83 – 40 per cent
controls vs 21 per cent treatment). Kaffman and Elizur (1979) in their
study of 2-10 year olds in Israeli Kibbutzim who were bereaved by the
Yom Kippur war and who were seen 1-6 months later, also found an incidence of 50 per cent behaviour changes.

Table 5. Bereaved children 1982

Age at Bereavement	N	None	Some	Regressive (Soiling Wetting, etc.)	Con-duct	Emotional	Other
				Behaviour changes since bereavement			
				Type			
0- 5 years	(15)	10	5	3	0	2	0
5- 8 years	(13)	5	8	1	3	3	1
8-11 years	(17)	9	8	0	4	4	0
11-16+ years	(35)	17	18	2	2	12	2
Total	(80)	41	39	6	9	21	3

We looked at the pattern of children crying about the dead parent, both around the time of the bereavement and later. Children who cried more also talked more about him and those children who did not cry also avoided talking. This was so at all ages but as few of the under-fives cried much, we looked separately at the over-fives and found that this association increased in significance (p = 0.07 all ages, 0.02 over-fives). Over-fives who cried more had fewer and less serious behaviour and emotional problems (p = 0.002). Treatment increased the crying scores and decreased behaviour problems.

Few of our children attended the funeral - predictably the older ones were more likely to. Funeral attendance was related to less and shorter lasting deviant behaviour, and increased crying.

More fathers died at home although there was no association between length of illness and place of death. If a parent died at home, the surviving parent was more depressed and the child's behaviour more disturbed.

Support for Bereaved Families

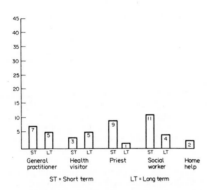

Figure 2.   Bereaved children 1982
(45 families)
Professional Support

What kind of support did our bereaved families receive? Both groups received poor support from professional care-givers - 17 families having none at all (see Fig. 2). Most people had help from a friend or relative but usually it was short-lived (see Fig. 3). Only 3 families had no non-professional support and 2 had no support from anyone. Asked what they would like, most people asked for temporary domestic help - only 2 had it and it preceded the death. Twenty five per cent of the control families found their way to other psychological help compared with none of the treatment families (excluding what we gave).

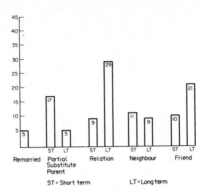

Figure 3.   Bereaved children 1982
(45 families)
Non-Professional Support

Did the people who accepted our intervention receive less support than
the treatment refusers?   We think it is unlikely.   Treatment acceptors
did not differ from the control group in the amount of support they
received and the controls did not receive any benefit from us.

Summary and Conclusions

We have of course no answers yet to the question of what factors might
prevent adverse outcome in bereaved children, in the long term.   However,
if crying for the dead parent and talking about him are evidence of
mourning - and we believe they are - then mourning is possible in
children, and its presence is associated with a better outcome in the
short term.

The ability to mourn appears, for children, to be associated with good
physical and mental health in the surviving parent, and a family intervention aimed at encouraging the expression of grief and family communication about the dead parent.

Widowed mothers seem more vulnerable to physical and mental ill health
than widowed fathers - perhaps because they receive less support from the
community and because they have more financial problems.   Neither age nor
sex of the child seemed related to outcome.   There was no relationship
between outcome and the sex of the child *vis-a-vis* the dead parent - at
least in the short term.

There are many deficiencies in this study - not least of which is direct
contact with the children at follow-up.   Nevertheless what is emerging is
it is possible to do for children what we know can be done for bereaved
adults: that is we can promote grief and by doing so decrease pathological outcomes - at least in the short term.

Acknowledgments

The Mental Health Research Fund supported this research which was sponsored by Cruse, 126, Sheen Road, Richmond, Surrey. We acknowledge our gratitude to them and to many colleagues for their advice and help; principally Dr. C. M. Parkes, Professor P. Graham, Dr. W. Kinston and Mr. J. Stevenson.

References

BIRTCHNELL, J. (1970) Case register study of bereavement. *Proceedings of the Royal Society of Medicine*, 64, 279-282.

BIRTCHNELL, J. (1972) Early parent death and psychiatric diagnosis. *Social Psychiatry*, 7, 202-210.

BLACK, D. (1981) Mourning and the family. In S. Walrond-Skinner (Ed.). *Developments in Family Therapy*, pp. 189-201. London, Routledge & Kegan Paul.

BLACK, D. and URBANOWICZ, M. A. (1983) *Family Intervention with Bereaved Children: a Research Report*. Manuscript submitted for publication.

BOWLBY, J. (1963) Pathological mourning and childhood mourning. *Journal of the American Psychoanalytic Association*, 11, 500-541.

BOWLBY, J. (1969, 1972, 1980) *Attachment and Loss* (three volumes). London, Hogarth Press.

BROWN, G. W. HARRIS, T. and COPELAND, J. R. (1977) Depression and loss. *British Journal of Psychiatry*, 130, 1-18.

HILL, O. W. (1969) The association of childhood bereavement with suicidal attempt in depressive illness. *British Journal of Psychiatry*, 115, 301-304.

KAUFFMAN, M. and ELIZUR, E. (1979) Children's bereavement reactions following death of the father. *International Journal of Family Therapy*, 1, 203-229.

PARKES, C. M. (1972) *Bereavement: Studies of Grief in Adult Life*. London, Tavistock.

PARKES, C. M. (1975) Determinants of outcome following bereavement. *Omega*, 6, 303-323.

PARKES, C. M. (1977) Evaluation of family care in terminal illness. In E. R. Pritchard (Ed.), *Social Work with the Dying Patient and the Family*, pp. 49-79. New York, Columbia University Press.

RAPHAEL, B. and MADDISON, D. (1976) The care of bereaved adults. In O. W. Hill (Ed.), *Modern Trends in Psychosomatic Medicine - 3*. London, Butterworths.

RICHMAN, N., STEVENSON, J. and GRAHAM, P. (1975) Prevalence of behaviour problems in three year-old children. *Journal of Child Psychology and Psychiatry*, 16, 277-287.

RUTTER, M. (1966) *Children of Sick Parents*. Oxford, Oxford University Press.

RUTTER, M., TIZARD, J. and WHITMORE, K. (1970) *Education, Health and Behaviour*. London, Longmans.

PART FOUR

Review Papers

CHAPTER 17

The Home Inventory: Rationale and Research

Robert H. Bradley

*Center for Child Development and Education, University of
Arkansas at Little Rock, Little Rock, Arkansas, U.S.A.*

Until recently there were few techniques available for accurately and
precisely measuring a child's home environment. The intention of this
paper is to describe briefly the development of one such instrument, the
Home Observation for Measurement of the Environment (HOME) Inventory, and
to review a number of studies that may help clarify its potential usefulness as an assessment tool.

Description of HOME Inventory

Currently there are two versions of the HOME Inventory, one for infants
(birth to 3 years) and one for pre-schoolers (age 3 to 6 years). The
instruments designed for assessing the homes of infants contains 45 items
clustered in six sub-scales. Sample items from each sub-scale are contained in Table 1.

The HOME Inventory designed for use with families of pre-school age
children contains 55 items clustered into eight sub-scales. Sample items
from the eight sub-scales are found in Table 2.

Information needed to score items on the Inventory is obtained through a
combination of observation and interview. It is administered in the
child's home with information supplied by the child's primary caretaker.
Administration takes approximately one hour. It requires that the child
be present and awake during the time of the home visit.

Psychometric Properties

Researchers reporting data on interrater reliability include Elardo,
Bradley, and Caldwell (1975), 90 per cent; Caldwell (1967), 94.6 per
cent; Ramey and Mills (1977), 92 per cent; Wulbert, Inglis, Kriegsmann,
and Mills (1975), 92 per cent; and Johnson, Kahn, Hines, Leler and
Torres (1976), 85 to 90 per cent. The interobserver agreement on coding
the HOME items is quite high (the average of the above figures is 89.6
per cent). This level of agreement is probably due to the fact that all
items are scores in a binary (Yes-No) fashion, which does not require any

rating of degree within an item.

Table 1. Sample items from the HOME Inventory - infant version

---

1. Emotional and Verbal Responsivity of Mother
   Mother responding to child's vocalization with a verbal response
   Mother caresses or kisses child at least once during visit

2. Avoidance of Restriction and Punishment
   Mother does not shout at child during visit
   Mother does not interfere with child's actions or restrict child's
      movements more than three times during visit

3. Organization of Physical and Temporal Environment
   When mother is away, care is provided by one of three regular substi-
      tutes
   Someone takes child into grocery store at least once a week

4. Provision of Appropriate Play Materials
   Child has some muscle activity toys or equipment
   Mother provides toys or interesting activities for child during
      interview

5. Maternal Involvement with Child
   Mother consciously encourages developmental advances
   Mother structures child's play periods

6. Opportunities for Variety in Daily Stimulation
   Father provides some caretaking every day
   Family visits or receives visits from relatives

Elardo *et al.* (1975) reported Kuder-Richardson-20 coefficients (KR-20)
for the infant scale, based on 176 cases, which ranges from 0.44 for sub-
scale VI, 'Opportunities for Variety in Daily Stimulation', to 0.89 for
sub-scale III, 'Organization of Physical and Temporal Environment'. The
KR-20 coefficient for the total scale was 0.89.

Bradley and Caldwell (1979) reported KR-20 coefficients for the pre-
school scale based on 117 families. They ranged from 0.53 to 0.83 for
the sub-scales and 0.93 for the total scale.

Studies Conducted at the Center for Child Development and Education

In 1969, Caldwell and her colleagues at the Center for Child Development
and Education, University of Arkansas, Little Rock, inaugurated a longitudinal observation and intervention study examining the relation of
home environments and day care to children's development. The partici-
pants were quite heterogeneous albeit the majority were from lower and
lower-middle income backgrounds. Approximately 65 per cent of the part-
icipants were black.

Table 2. Sample items from the HOME Inventory - pre-school version

1. Stimulation Through Toys, Games, and Reading Materials
   Record player and at least five children's records
   Family buys a newspaper daily and reads it

2. Language Stimulation
   Parent teaches child some simple manners - to say, 'Please', 'Thank
   you', 'I'm sorry'
   Mother uses correct grammar and pronunciation

3. Physical Environment - Safe, Clean and Conducive to Development
   Building has no potentially dangerous structural or health defect
   There is at least 100 square feet of living space per person in the
   house

4. Pride, Affection and Warmth
   Parent holds child close ten to fifteen minutes per day
   Mother spontaneously praises child's qualities or behaviour twice
   during visit

5. Stimulation of Academic Behaviour
   Child is encouraged to learn colours
   Child is encouraged to learn to read a few words

6. Modeling and Encouragement of Social Maturity
   Some delay of food gratification is demanded of child
   Child is permitted to hit parent without harsh reprisal

7. Variety of Stimulation
   Child has been taken by a family member to a scientific, historical or
   art museum within the past year
   Child eats at least one meal per day, on most days, with mother (or
   mother figure) and father or (or father figure)

8. Physical Punishment
   Mother does not use physical restraint, shake, grab, or pinch child
   during visit
   No more than one instance of physical punishment occurred during the
   past week

A series of publications involving this longitudinal study first appeared
in 1975. In the first study, 77 children and their families were
included (Elardo et al., 1975). The homes of the children were visited
and the HOME Inventory was administered when the children were 6-, 12-,
and 24-months-old. The children were also given the Bayley Scales of
Infant Development at these points and the Stanford-Binet Intelligence
test at age 3. The predictive validity of the Bayley Scales was contrasted with that of the HOME Inventory.

The Mental Development Index (MDI) from the Bayley Scales, measured at age one, correlated 0.32 (p < 0.01) with Binet IQ performance. By contrast, the multiple correlation between HOME sub-scale scores and 3-year IQ was computed at 0.59 (< 0.01), thus indicating that the HOME is a more effective predictor of IQ than the Bayley (see Table 3).

Table 3. Correlations between HOME scores and 36-month IQ

HOME sub-scales	Time of HOME assessment		
	6 months	12 months	24 months
1. Responsivity	0.25	0.39	0.50
2. Acceptance	0.24	0.24	0.41
3. Organization	0.40	0.39	0.41
4. Toys	0.41	0.56	0.64
5. Involvement	0.33	0.47	0.55
6. Variety	0.31	0.28	0.50
Total Score	0.50	0.55	0.70
Multiple correlation	0.54	0.59	0.72

In a follow-up study, Bradley and Caldwell (1976) found that the strong relation between HOME scores and IQ persisted. The multiple correlation between 6-month HOME scores and 54-month IQ scores was 0.50 (p < 0.01); the multiple correlation between 24-month HOME scores and 54-month Binet scores was 0.63 (< 0.01).

Elardo, Bradley and Caldwell (1977) investigated the relation between HOME scores in the first 2 years of life and language competence as measured by the Illinois Test of Psycholinguistic Abilities (ITPA) at age 3 years. Multiple correlations between 2-year HOME scores and 3-year ITPA scores were 0.57 for blacks and 0.74 for whites. In contrast with results for whites, only the 24-month HOME scores were predictive language competence among blacks. Furthermore, neither organization of the environment nor material involvement was as highly correlated with ITPA performance among blacks as whites. Some slight sex differences were also noted, with a stronger relation (non-significant) observed for females. Four of the six HOME sub-scales measured at 24 months showed higher correlations with language for females.

Recent studies conducted at the Center have sought to delineate more fully the relation between performance on the HOME Inventory and children's development. In one study, Bradley, Caldwell and Elardo (1977) investigated the relation among home environment, social status, and IQ for 105 children. Their findings showed that the HOME Inventory predicted 3-year IQ scores about as well as the combination of HOME and four SES indices (mother's education, father's education, occupation of head of household, amount of crowding). By comparison, there was generally a loss in predictive power when the SES variables were used by themselves. The most dramatic difference was among a black-only sub-group. In this group, the combination of HOME and SES accounted for almost three times as much variance as did SES alone (34 per cent *vs.* 12 per cent). The relatively high correlations obtained between HOME and IQ indicate that subtests of HOME are tapping aspects of the early socializ-ation of intelligence in both black and white homes, although the pattern of relations between HOME and IQ seems somewhat different for the two groups. As with ITPA results, correlations between HOME and IQ were higher for females than males (0.79 *vs.* 0.65).

The final study reported by the Little Rock group was a theoretical investigation of early environmental action. At issue was the observed strong correlation between early experience and later mental-test scores. Do such correlations indicate that early experience has unique salience for cognitive attainment? Alternatively, is the strong relation between early experience and later IQ primarily attributable to the fact that early experience is highly correlated with later experience (i.e. the quality of a child's environment remains stable and it is cumulating experience that makes the difference?) In an effort to examine these alternatives, a series of partial correlations was computed. Six-month HOME scores were correlated with 3-year IQ scores, with 12-month HOME scores partialed out. Similarly, 12-month HOME scores were correlated with 3-year IQ scores, with 6-month HOME scores partialed out. The results generally indicated that the 6-month HOME scores offered no unique prediction of IQ, whereas the residual correlation between 12-month HOME scores and IQ were significant. Some sex differences were noted in these correlations but most were non-significant.

Studies Conducted by Other Researchers

Health-related outcomes

The HOME scale was intended for use in assessing homes to identify those which pose a risk to a child's development. The efficiency of the HOME scale as a screening instrument has been explored in a variety of studies (see Bradley and Caldwell, 1978). The earliest, by Cravioto and DeLicardie (1972), was a prospective longitudinal study of a total group of 229 Mexican infants. Extensive environmental, health, and develop-mental data were gathered on all children, including HOME assessments twice yearly up to age three and once yearly thereafter. Of the 229 infants, 19 were identified as having experienced severe clinical mal-nutrition some time prior to age 30 months (with most of the cases occur-ring between the ages of one and three). After the 19 index cases of malnutrition had been identified, Cravioto and DeLicardie selected from the remaining 210 children a matched sample of 19 children for a compari-son group. The investigators examined the six month HOME scores of the two groups. The results indicated that the children who developed mal-nutrition were living at age six months in homes much lower in stimulation than were matched comparison children. When the homes were assessed again at 48 months, the picture was essentially the same.

The HOME Inventory was also employed in the Chase and Martin (1970) study
of undernutrition and child development. Nineteen children with a
primary diagnosis of generalized undernutrition provided the chief focus
of the investigation. The mean HOME scores of these children was six
points lower than the mean HOME scores of nineteen control children from
similar SES backgrounds.

The studies of malnutrition inaugurated a series of studies showing the
relation of HOME to health-related outcomes. Milar *et al.* (1980) examined
the relation between HOME scores and another health-related problem, lead
burden. Their study involved 52 children 10 to 73 months old. The
fifty-two children included twenty-six matched pairs (high lead burden
vs. low lead burden). Children in the two groups were matched for sex,
SES, and age. Results indicated lower scores for high lead burden
children on two sub-scales, Responsivity of Mother and Maternal Involvement. These two sub-scales were also related to maternal IQ. The total
HOME scores was correlated 0.60 with maternal IQ.

For years it has been recognized that many failure-to-thrive children
have no apparent organic basis for their condition. In an effort to more
fully delineate the psychiatric basis for the syndrome, Pollitt, Eichler
and Chan (1975) employed the HOME Inventory together with other measures
of the child's family environment for 19 index cases of failure-to-thrive
children and their matched controls. A shortened version of the HOME was
used for each case as were a few items from the Childhood Level of Living
Scale. Items clustered into three categories: development and vocal
stimulation, emotional climate, and reliable evidence of affections.
Results showed that mothers of index cases of failure-to-thrive displayed
less physical and verbal interaction with their children, were less
likely to praise, kiss, or caress their children, but were more likely to
scold, express annoyance, or slap their children.

Developmental Outcomes

Wulbert *et al.* (1975) examined the relationship between early environment
and language delay. These researchers identified a group of pre-school
children with delayed language development but who showed a high probability of having normal intelligence. The home environments of normal
children were also compared to those of children with a developmental
disability for which psychosocial causation would not be suspected,
Down's Syndrome. Results of their study revealed that the children with
a language disability did in fact live in a home environment which
differed markedly from that of the normal and the Down's Syndrome groups.

The Stanislawski (1977) investigation represents similar attempts to
evaluate the screening efficiency of the HOME scale. The ability of the
HOME to discriminate among three populations of children (developmentally
disabled, developmentally delayed, and developmentally normal) was
explored. The developmentally disabled group included children whose
developmental problems were attributable to neurological factors. The
developmentally delayed group included children whose problems did not
appear to result from physical conditions. Results showed that the HOME
scale differentiated between the environments of delayed children and the

environments of the other two groups. The mean score for the delayed
group was 32.7 as compared to means of about 40 for the other groups.

Siegel (1981) reports on a study of 148 mostly lower class infants from
Hamilton, Ontario who were part of a longitudinal investigation of preterm (birthweights under 1500 grams) and fullterm babies. The Bayley
scores during the first year of life showed moderate correlation to
Reynell language scores at age two (0.3 to 0.5). The 12 month HOME
scores generally showed low to moderate correlations with both Reynell
language scores and Bayley scores (0.2 to 0.4), the strongest relation
being that for Provision of Appropriate Play Materials. Siegel (1981)
also analyzed her data to establish the accuracy with which early infant
tests and HOME scores could predict developmental delay. She divided
children into four groups for the purpose of this analysis: (a) True
negatives were children who received scores of $\geq$ 85 on the Bayley at two
years and also at the early period, four, eight, twelve, or eighteen
months, that is they did not show developmental delay; (b) True positives
received scores of < 85 at two years and also at four, eight, twelve, or
eighteen months, that is they did show developmental delay; (c) False
negatives received scores of $\geq$ 85 at two years, but scores of < 85 at
four, eight, twelve, or eighteen months, that is they did not score in the
risk range at infancy but were delayed at two years; and (d) False
positives received scores of < 85 at two years by scores of $\geq$ 85 at four,
eight, twelve, and eighteen months and thus they scored in the risk range
in infancy but were not delayed at two years. A similar pattern was also
followed with the Reynell. Siegel (1981) concluded that: 'Infants who
were performing in the risk range early in development but whose subsequent development at two years was normal, the false positives, came
from more stimulating environments as measured by the HOME scale ....
In addition, infants who were not detected as being at risk early in
development, but showed developmental delay at two years, the false
negatives, came from homes which may not have provided sufficient stimulation to overcome the delay'.

Among the most recent studies investigating the predictability of the
HOME Inventory is one reported by Piper and Ramsay (1980) involving 37
Down's Syndrome infants. The infants were followed for a six month
period (mean age at entry: 8.9 months). Changes in their mental developmental over this period, as measured by the Griffiths Mental Developmental
Scales, were correlated with initial scores on the HOME Inventory.
Results showed that three HOME sub-scales, Organization of the Environment, Variety in Daily Stimulation, and Maternal Involvement with Child,
were significantly related to the Griffiths Personal/Social Scale. A
discriminant analysis composed of these three sub-scales differentiated
the infants into two groups according to the group was associated with a
better organization for the environment.

VanDoorninck et al. (1977) completed a long term study of the screening
efficiency of the HOME. They found that 43 per cent of the children from
lower-class families had school problems, including low scores in achievement tests, low grades, and poor performance in reading and math. Only
7 per cent of the higher social class had children with such school problems. In their sample, 56 per cent of the low SES children had no
reported school problems. These low SES children had no reported school

problems. These low SES, high achievement families would have been need-
lessly identified and 'assisted' with supplemental programs. These
investigators noted that the overinclusion of the low SES children in the
high risk group could have been avoided to a large extent if HOME scores
would have been employed to classify children at risk. When twelve month
HOME scores were used, prediction was much more accurate (VanDoornick *et
al.*, 1977). Sixteen of twenty-four children whose families received low
HOME scores (67 per cent) developed significant school problems. By comparison, 81 per cent (42 of 52) children whose families received high
HOME scores had no apparent school problems.

In a sophisticated investigation of environmental effects of educational
effects of educational and cognitive attainment, Jordan (1976) used three
means of assessing environmental quality: SES, the Home Inventory, and
the Coddington Scale, which measures the amount of change in a child's
life. At age 5, the 165 St. Louis children who took part in the longitudinal study were also assessed with the Wide Range Achievement Test
(WRAT), reading subtest, and the Raven's Coloured Progressive Matrices, a
non-verbal measure of cognitive capability. An interaction regression
procedure was used to examine how the various components of the child's
environment interacted to affect performance on the two outcome measures.
All three environmental measures showed strong relations with cognitive
performance. Perhaps more important, interactions were observed between
the three environmental measures in terms of their effect on cognitive
competence. Certain aspects of the environment seemed significantly
related to the criterion-developmental measures only when certain other
environmental measures reached a particular level. To be more specific,
the WRAT scores of children with low SES were significantly related to the
HOME scores. Based on results of another interaction regression analysis,
Jordan (1978) concluded that: 'the pattern of elements within homes
(especially the HOME scores) exerts an influence on language development
greater than that of any other factor in the complex of influences
chosen for the study'.

                           Pre-School HOME

Relatively fewer studies have been published using the pre-school version
of the HOME Inventory. The most extensive data available on the pre-
school version are reported in Bradley and Caldwell (1979). The study
involves 117 pre-school age children and their families (62 per cent
black). Families represented diverse socioeconomic backgrounds with a
disproportionate number from lower to lower middle class. Assessments of
the home environment at age three showed moderate correlations with IQ at
age three (0.2 to 0.5) with the highest correlation being for Toys,
Games, and Reading Materials (0.47) and Variety of Stimulation (0.45).
As Table 4 shows, the same level of relation was observed between three
year HOME scores and IQ assessed at age 4½ years. The total HOME score
was correlated 0.54 with IQ. HOME assessments at 4½ years also showed
moderate correlations with IQ. The strongest correlations were for Stimulation of Academic Behavior (0.47), Toys, Games, and Reading Materials
(0.55), and Variety of Stimulation (0.51).

Recently Bradley and Caldwell (1981) reported on a study of 60 black pre-
school children and their families (30 male, 30 female). The children
were mostly from lower to lower middle class backgrounds. In the case of
black females, generally moderate correlations were observed between HOME
sub-scale scores. The two HOME sub-scales showing the highest correlations were Toys, Games and Reading Materials, (0.5) and Pride, Affection, and Warmth, (0.05). When maternal education and child IQ were out
of the HOME-achievement test relationship, little significant residual
effect was observed. A somewhat different pattern of relations was
obtained for black males. Specifically, four of the HOME sub-scales
demonstrated significant relations with achievement: Toys, Games and
Reading Materials of Academic Behaviour (0.47). Unlike the situation
with black females, when maternal education and pre-school IQ were
partialled out of the HOME-achievement test relation, significant
relations remained. HOME scores contributed significantly to prediction
of school achievement beyond what could be predicted from child IQ and
maternal education information.

A recent study of the HOME scores of methadone-treated and matched non-
drug dependent mothers revealed the generality of the relation of HOME to
health and development outcomes (Strauss et al., 1979). There were 31
drug-exposed and 27 comparison cases, all black. Children with higher
General Cognitive scores on the McCarthy Scales came from homes that
scored higher on two HOME sub-scales: Physical and Language Stimulation,
and Non-Restrictive or Punitive. More importantly, a multivariate ANOVA
showed no significant differences between the methadone-treated mothers
and comparison mothers on the HOME. However, significant univariate
effects were obtained for physical and language stimulation, physical
punishment, and encouragement of independence sub-scales.

These studies attest to the HOME's potential usefulness in identifying
home environments associated with clinical malnutrition, with retarded or
above average mental development, with abnormal growth, and with poor
school performance. Each of the studies cited has limitations stemming
from both the sample and the research design employed. Additional cross-
validation studies should be conducted using different populations of
families and different ranges of IQ scores. However, HOME has been used
successfully in a variety of settings outside the United States, including Canada, Mexico, Guatemala, England, Japan, and Argentina. Moreover,
it has been used with a variety of ethnic groups within the United States,
including whites, blacks, Mexican-Americans, and other Spanish-speaking
Americans. It has been used effectively in urban, suburban, and rural
settings, and has been employed with children with special problems,
including Down's syndrome, low birthweight, language impairment, and drug
dependency.

References

BRADLEY, R. and CALDWELL, B. (1976) The relationship of infants' home
    environments to mental test performance at fifty-four months: a
    follow-up study. Child Development, 47, 1171-1174.
BRADLEY, R. and CALDWELL, B. (1978) Screening the environment. American
    Journal of Orthopsychiatry, 48, 114-130.

BRADLEY, R. and CALDWELL, B. (1979) Home observation for measurement of the environment: a revision of the pre-school scale. *American Journal of Mental Deficiency*, 84, 235-244.

BRADLEY, R. and CALDWELL, B. (1981) The HOME Inventory: a validation of the pre-school scale for black children. *Child Development*, 52, 708-710.

BRADLEY, R., CALDWELL, B. and ELARDO, R. (1977) Home environment, social status and mental test performance. *Journal of Educational Psychology*, 69, 697-701.

CALDWELL, B. (1967) Descriptive evaluation of development and developmental settings. *Journal of Pediatrics*, 40, 46-54.

CHASE, H. and MARTIN, H. (1970) Undernutrition and child development. *New England Journal of Medicine*, 282, 932-939.

CRAVIOTO, J. and DeLICARDIE, E. (1972) Environmental correlates of severe clinical malnutrition and language development in survivors of Kwashiokor or Marasmus. In Pan-American Health Organisation, *Nutrition: the Nervous System and Behaviour*, Scientific Publication No. 251). Washington, D.C.

ELARDO, R., BRADLEY, R. and CALDWELL, B. (1975) The relation of infant's home environment to mental test performance from six to thirty-six months: a longitudinal analysis. *Child Development*, 46, 71-76.

ELARDO, R., BRADLEY, R. and CALDWELL, B. (1977) A longitudinal study of the relation of infants' home environments to language development at age three. *Child Development*, 48, 595-603.

JOHNSON, D., KAHN, A., HINES, R., LELER, H. and TORRES, M. (1976) Measuring the learning environment of Mexican-American families in a parent education program. Paper presented at the annual meeting of the American Educational Research Association, San Francisco, California.

JORDAN, T. (1976) Measurement of learning and its effects on cognitive and educational attainment. Paper presented at the annual meeting of the American Educational Research Association, San Francisco, California.

JORDAN, T. (1978) Influences on vocabulary attainment: a five year prospective study. *Child Development*, 49, 1096-1106.

MILAR, C., SCHROEDER, S., MUSHAK, P., DOLCOURT, J. and GRANT, L. (1980) Contributions of the caregiving environment to increased lead burden of the children. *American Journal of Mental Deficiency*, 84, 339-394.

PIPER, M. and RAMSAY, M. (1980) Effects of early home environment on the mental development of Down syndrome infants. *American Journal of Mental Deficiency*, 85, 39-44.

POLLITT, E., EICHLER, A. and CHAN, C. (1975) Psychosocial development and behaviour of mothers of failure-to-thrive children. *American Journal of Orthopsychiatry*, 45, 525-537.

RAMEY, C. and MILLS, P. (1977) Social and intellectual consequences of day care for high-risk infants. In R. Webb (Ed.), *Social Development in Childhood*, pp. 79-110. Baltimore, Johns Hopkins University Press.

SIEGEL, L. (1981) Home environmental influences on cognitive and language development in preterm and fullterm infants. Paper presented at the bienniel meeting of the Society for Research in Child Development. Boston, Massachusetts.

STANISLAWSKI, E. (1977) *A comparison of the DDST and HOME for Developmental Assessment with Three Populations of Young Children.* Unpublished master's thesis, University of Wisconsin.

STRAUSS, M., LESSEN-FIRESTONE, J., CHAVES, C. and STRYKER, J. (1979)
    Children of methadone-treated women at five years of age. *Pharma-
    cology, Biochemistry and Behaviour*, 2, (Supplement), 3-6.
VAN DOORNINCK, W., CALDWELL, B., WRIGHT, C. and FRANKENBURG, W. (1977)
    The relationship between the 12-month inventory of home stimulation
    and school competence. Paper presented at the bienniel meeting of
    the Society for Research in Child Development, Denver, Colorado.
WULBERT, M., INGLIS, S., KRIEGSMANN, E. and MILLS, B. (1975) Language
    delay and associated mother-child interactions. *Developmental Psy-
    chology*, 2, 61-70.

Table 4. Correlations between HOME scores for families with pre-school age children and mental test performance

Sub-scales	3 year HOME vs. 3 year IQ	3 year HOME vs. 4½ year IQ	4½ year HOME vs. 4½ year IQ	5-6 year HOME vs. 6-10 year IQ
	N = 91	N = 46	N = 51	N = 34
I. Stimulation Through Toys, Games and Reading Materials	0.47†	0.48†	0.55†	0.50†
II. Language Stimulation	0.39†	0.37*	0.40†	0.30
III. Physical Environment	0.25*	0.31*	0.22	0.23
IV. Pride, Affection and Warmth	0.43†	0.37*	0.27	0.32
V. Stimulation of Academic Behaviour	0.29†	0.41†	0.47†	0.28
VI. Modeling and Encouraging of Social Maturity	0.37†	0.17*	0.21	-0.15
VII. Variety of Stimulation	0.45†	0.47†	0.51†	0.36*
VIII. Physical Punishment	0.23*	0.32*	0.08	0.15
Total Score	0.55†	0.54†	0.58†	0.58†
Multiple Correlation	0.61†	0.58†	0.62†	0.67*

*p < 0.05
†p < 0.01

CHAPTER 18

The First Years: Pre-school Children and Their Families in the Inner City

Stephen Wolkind

Family Research Unit, London Hospital Medical College, London

Inner city areas provide a far from ideal setting in which to bring up children. Housing problems may be acute, schools can have high rates of teacher turnover and other difficulties, unemployment amongst parents will be common and resources for children few. With this well-described picture it is not surprising that rates of psychiatric disorder are high amongst children, both in absolute terms and in comparison with more favoured areas (Rutter *et al.*, 1975). Though common sense suggests that this should be the case, the actual reasons for the raised morbidity are not necessarily easily determined. Certain factors such as the ethos and morale of the school attended may impinge directly upon the child (Rutter *et al.*, 1979). With probably the majority of other factors, it seems likely that they are not acting immediately upon the child, but that their effects are being mediated through the family. Thus in the study quoted above describing differential area rates of disorder, the reasons for these differences were not necessarily related directly to characteristics of the areas. What seemed to be the case was the fact that various family characteristics such as maternal depression or poor parental relationships were associated in both types of area with child disorder. In the deprived area these adverse characteristics were much commoner.

For clinicians working in a deprived area, findings such as these can pose a number of dilemmas. Some would feel that they could be usefully employed seeking social change. Even if the possibility existed of clinicians producing change, we do not, in reality, know how any particular change would actually affect children. Remaining within the clinical setting, it is clear that facilities will rarely allow more than a small minority of children to be seen. Even if these were increased, many types of treatment were designed for use in families with few material difficulties and with adequate social supports. They might be totally inappropriate for those facing major deprivation. The obvious answer in such circumstances should lie in prevention, to develop strategies which could allow the identification of problems before they have become established or perhaps even before they have arisen. For this to be successful it is essential that we develop models which can explain why difficulties arise and, even more importantly, how they become maintained. In addition, it is necessary to identify target groups who will be

particularly vulnerable. Such issues have been explored over a number of
years in the Psychiatric Unit of The London Hospital Medical College.
The London serves a deprived area in the East of the City, the traditional East End of London. The work completed has involved both action
research and non-intervention studies of young children and their
families.

Action Research

The first move into pre-school work was the establishment in 1969, by
Desmond Pond, of the Pre-School Treatment Unit. This unit had as its aim
the attempt to determine the most appropriate type of facilities for disturbed under 5's living in disadvantaged families. The initial focus for
intervention was the mother-child relationship (Lindsay-German and
Coleman, 1971), with both mother and child attending the unit together.
Various disadvantages became apparent with this approach. The most
seriously disturbed children tended to have the least motivated mothers.
A follow-up of children treated in this way showed some improvements in
the home, but continuing problems when the child reached school (Mitchell,
Rothwell and Burtenshaw, 1975). As a result of these findings, the
regime was changed to provide an individually tailored programme designed
to deal with each child's cognitive, social and emotional deficits
(Coleman *et al.*, 1977). A further result of the follow-up study was the
awareness that it was possible to detect at age 3 or less children who
would later have difficulties in school. These findings led on to the
establishment of non-intervention studies, to seek the reasons for this
chronicity and determine points where limited intervention might be effective.

Non-Intervention Studies

An initial study of 3-year-olds within the community demonstrated that
approximately 20 per cent showed pictures of handicapping disorder and
that even at this young age the dichotomy between conduct and emotional
disorder could be seen (Wolkind and Everitt, 1974). A follow-up of these
children to age 5 showed moderate continuity of disorder in the home, but
at 5 little relationship between behaviour in the home and the school
(Coleman, Wolkind and Ashley, 1977). The next step of the work was the
setting-up of a longitudinal study, one which would follow-up a group of
children and young families from an even earlier stage.

The Longitudinal Study - The Sample

The sampling frame for the study comprised all British-born women, living
within the target borough, who in 1974-5 were booked into the antenatal
clinics of The London and were expecting their first babies. The cover-
age of the borough, by the hospital, is very comprehensive, and well over
95 per cent of primiparous women would be booked there. The sample was
predominantly Caucasian, but with approximately 10 per cent being black
or of mixed race. The restriction of the study to British-born women was
designed to exclude those in the local Bangladeshi community, many of

whom had, at that time, only a limited knowledge of English. Once identified, each woman was given, at the time of booking, a brief screening
interview. This was used in two ways. The code number of each interview was used to select a random sample, and its contents to select
women whom, it was hypothesized, would have higher than average rates of
difficulties with their children. The structure of the sample is shown
in Figure 1.

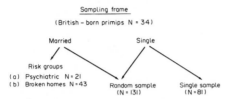

Figure 1. The longitudinal study - sampling frame

A random sample of 131 women was selected over the year. In addition all
single women, of whom 70 per cent were teenagers, comprised a risk group.
Two groups of married women were also selected as being a risk, those
with a previous history of psychiatric disorder and those coming from
broken homes. It was clearly possible for a woman to be selected for
random and risk samples. This was acceptable as each was to be used
differently. The random sample would be used to give the prevalence and
patterning of difficulties within a representative group. The risk
groups would provide pools in which, if riskness were confirmed, and high
rates of difficulties found, a detailed examination of the reasons for
this could be undertaken. Fuller details of the criteria and rationale
behind the concept of 'risk' can be found in Wolkind and Zajicek (1981).

Methods

Those women selected were seen at various intervals (Fig. 2).

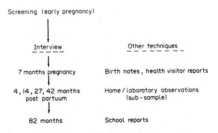

Figure 2. The study - methods

Semi-structured interviews were used, with interviewers being rotated so that no women were seen consecutively and only rarely ever by the same interviewer. Information collected included child behaviour, family relationships, maternal health, social data and child care practices and attitudes. For certain measures standardized instruments tested by other workers were used, e.g. child behaviour (Richman and Graham, 1971), maternal mental health (Rutter *et al.*, 1975), the marital state (Quinton, Rutter and Rowlands, 1976). A randomly selected sub-sample was also observed using ethologically-based observational methods (Hall, Pawlby and Wolkind, 1979) at home at 4 and 14 months and in a laboratory at 27 and 42 months.

Results

This study has revealed not only the problems, but also many positive aspects of family life in the inner city. On the positive side was a picture of the majority of young mothers being proud of their children and often, despite considerable material difficulties, coping well with parenthood. Most were supported in this by their husbands. On the negative side the minority affected by various problems was, for certain factors, worryingly high. Perhaps the most outstanding example was in depression amongst the mothers where almost a quarter were handicapped in their everyday functioning by this and a further 10-15 per cent had unpleasant symptoms without handicap (Wolkind, Zajicek and Ghodsian, 1980). Many in the sample were experiencing marital problems and the proportion increased as the study progressed. It will be of no surprise that the results of the study have produced no comprehensive and overall model to explain the variations seen amongst the sample. Nevertheless, as the analysis has continued a number of major themes have emerged and by examining the random and various risk groups these will be explored.

Social Support and Adult Relationships

The importance of current social support during adult life is a topic that is currently receiving considerable attention (e.g. Parkes and Stevenson-Hinde, 1982). Previously most emphasis was put on experience and relationships during an individual's childhood as the cause for later problems in areas such as parenting. Our results support the importance of current relationships, though it may well be that earlier events increase or decrease a woman's chances of these being satisfactory. This theme can be illustrated by examining the results for two of our risk groups, namely single mothers (Kruk and Wolkind, 1983) and those mothers who, during their own childhood, had, in addition to having come from a broken home, been in local authority care (Wolkind and Kruk, in press).

The first analyses suggested that both groups shared many similar characteristics. Each contained a high proportion of teenagers. They were more likely to come from large families with a father in an unskilled occupation. During pregnancy they both gave grounds for concern. Compared with the random sample they were less likely to have planned or initially wanted the baby. They were more likely to have smoked and had less realistic expectations of motherhood and of the child they were

expecting. After the birth and throughout the course of the study, both
groups were materially disadvantaged, in terms of general amenities and
housing. Here, however, the differences stopped. The single sample,
irrespective of their age at the birth, or whether or not they later
married, did no worse on any psychological measure than the predominantly older, initially married women, in the random sample. This applied
to both mother and child. In marked contrast the in-care group did very
badly. The mothers had consistently high rates of depression and they
were more likely to be in poor marriages. Their children were disadvantaged on a wide variety of measures. They started life with a significantly lower birthweight. On a wide range of behavioural measures they
showed high rates of difficulties in both the home and the school. At
four months, on observational measures, their mothers interacted far less
with them (Wolkind, Kruk and Hall, 1983).

An initial explanation for the different outcomes appeared to lie in the
childhood experiences of each group. The in-care women, by definition,
came from broken homes, where family failure had reached a point such that
they had to be cared for by a local authority (even though in many cases
this was for only a brief period during adolescence). Their memories of
their childhood were consistently negative and they described unhappy
experiences and relationships. The single women, in contrast, looked
back on their childhood with affection. These early experiences did not,
however, seem to explain the outcome. By looking at within group differences *current* relationships seemed of far greater importance. The good
outcome for the single group appeared to relate to the strong support
they received from their mothers during and after the pregnancy. This
seemed to have helped the women through the critical transitional phase
of early motherhood. Such support was generally lacking for the in-care
women. When it was present the outcome was better.

The Contribution of the Child

The effects of children upon their caretakers have been well documented
(Bell, 1974). It, therefore, seemed essential to include in the study
measures which could assess variations between the children and which
were independent of maternal perception. Two major measures used were
the Brazelton Neonatal Assessment (Brazelton, 1973) performed at six days
on the children in the observational sub-sample, and an interview-based
measure obtained at four months on the child's temperament. The method
used to assess temperament was based upon detailed questioning, initially
concerned with infants' behaviour on the day before the interview. This
was then broadened out to cover the previous week and then month. Ratings
were made on the interviewer's assessment of the child, according to pre-
determined definitions rather than on the mothers' perception. Validity
checks suggested that this did produce a rating independent of the
mother's feelings (Wolkind and De Salis, 1982). It is fair to say,
however, that within a sample characterized by both a high level of disadvantage *and* great variation in the degree of disadvantage, we did not
expect child variations to contribute a great deal to the picture. Our
hypothesis was that social factors would blanket out the child variability. This proved not to be the case.

At the end of the Brazelton assessment an evaluation was made as to
whether the baby should be regarded as 'atypical'. This was based on the
presence of various behavioural characteristics such as excessive tremul-
ousness or drowsiness, a weak cry or sudden changes from vigorous crying
to sleep ('state shooting'). At 27 months the laboratory observational
data was used to determine whether the infant showed evidence of non-
optional behaviour. This comprised for two-thirds of such children, a
timid, clingy, withdrawn picture. The remainder showed over-excitable,
aggressive behaviour, in some cases combined with bouts of withdrawal and
timidity. This assessment of non-optimal behaviour was very significantly
associated with an atypical rating at six days (Hall *et al.*, 1979). No
obvious biological or social characteristics could be found to explain
the Brazelton variations, though 'atypical' babies were of slightly lower
birthweight.

With the measure of temperament a wide range of descriptions were
obtained. On an 'easy/difficult' dimension an almost normal distribution
was found, with, at the extremes, some babies being noticeably regular,
of good mood and with low intensity, others being quite the opposite.
These variations were found to relate strongly to the number of behaviour
problems shown by the child at 42 months. A striking point, however, was
the way in which at this later time early temperament interacted with the
current mental state of the mother (Wolkind and De Salis, 1982). In the
total random sample, maternal depression at 42 months related strongly to
child behaviour problems at that time. Looking within the group this
did, however, depend on the child's earlier temperament. Thus, maternal
depression was associated with greater behaviour problems, only in those
children who had been in the two extreme quartiles of the temperamental
scale. Children in the two intermediate quartiles appeared later to be
unaffected by depression in their mothers. Thus, although there were
exceptions, a high level of behaviour problems at 42 months appeared to
require the combination of a particular temperament *and* a depressed
mother.

The possible effects of the child upon its mother was also seen in this
analysis. At 4 months infant temperament was unrelated to maternal
mental state, though mothers with temperamentally difficult children
reported more tiredness at that time. At the second post-partuum interview, conducted at 14 months, a number of mothers who had never previously
had any form of psychiatric disorder were rated as being depressed. A
disproportionate number of them had babies who had been rated as temperamentally 'difficult' at the previous interview.

Vicious Circles

The high rate of maternal depression in the sample was described above.
Perhaps even more worrying than the rate itself was the evidence for a
considerable degree of chronicity (Wolkind, Hall and Pawlby, 1977). This
can be well illustrated with that group of women defined as being at risk
because of their history of psychiatric difficulties occurring before the
pregnancy. At each stage of the study at least 50 per cent and more
usually at least 70 per cent had handicapping depression. It could be
suggested that this was due to personality disorder making these women

prone to depression throughout adult life. There is an alternative hypothesis.

Depression during pregnancy had no prognostic significance (Zajicek and Wolkind, 1978). After this stage, however, once a woman became depressed, her chance of remaining within the handicapped group was as high as that of the pre-pregnancy affected group. It seemed that in each case similar mechanisms were at work. An analysis of the 4-month interview data was conducted in order to determine why certain women experienced their first ever depression at that time (Zajicek and Wolkind, 1983). The only positive factors were the baby being born in a poor state and a deterioration in the quality of the marriage. We hypothesized that the anxiety about a baby causing concern could lower a woman's self esteem and precipitate depression (in a very similar way to that described above for 14-month depression and early infant temperament). It was not possible to determine the direction of the link between depression and the state of the marriage, but it was noticeable that it was found at all stages of the study. A further point was the association between maternal depression and child behaviour. During the later stages this behaviour concerned problems, at earlier stages, delays. For example, the children of depressed mothers were slower in attaining night-time bladder control (Zajicek and De Salis, 1979). At 4 months we found that they were less likely to be sleeping right through the night. It seems less important to discuss cause and effect than to think of a series of vicious cycles in which one problem attracts another which worsens the first and so on. A waking baby would have a significance for a depressed mother in a poor marriage quite different to that for one in more favourable circumstances. It seemed as if once depressed either before or after the pregnancy, it was extremely difficult for a woman and her family to 'escape' from the cycle. Using child behaviour problems as a starting point it was noticeable how, at each interview, the number of family and social factors associated with them, increased (Ghodsian, Zajicek-Coleman and Wolkind, 1983). A coalescence of difficulties was occurring.

Overview

Taken together, these different themes suggest that we are seeing, in this population, the way in which social, psychological and biological factors can combine and result in a child psychiatric disorder. This problem will, in turn, affect many of the contributing factors. The links over time are often exceedingly complex and show how simple models are not plausible. As an example, we attempted to examine the link between early maternal depression and later child problems (Ghodsian, Zajicek and Wolkind, 1984). A strong association for virtually all stages was found, but with the continuity of depression it was necessary to control for current maternal depression. When this was done, some, but not all of the associations, disappeared. It was then necessary to look for other factors which related both to earlier depression and later behavioural problems. Some, including the birth of a second sibling or overcrowding, were found. When these were controlled for more associations disappeared. These findings demonstrated how it was not possible to think of a mother-child relationship in isolation. It was affected by social and other family factors.

A further example can be seen with birthweight. This was found, in the observational sub-sample, to relate to the child's language ability at 27 months (Pawlby and Hall, 1979). Birthweight also related to various maternal factors. It was lower in babies born both to mothers who had been in care and those who were depressed during pregnancy (Wolkind, 1981). It linked with atypical signs on the Brazelton and indirectly with later behaviour in the laboratory. Taken together these findings suggest that the effects of a biological factor cannot be understood outside of its wider social context.

Implications

These last findings, when combined with the high rates of family, maternal and child problems present a bewildering picture. We feel, however, that the lack of simple findings is of considerable importance. There was no evidence for any single biological factor or psychological damage causing irreversible difficulties in either mothers or children. It seems that in looking at the development of these young families there were numerous points at which the course could change for good or bad. In terms of intervention the best lead comes from the comparison of single and in-care mothers. Continuing support from a concerned adult seemed to determine the outcome. The question for clinicians is whether, when that support is not available within the family, could it be provided by outsiders. It might well be that this is the case, and this suggests that a variety of evaluated interactions would be justified. These could involve volunteers as well as primary care workers. Such attempts would be worthwhile. Though the majority of the sample did well, the degree of distress and frustration in the minority was too great to be acceptable.

Acknowledgments

The work described in this paper was initiated by Professor Sir Desmond Pond. I and the colleagues I have quoted owe him a great debt for his continuing inspiration and help. The longitudinal study was generously funded by the MRC and SSRC.

References

BELL, R. Q. (1974) Contributions of human infants to care giving and
    social interaction. In M. Lewis and L. A. Rosenblum (Eds.), *The
    Effect of the Infant on its Caregiver*, pp. 1-20. London,
    John Wiley.
BRAZELTON, T. B. (1983) *Neonatal Behavioral Assessment Scale*, Clinics in
    Developmental Medicine, No. 50. London, Spastics International
    Medical Publications.
COLEMAN, J., BURTENSHAW, W., POND, D. and ROTHWELL, B. (1977) Psycho-
    logical problems of pre-school children in an inner urban area.
    British Journal of Psychiatry, 131, 623-630.
COLEMAN, J., WOLKIND, S. N. and ASHLEY, L. (1977) Symptoms of behaviour
    disturbance and adjustment to school. *Journal of Child Psychology and
    Psychiatry*, 18, 201-208.

GHODSIAN, M., ZAJICEK-COLEMAN, E. and WOLKIND, S. (1983) *A Comparative Study of Social and Family Correlates of Child Behaviour Problems.* Submitted for publication.

GHODSIAN, M., ZAJICEK, E. and WOLKIND, S. (1984) A longitudinal study of maternal depression and child behaviour problems. *Journal of Child Psychology and Psychiatry*, 25, 91-110.

HALL, F., PAWLBY, S. J. and WOLKIND, S. N. (1979) Early life experiences and later mothering behaviour: a study of mothers and their 20-week-old babies. In D. Shaffer and J. F. Dunn (Eds.), *The First Year of Life*, pp.153-174. Chichester, John Wiley.

KRUK, S. and WOLKIND, S. N. (1983) A longitudinal study of single mothers and their first children. In N. Madge (Ed.), *Families at Risk*, pp. 119-140. London, Heinemann.

LINDSAY-GERMAN, J. and COLEMAN, J. (1971) The Oxford House Day Unit, *British Hospital Journal and Social Service Review*, April, 714-716.

MITCHELL, W., ROTHWELL, B. and BURTENSHAW, W. (1975) Mothers and their disturbed pre-school children: an intervention study. *Child: Care, Health and Development*, 1, 389-396.

PARKES, C. M. and STEVENSON-HINDE, J. (Eds.) (1982) *The Place of Attachment in Human Behavior.* New York, Basic Books.

PAWLBY, S. J. and HALL, F. (1979) Evidence from an observational study of transmitted deprivation among women from broken homes. *Child Abuse and Neglect*, 3, 844-850.

QUINTON, D., RUTTER, M. and ROWLANDS, O. (1976) An evaluation of an interview assessment of marriage. *Psychological Medicine*, 6, 577-586.

RICHMAN, N. and GRAHAM, P. J. (1971) A behavioural screening questionnaire for use with three-year-old children. *Journal of Child Psychology and Psychiatry*, 12, 5-30.

RUTTER, M., MAUGHAN, B., MORTIMORE, P. and OUSTON, J. (1979) *Fifteen Thousand Hours: Secondary Schools and Their Effects on Children.* London, Open Books.

RUTTER, M., YULE, B., QUINTON, D., ROWLANDS, O., YULE, W. and BERGER, M. (1975) Attainment and adjustment in two geographical areas III. Some factors accounting for area differences. *British Journal of Psychiatry*, 125, 520-533.

WOLKIND, S. N. (1981) Pre-natal emotional stress-effects on the foetus. In S. N. Wolkind and E. Zajicek (Eds.), *Pregnancy: A Psychological and Social Study*, pp. 172-194. London, Academic Press.

WOLKIND, S. N. and EVERETT, B. (1974) A cluster analysis of the behavioural items in the pre-school child. *Psychological Medicine*, 4, 422-427.

WOLKIND, S. N. and KRUK, S. (In press) From child to parent. Early separations and the transition to parenthood. In A. R. Nicol (Ed.), *Lessons from Longitudinal Studies.* Chichester, Wiley.

WOLKIND, S. N. and De SALIS, W. (1982) Infant temperament, maternal depression and child behaviour problems. In M. Rutter (Ed.), *Temperamental Differences in Infants of Young Children.* (Ciba Symposium, No. 89). London, Pitman.

WOLKIND, S. N. and ZAJICEK, E. (1981) *Pregnancy: A Psychological and Social Study.* London, Academic Press.

WOLKIND, S. N., ZAJICEK, E. and GHODSIAN, M. (1980) Continuities in maternal depression. *International Journal of Family Psychiatry*, 1, 167-181.

WOLKIND, S. N., HALL, F. and PAWLBY, S. J. (1977) Identification in
    pregnancy of the 'At Risk" mother. In P. Graham (Ed.), *Epidemio-
    logical Approach in Child Psychiatry*, pp. 107-124 . London, Academic
    Press.
WOLKIND, S. N., KRUK, S. and HALL, F. (1983) The Family Research Unit
    Study of women from broken homes: What conclusions should we draw?
    In A. White Franklin (Ed.), *Family Matters*, pp. 32-42 . Oxford,
    Pergamon.
ZAJICEK, E. and De SALIS, W. (1979) The Family Research Unit study of
    child development. IV. Depression in mothers of young children.
    Child Abuse and Neglect, 3, 833-835.
ZAJICEK, E. and WOLKIND, S. N. (1978) Emotional difficulties during and
    after the first pregnancy in a sample of married women. *Journal of
    Medical Psychology*, 51, 379-385.
ZAJICEK, E. and WOLKIND, S. N. (1983) Depression in women four months
    after the birth of a first child. (Submitted for publication)

CHAPTER 19

Stress-resistant Children: the Search for Protective Factors

Norman Garmezy*

Department of Psychology, University of Minnesota,
Minneapolis, Minnesota 55455, U.S.A.

Introduction

The concept of risk has a centuries-old history; by contrast, the importance of 'protective factors' has only come into prominence in recent
years. The notion of 'risk' had its beginnings in the field of marine
insurance. Centuries ago, when sea travel was dangerous, venturesome men
evaluated the hazards of voyages and in bargaining sessions arrived at an
agreement on premium payments as a hedge against the possibility of dis-
aster that would repay for loss. Such evaluations called for two
decisions: What was the possibility of success or failure of the seagoing
mission? Which factors - human, mechanical, navigational - were important in determining such a possibility?

It was a long historical step from those early mercantile origins to the
science of *epidemiology*, but the transition was successfully achieved.
Epidemiology deals with the incidence and distribution of diseases and
the determination of factors that control the presence or the absence of
such conditions. Through epidemiology the concept of 'risk' became
attached to medicine, and elements of the centuries-old meaning of the
term were transformed. The impersonal 'hazards' of financial loss became
the personal hazard of loss of health through the onset of disease and
other debilitating conditions: 'possibility' became the statistics of
probability, to be determined by actuarial data whenever available; and
'danger' became the predisposition for disease that arose out of biological factors, often in combination with adverse circumstances including unhealthy or pathogenic environments.

Epidemiology has been described by one of its leaders, Johns Hopkins'
Professor Ernest Gruenberg (1981), as:

> 'The basic science of public health practice and preventive medicine
> whose traditional focus of inquiry is framed by three questions that
> must be directed to any disease or disorder:

- Who gets sick? Who doesn't?
- Why? (What are the 'risk' factors?)
- What can we do to make the sickness less common?' (pp. 8-9)

Data-based answers to these questions have produced scientific advances in understanding the precursors to many forms of disease. Once these have been discovered, methods of preventive intervention have been developed leading to a reduction in the incidence and prevalence of disorder.

These three questions have relevance for the investigation of risk and protective factors in the major mental disorders (Regier and Allen, 1981). 'Who gets sick?' emphasizes the research effort needed to identify those factors that appear to predispose some individuals to a particular psychiatric disorder. 'Who doesn't?' reflects parallel effort to search out protective and emeliorating factors to account for the many individuals who, despite sharing the risk potential of those who have become ill, continue to make healthy adaptations. 'Why?' reflects the need to understand the mechanisms or processes that account for the transition from an illness-free state to a full-blown psychiatric disorder. And finally, 'What can be done about it?' focuses upon the significant preventive intervention activity that follows the identification of the population at risk and the mechanisms underlying the disorder. Here the effort is made to introduce (wherever possible) the newly discovered protective factors to test whether these can serve as 'inoculants' against breakdown.

This sequence of tasks presents a heavy challenge to researchers in psychopathology. There are those who see mental disorders such as antisocial personality, schizophrenia, and the affective disorders as having, in part, some portion of developmental continuities reflected in their actualization. However, the difficult task is the speculative nature of identifying early risk factors that show continuities from childhood into adulthood. This and related difficulties have been described in a series of articles published in recent years (See Garmezy, 1977, 1978a, 1978b).

It would be inappropriate to leave the impression that the developmental study of risk is simply an imprecise pioneering venture in which inquiry and experimentation is built exclusively on speculation and guesswork. Quite the contrary.

In recent years there has been an expansion of research with children who are presumed to be at risk for future psychopathology. The prediction of persistent anti-social disorder has been a favorite target for risk researchers. Numerous volumes (e.g. Bennett, 1959; Glueck and Glueck, 1950; Hutchings and Mednick, 1974; McCord, McCord and Zola, 1959; Morrison, 1978; Robins, 1966; Rutter, 1977; West, 1977; West and Farrington, 1973) bear witness to the power of predictive factors studied in childhood that project a heightened probability of maintained antisocial behavior in adolescence and adulthood. Such factors have included family background, parental maladaptation, individual personality dispositions, potential hereditary influences, deprived ecological settings, and societal-institutional indices. Although not all agree (Hirschi, 1969) with regard to the predictive power of these variables and the

repeated cautions that one is dealing with correlational factors and not
etiological ones (West, 1977), the majority of investigators would tend
to agree that there are reliable 'risk' indices that strengthen the prediction of anti-social behavior.

Another area that has had a long history of research associated with risk
factors is the study of infants who are at biological, genetic or psychosocial disadvantage (e.g. Bierman and Streett, 1982; Ellis, 1975; Field,
1979, 1980; Jekel et al., 1975; Ryan and Schneider, 1978; Sacker and
Meuhoff, 1982; Sameroff and Chandler, 1975; Sawin et al., 1980; Schwartz
and Schwartz, 1977; Scott, Field and Robertson, 1981; Shaffer et al.,
1978; Sugar, 1976; Tjossem, 1976; Zlatnick and Burmeister, 1977). The
literature on psychosocial risk alone is so extensive that a volume
devoted to risk factors arising from infant-environment transactions provides a final chapter of 34 closely printed pages designed to serve as a
guide to recent research in the framework of a taxonomy of various types
of social risk factors (Sawin et al., 1980).

More recent newcomers to risk research with children are studies devoted
to two of the most severe of the major mental disorders - schizophrenia
and the major affective disorders (Regier and Allen, 1981). Risk for
schizophrenia has a history (Garmezy and Streitman, 1974) with tracings
back to the 1920's, but the more systematic research efforts are reflected in contributions of multiple investigators whose work was sparked by
the seminal experimental/longitudinal efforts of Mednick and Schulsinger
(1968, 1970). What risk researchers themselves have now termed the
'first generation' studies have been gathered together in a large single
volume that will soon be published (Watt et al., in press).

By contrast with the output of research into risk for anti-social and
schizophrenic pathology is the far more neglected study of children who
are at risk for the affective disorders. However there are studies now
underway in several laboratories and more will follow given the growing
research attention that is now being directed to the antecedents of adult
affective disorders (Beardslee, Keller and Shapiro, 1979; Orvaschel,
Weissman and Kidd, 1980; Radke-Yarrow and Zahn-Waxler, in press;
Weissman, Paykel and Klerman, 1972; Zahn-Waxler, 1981).

The Significance of Studying Risk and Protective Factors

The toll taken by mental disorders is not only a heavy one for the affected individuals, but its repercussions are felt in families and communi-
ties. Recent progress in the treatment of the major mental disorders
with pharmacological and psychosocial methods present a hopeful sign for
the future. However, the ultimate resolution of the problem of mental
illness lies in the determination of necessary predispositional qualities
and those potentiating factors that activate such predispositions to produce the symptom patterns of the various major mental disorders. Until
we gain this scientific knowledge, treatments can only be directed at
those who have already suffered a major breakdown in personal and social
functioning. Preventive interventions, whether of a primary or secondary
type, are most likely to be successful when we understand etiologic
agents and the pathogenic processes they elicit.

Until recently, psychiatric research has been concentrated on adult
patients who are already disordered. Although potential risk factors can
be suggested by retrospective inquiry, attempts to reconstruct significant elements in a patient's early life history is dependent upon the
faulty and often biased memory processes of adult patients and family
members. Unfortunately such methods of inquiry are fraught with error
(Radke-Yarrow, Campbell and Burton, 1970), a methodological shortcoming
which does not necessarily eliminate this important scientific question:
Can the focus on the adult patient provide clues about possible risk and
(even) protective factors? The answer is a cautious and circumscribed
'yes'. A backward look can suggest clues that can then be investigated
in children or adolescents who are presumed to be at risk for the mental
disorder exhibited by a patient, but who as yet show no behavioral signs
of being so affected. Were one to look at positive outcome cases (i.e.
patients who recover) *vs.* those who fail to recover or who relapse and
return to hospital the former may provide hypotheses about possible protective factors, and the latter may afford insights into more powerful
and more intransigent risk factors that are not necessarily associated
with the onset and maintenance of a particular psychiatric disorder.

An example drawn from schizophrenia research suggests the tenability of
such an approach. British psychiatric investigators (Leff, 1976; Vaughn
and Leff, 1976a; Vaughn and Leff, 1976b) have studied chronic schizophrenics discharged from the mental hospital with a critical issue in
mind. Who relapses? Who stays out? One answer appears to lie in the
specific characteristics of the emotional climate of the family to which
the patient has returned from the hospital. Research indicates that many
of those who relapsed and had to be rehospitalized had returned to homes
characterized by excessive criticism and emotional overinvolvement
directed to the ex-patient. (To these attributes the investigators
assigned the term, 'expressed emotion': EE). Another strong risk factor
has been the patient's failure to maintain a prescribed drug regime.
Both factors are correlated and can be viewed as serving possible risk
and potentiating functions. What of protective factors? These too seem
to be present in the picture: drug maintenance for one, and training
patients in social skills for another, apparently serve the function in
the former of dampening reciprocal emotional responses, and in the latter
of developing skills in the patient that can draw the person away from
the home and the critical rejecting behavior of family members.

What is of particular interest for the concept of risk is that these same
family attributes have also been studied as a component part of the
Rodnick-Goldstein Adolescent Risk Project conducted at UCLA. In that
research context so different in terms of geographical locale, patient
status, cultural setting, and investigative group, disturbed but non-
psychotic adolescents exposed to a comparable affectively distorted
family milieu heightened the probability of a later onset of schizophrenia and related conditions (Rodnick *et al.*, 1982). The fact that a
degree of continuity may exist between precursor factors that enhance or
reduce vulnerability to the later onset of schizophrenia with those that
enhance or reduce vulnerability to relapse suggests that expressed
emotionality in families may be one possible risk factor in the
pathogenesis of schizophrenia.

Predisposition and potentiation have always played central roles in psy-
chopathologists' orientation to etiology and symptomatology in the major
mental disorders. Protective factors - the inhibitors of pathogenic processes - have played a negligible role either in theory construction or
in the empirical researches of psychiatric investigators.

It is not presumptious to suggest that the next decade will witness a
surgent growth of interest in the study of resiliency and stress-
resistant components of persons presumed to be at risk for later
disorder - and that such investigations will be of importance whatever
the theoretical model used to explain the origins of mental illness.

It is appropriate to consider one way that would permit us to enrich our
understanding of factors that predispose persons to the development of
mental disorder. This would be to contrast groups considered to be at
risk for such disorders but whose outcomes prove to be markedly dis-
parate - some traversing a road to incompetence, maladaptation and symptom formation, as opposed to others who move toward mature, competent,
and adaptive functioning.

There is now the beginnings of a literature aimed at the identification
of these latter groups, the so-called stress-resistant children for whom
predictions of deleterious outcomes prove inappropriate. Risk research
in the four domains cited - infancy, anti-social disorder, schizophrenia
and the affective disorders - validate a claim that such children exist
and can contribute to our understanding of protective factors. What is
surprising is not the existence of such children but rather the neglect
and lack of attention paid them by competent researchers and competent
clinicians.

Michael Rutter (1979) took a similar position when he wrote:

> 'There is a regrettable tendency to focus gloomily on the ills of
> mankind and on all that can and does go wrong. It is equally unusual
> to consider the factors or circumstances that provide support, pro-
> tection or amelioration for the children reared in deprivation ....
> Would our results be better if we could identify the nature of pro-
> tective influences? I do not know, but I think they would. The
> potential for prevention surely lies in increasing our knowledge and
> understanding of the reasons why some children are not damaged by
> deprivation' (p.49).

These were the opening sentences of a chapter that appeared in a volume
devoted to competence in children in the context of primary prevention of
psychopathology (Kent and Rolf, 1979). Rutter's closing paragraph
offered a view of a scientific agenda for the future:

> 'The exploration of protective factors in children's responses to
> stress and disadvantage has only just begun. We are nowhere near the
> stage when any kind of overall conclusions can be drawn. What is
> clear, though, is that there is an important issue to investigate.
> Many children do *not* succumb to deprivation, and it is important that
> we determine why this is so and what it is that protects them from
> the hazards they face. The scanty evidence so far available suggests

that when the findings are all in, the explanation will probably
include the patterning of stresses, individual differences caused by
both constitutional and experiential factors, compensating experiences outside the home, the development of self-esteem, the scope and
range of available opportunities, an appropriate degree of environmental structure and control, the availability of personal bonds and
intimate relationships, and the acquisition of coping skills' (p.70).

In the section that follows some representative examples are presented of
those beginnings to which Rutter alluded.

The Search for Protective Factors

Searching for protective factors in children under stress is a 'catch-as-
catch-can' situation. There is no single source or even multiple sources
to which one can turn. The search tends to be elusive but gratifying
once a study or a project is located that is explicit with regard to
children who cope effectively with adversity. But it isn't coping alone
that will suffice to provide clues to protective factors. Investigators
of children who cope successfully in stressful circumstances must not
merely identify such children but also search out the correlates of their
adaptive behaviors. These correlates can extend to personality dispositions, parental attributes, situational and cultural contexts, family
milieu, significant supportive figures and institutions, etc. Stage 1,
then, in the search for protective factors would be the identification of
children at risk who demonstrate good coping abilities. Stage 2 constitutes the search for the correlates of such adaptive behaviors in the
child, the family, and the various situational contexts in which
resilient behavior is observed. There is a growing scientific literature
of Stage 1 studies, appreciably fewer Stage 2 studies, and fewest of all
are the critically important Stage 3 studies. This third stage would
involve the systematic search for the *processes* and *mechanisms* that under-
lie the manifestations of stress-resistant behavior in children.

So for now one searches for clues to resiliency across diverse studies
whatever their heterogeneity with regard to types of stressors, child
cohorts, investigative modes, and measures of adaptation. This scarcely
seems to have the procedural rigor that would lead one to anticipate a
satisfactory identification of protective factors that may be implicated
in stress-resistance. Yet, a search does reveal a certain degree of con-
formance in the findings, as is evident from a diverse set of studies
that provide information about the correlates of adaptive behavior of
children in adversity.

1.   The first, epidemiological in content and form, are the studies
conducted by Rutter and his colleagues on the Isle of Wight and in an
inner London borough (Rutter, 1979). These investigators isolated six
family variables that they found to be associated with a heightened
prevalence of psychiatric disorders in children: (1) severe marital discord; (2) low social status of the family; (3) overcrowding or large
family size; (4) paternal criminality; (5) maternal psychiatric disorder;
and (6) admission of the child into the care of local authority. The
rates of psychiatric disorder in the children proved to be a function of

the *number* of familial risks to which a child had been exposed. A single stress, even if chronic, produced rates no greater than those of children who were not exposed to any of the risk factors. However, the presence of two or three concurrent stressors resulted in a fourfold increase in the rate of psychiatric disorder, while four or more produced a tenfold increment.

What of resilience or stress-resistance? Rutter and his colleagues identified a number of risk reducers among which were these: positive temperament factors: gender (girls proved to be less vulnerable than boys); the presence, even in a home marked by parental strife, of a parent whose relationship to the child was marked by warmth, affection and the absence of severe criticism, and supportiveness; and the socializing influence of a positive school environment that had as its ethos teacher/administrator concern for the growth and well-being of the child (Rutter *et al.*, 1979).

Examining this list of potential protective factors, suggests the operation of three broad categories of variables: (1) personality dispositions of the child; (2) a supportive family milieu; and (3) an external support system that encourages and reinforces a child's coping efforts and strengthens them by inculcating positive values.

2.   Study 2 is a longitudinal study of 30 years duration by a group of dedicated investigators led by Dr. Emmy Werner. The site of their study was the Island of Kauai, one in the chain of the Hawaiian Islands. Three volumes spaced 11 years apart have traced the project and its findings: *The Children of Kauai* (Werner, Bierman and French, 1971); *Kauai's Children Come of Age* (Werner and Smith, 1977); and the concluding volume of the trilogy whose title expresses the theme of this presentation, *Vulnerable but Invincible: A Study of Resilient Children* (Werner and Smith, 1982).

The stressors of this study were somewhat different from the preceding one. Werner, in the first volume, identified the inauspicious beginnings of her infant cohort whose presumed vulnerabilities were suggested by their exposure initially to perinatal stress, followed by poverty, family instability, limited parental education, and in some cases serious mental health problems of the parents.

In the third volume the investigators have compared a group of so-called 'resilient' children with peers who were coping inadequately. The variables that discriminated between the groups included factors such as these: the 'resilients' had better relationships with their parents, who were less frequently absent from the home; the family milieu was marked by parental support, family closeness, rule setting, discipline, and a respect for individuality. Resilient children had better health histories, recuperated from illnesses more quickly, were rated in infancy and in childhood as 'active', 'socially responsive', 'autonomous', and given to a more 'positive social orientation'. The resilient girls had fewer teen marriages, less teen-age pregnancies, and fewer accidents. In these factors and others not cited here one can perceive the personal dispositional attributes of the resilient ones and the positive family milieu that characterized their world. But beyond these factors was their skill in identifying and selecting resilient models and sources of

support in peers, older friends, ministers, and teachers to whom they
could turn when needed.

3.   An additional longitudinal study of importance is the 14-year program of research conducted by Jeanne and Jack Block of the University of
California, Berkeley focused on the development of ego resilience from
the pre-school years to late adolescence (Block and Block, 1980). The
Blocks too have noted that the antecedents of resilience are likely to be
found in genetic and constitutional factors as observed in the way the
infant responds to environmental change, can be comforted, equilibrates
physiological responses, and modifies sleep-wakefulness states. A second
group of factors likely lies in the nature of the families. In an
earlier search for continuities Jack Block reported that ego-resilient
children have parents who are competent, loving, compatible, patient,
integrated, and have shared values; ego-brittle children come from homes
marked by discord and conflict (Block, 1971).

Space constraints force an abridgement of the results of several other
investigations. Library research conducted by Nuechterlein (1970) and
the author (Garmezy, 1981) for studies (many unpublished but available
through the Educational Resources Information Center) describing the
attributes of competent Black children reared in poverty in America's
inner city ghettos generated a review of the correlates of competence in
minority children who had known economic and social disadvantage. By
this time the litany of virtues of such children has a familiar sound.
On the personality side the children were described as socially
responsive, active, sensitive, lacking in sullenness and restlessness,
intelligent and cooperative, enjoying a positive view of self and evident
self-esteem. Family intactness was not an identifying factor but in the
single parent homes mother was active, concerned for the child's competency, assisted with homework and recognized and reinforced her child's
interests, goals and striving for self-direction. From a physical standpoint the family household was marked by neatness, a lack of clutter, and
the presence of books. Several studies indicated that in the lives of
these children there was at least one adequate significant adult who was
able to serve as an identification figure. In turn the achieving young-
sters seemed to hold a more positive attitude toward adults and authority
figures in general.

Once again a triad of factors appear: dispositional attributes, family
cohesion and warmth, and support figures available in the environment.

Still another research program provides additional insights into children
under stress. Wallerstein and Kelly (1980) have directed their clinical
research to a massive and growing psychosocial problem that exists not
only in the United States but in many other parts of the world as well.
This is the problem of divorce, with all of its stress-inducing effects
on children. Their volume details the results of a five-year longitudinal
study of such children. In a chapter (13) of that volume the authors
report the adaptations of children when evaluated at the five-year mark.
In describing those children who had 'enhanced, or consolidated, or continued in their good developmental progress following the divorce' as
well as others who 'deteriorated, moderately or markedly' they can find
no single theme in the lives of those in either group. Rather they note

one is confronted with:

> ' ... a set of complex configurations in which the components came
> together in varying combinations in the individual life of each
> child. Some of the components are the family relations, others are
> those in the social surrounding, and all react on the resources or
> the frailties of the particular child at a particular time in his or
> her growing-up period' (p.206).

The components of the divorce experience that affected positive outcomes
at the 5-year point were these:

(1) The extent to which the parents were able to resolve and reduce
their conflict and anger;

(2) The course of the custodial parent's treatment of the child and the
resumption of good parenting in the home;

(3) The extent to which the child did not feel rejected by the non-
custodial or visiting parent and the maintenance of that regular
relationship over time;

(4) The range of personality assets and deficits which the child
brought to the divorce including the child's history within the
pre-divorce family and the capacity to make use of his or her
resources within the present, particularly intelligence, the
capacity for fantasy, social maturity, and ability to turn to peers
and adults;

(5) The availability to the child of a supportive human network;

(6) The absence of anger and depression in the child;

(7) The sex and age of the child (p.207).

The triad of contents again appears but as any excellent clinician would
anticipate there is unlikely to be a specific configuration for copers
and another for non-copers. Configural patterns can be expected to vary
and to change with time as a function of the child's developmental status
and the situational changes brought about by a family's dissolution. But
in broad outline, attributes of the child, the family and support networks
are powerful determiners of the adequacy with which the child copes when
confronted with the rupture of his or her family.

Still another area of research is one with which the author has been
associated - the vulnerability of children to mental disorder and the
concept of risk. There have been many research programs focused on
children born to schizophrenic parents, particularly mothers. The
results of many of these research programs that have been conducted in
various countries of the world will be available shortly in a compendium
soon to be published (Watt *et al.*, in press).

One of the most extraordinary contributions to our knowledge of the adult
outcomes of such children at risk comes not from the more traditional
experimental type of risk studies, but rather from a 20 year longitudinal
study of 208 schizophrenic probands conducted by Professor Manfred Bleuler
(1978) and published in English under the title *The Schizophrenic*

Disorders: Long-term Patient and Family Studies.

In the course of his 20 years of research with the probands, 104 of
Bleuler's patients married and had 169 offspring. An additional 15
children were born out of wedlock. Of these 184 children only 10 were in
time diagnosed as definitely schizophrenic and five of these ten recovered
before the research was concluded. Three-quarters of the children were
mentally sound in adulthood, 120 of the 143 children who were older than
20 years of age at the time of the study's completion were found to be
working in jobs that exceeded expectations based on their level of training and education; and all but 10 children exceeded the paternal occupa-
tional level. Eighty-four per cent of the offspring who had married had
happy and successful marriages.

Bleuler was well aware of the many stressors to which these offspring had
been exposed. The realities which he witnessed led him to write that:
'the accomplishments of these children were remarkable when one considers
their handicaps - the emotional suffering, social ostracism, and economic
disadvantages to which their parents' psychoses subjected them'.

Bleuler came to know these children extremely well and that knowledge
enabled him to write this moving passage about his patients' offspring
(Bleuler, 1978):

> 'I ... became acquainted with the majority of mine as the physician
> of their parents. Many of these probands' children I had to counsel
> professionally, principally because of the distress that the psycho-
> sis of their parents had caused them. I shared with these children
> their concern for the sick parents when things went bad for them -
> and their joy and pleasure when their parents improved. I have often
> seen these probands' children weep. I have met them on the stairs
> and in the halls of the clinic, bearing flowers and gifts as they
> went to visit their parents. And I saw them again repeatedly, some-
> times years apart, or heard of them and their fates for years, while
> visiting other patients. From this different way of meeting them I
> was bound to come up with a different evaluation of their personali-
> ties. Personality phenomena that appeared to an exclusively scient-
> ific investigator to be firmly set prototypes of eccentrics or psy-
> chotics, appeared to me as the physician (and sometimes as a personal
> friend as well) of the probands' children, much more as perfectly
> natural behavior patterns for a healthy individual undergoing diffi-
> cult circumstances in connection with his family. In the course of
> their purely scientific interest, the earlier investigators aimed
> specifically at deviant personality characteristics. I searched for
> these, too, but I saw primarily also the good and normal aspects. I
> saw how children worried about their parents, how they struggled
> against it when their parents were to be transferred to other clinics
> because, perhaps, visiting them would be more difficult then. I
> found out how many of these children of my patients made economic
> sacrifices or interrupted their professional training in order to
> help their parents, or how a son might undertake to manage the house-
> hold to take the place of his hospitalized mother. A school-age girl
> cleverly evaded the truant officer in order to be able to care
> devotedly for her smaller siblings necessarily neglected by the sick

mother. And I saw frequently, too, how these children were confused
in their relations to the opposite sex, because of the schizophrenia
of their father or mother. Invariably they felt guilty toward a love
partner; they worried whether, faced with the probability of becoming
ill or of their future offspring becoming ill, marriage would be a
responsible step to take. What appeared to be a form of schizoid
autism in an erotic situation, without knowing their internal suffer-
ings, was actually the understandable, rather dramatic reaction of a
warm-hearted, sensitive human being. In short, it was inevitable
that I should find considerably more mentally sound and fewer psycho-
paths than I would have, if I had seen my probands' children in but a
single interview and only for the purpose of scientific inquiry'.
(pp. 380-381)

No wonder then that Bleuler was led to comment in the closing paragraphs
of his description of these offspring:

' ... it must be emphasized, that only a minority of the children of
schizophrenics are in any way abnormal or socially incompetent. The
majority of them are socially competent, even though many of them
have lived through miserable childhoods, and even though there are
reasons to suspect adverse hereditary taints in many of them. Keeping an eye on the favorable development of the majority of these
children is just as important as observing the sick minority. It is
surprising to note that their spirit is not broken, even of children
who have suffered severe adversities for many years. In studying a
number of the family histories, one is even left with the impression
that pain and suffering has a steeling - a hardening - effect on the
personalities of some children, making them capable of mastering
their lives with all its obstacles, in defiance of all their disadvantages'. (p. 400)

In preparing this article, the author wrote a letter to Professor Bleuler
seeking to elicit from him speculations as to what protective factors he
believed may have operated to produce so many positive outcomes in his
cohort of offspring of schizophrenic parents. The letter indicated a
belief that those who have had the opportunity to observe at length the
positive adaptations of stressed children were likely to be able to provide hypotheses related to resilience that would be needed for future
research on stress-resistant children.

Professor Bleuler's reply was a lengthy one and included a detailed case
history of a young woman named Vreni (which will appear in the Watt *et
al.*, in press).

In brief, Vreni presents an almost classical picture of a child exposed
to chronic adversity. Her mother was addicted to drugs, the father an
emotionally unstable alcoholic. To Vreni, at age 14, fell the task of
caring for a 13-year-old brother, a 12-year-old sister, 6-year-old twins
and a mentally and physically ill father. So distressed was Professor
Bleuler with these adverse circumstances that he dispatched a welfare
worker to the home who returned to report that 'the household was kept in
perfect order by Vreni, the smaller children were well, happy, well fed,
well dressed, went regularly to school and their teachers had no

complaints as regards their behaviour'.

At the same time Vreni visited her mother regularly in the hospital,
brought her fresh clothes, accompanied her on walks near the Clinic. She
had hoped to be a nurse and Dr. Bleuler arranged for her to be tutored to
make up for her educational deficiencies. After she had been accepted
into a nursing school and with her goal close to reality, she returned to
Bleuler in tears with the realization that she could not study and simul-
taneously care for her younger siblings and sick father.

Vreni at age 22 married a kind-hearted man who devotes 'all of his free
time to the family'. There are now two healthy children and the family
circle is a happy one. Bleuler reports that he has maintained touch with
her and her family. Her household is well cared for, she sees to it that
her children are well educated and she and her husband maintain 'a cordial
and warm atmosphere in the home'.

If Professor Bleuler had stopped at this point, Vreni would have joined a
legion of other case studies that give substance to an observation that
Karl Popper once made that the study of man is the study of the unantici-
pated consequences of expectable events.

But the function of a case study is not to provide drama but insight
through the elaboration of researchable hypotheses. Professor Bleuler in
his letter provided just such a key.

> 'It is not speculation but a fact that these children who have devel-
> oped well had found - like Vreni - living conditions in which they
> could apply their gifts and interests in an active way that corres-
> ponded with their personality.
>
> Why has Vreni become a very healthy and very happy wife and mother,
> in spite of a childhood which became so threatening soon after baby-
> hood?
>
> Or should the question be asked the other way around? Is she healthy
> and happy on account of a threatening childhood? To point to an (in-
> born personality) disposition in this connection is far from satis-
> factory. Nothing demonstrates that she had any particular disposition.
> She is certainly not a 'superkid'. Her IQ is average, she lacks
> particular interests or talents, she is not gifted in any particular
> way. One could point out the fact that the living conditions of the
> child only became impaired after babyhood. As far as we can conclude,
> however, from anecdotal experience we are tempted to say: Life gave
> her a rare chance in her childhood: The chance to do what she liked
> to do and was able to do. She loved and still loves children, she
> was proud to be able to care better for her sick father and for the
> youngsters than was her mother; and she was able to take over her
> mother's duties with a good heart and a practical skill. On the
> other hand she was not interested in school. *It seems that stress-
> ful, difficult childhood conditions are not felt as too stressful and
> as too difficult if they offer the opportunity to the child to ful-
> fill a great task which the child likes to and is able to fulfill*
> (present author's italics).

Such a statement seems too simple and too self-evident to be interesting. However it might have some importance. Perhaps we can help to manipulate the living conditions of a child in stressful and threatening conditions in such a way that the child can find a great and appropriate task. I could speak of experiences which suggest that such a manipulation might perhaps play a role in the prevention of schizophrenic psychoses. Until now, these experiences are merely anecdotal. Perhaps studies of high risk children will contribute more to this problem than anecdotal experience.

We can even go one step further: We all complain that living conditions for children have become unfavourable in modern civilization, in large cities, in small apartments, before a television set, distant from everything which is natural, distant from earth, distant from gardening and agriculture, distant from caring for each other. Anecdotal experiences similar to the one I have presented might give us some hints in our endeavors to propose conditions for children in which they might find a great and satisfactory task appropriate to their nature'.

Professor Bleuler's observations point to a psychological construct that has received too little attention. It is quite different from a companion construct that has received infinitely greater attention. There are very few who are unacquainted with Seligman's concept of *learned helplessness* (Seligman, 1975; Garber and Seligman, 1930). Rooted initially in animal experimentation, Seligman's paradigm is based on observations of the behavior of dogs when placed in a shuttle box compartment in which they were exposed to uncontrollable and inescapable shock. The translation of the construct into human behavior, particularly as an explanation for depression has brought learned helplessness to a level of high popular appeal. As a perceived analogy it has been attached to situations of separation and loss, lack of self-esteem, academic failure, and persuasive manifestations of incompetence which are not rooted necessarily in ability or talent deficits. This brief and inadequate summary may serve to point out that learned helplessness is the language of failure, of disability, and of self-perceived incompetence.

But this essay is one that emphasizes the language of children's success, of their overcoming of adversity, of their potential for adaptation and self-sufficiency. There is an applicable construct to such behavioral phenomena, but it is one that has gained little or no attention in keeping with that recurrent paradox that many of those in the *mental health* professions are more wedded to psychopathology than to well-being, to concern with those who fail rather than to those who succeed, to children who capitulate to stress rather than to those who resist its debilitating effects.

In 1978 Rachman published a volume titled, *Fear and Courage* in which he elaborated a concept he termed *required helpfulness*. A subsequent article (Rachman, 1979) provided a capsule description of the concept:

'The concept was introduced in recognition of the fact that people who are required to carry out dangerous/difficult tasks that are socially desirable, often manage to do so effectively and without

strain ... required helpfulness refers to dangerous/difficult acts
that are performed in response to social requirements - in order to
reduce or prevent other people from experiencing serious discomfort.
Under the incentive of high social demands, helpers often act more
effectively and more persistently than at other times. The execution
of successful acts of required helpfulness may lead to enduring
changes in the helper himself'. (p. 1)

This is 'therapy through helping others' and its consequences include
increased competence in the helper, markedly heightened morale and a
marked increment in motivation and persistence, a heightened probability
of successful accomplishment of one's tasks, a greater toleration of discomfort evoked by its performance, and the acquisition of new skills that
lifts the level of performance past its previous asymptote.

'It is probable,' noted Rachman, 'that in addition to the formally-
provided training for helping ... execution of the required tasks,
followed by the appropriate feedback, will lead to the growth of new
coping skills'. (p. 4)

The parallel of these observations to those of Dr. Bleuler seems evident.
His perception that a confluence of a requisite task needed to help
another, that a child at risk is called upon to fulfill and which he can
perform, makes stressful, difficult childhood conditions less stressful
and less difficult. Rather than leave such required helpfulness to
chance Bleuler raises the question of utilizing 'required helpfulness' as
a technique of intervention for enhancing the strengths of children at
risk, when he writes: 'It might happen that we can help to manipulate the
living conditions of a child in stressful and threatening conditions in
such a way that the child does find a great task appropriate to him'.
The elements suggested by this formulation is that an important task
successfully achieved that meets the needs of others adds a counterforce
of predictability and (above all) controllability that strengthens the
resilience and the ego resources of the child.

There are parallels to this in other areas of our psychological literature. In the study of prosocial behavior in children social competence
bears a positive relationship to such behavior. Altruism in adolescents
is correlated with emotional stability and social relations. High ego
strength and peer judgments of altruism are correlated. Block (1971) has
reported significant positive correlations between ego-resiliency and
children's helpful, considerate behavior. Affiliativeness, social
responsibility and emotional stability also relate to prosocial
behaviors. (Reported in Radke-Yarrow, Zahn-Waxler and Chapman, 1984).

Radke-Yarrow and Zahn-Waxler (1984) have reported signs of prosocial
behavior in young children of severely depressed parents in which some
offspring manifest 'sensitive caring behavior toward the sick parent'.
Altruistic behavior such as this made manifest under conditions of adversity has not been provided for in typical developmental theories of
childrearing. What, it is important to ask, are the roots of prosocial
behavior? The study of such behaviors in children who are at risk may
add not only to basic research in developmental psychopathology but also
to the basic science of developmental psychology.

There are also available anthropological accounts that provide cross-
cultural data in support of this concept of required helpfulness applied
to children's work on behalf of family. (Whiting and Whiting, 1975)
Weisner and Gallimore (1977) have provided a substantial review of the
child as an effective sibling caretaker, acting in a parental surrogate
role.

There are problems of pressing significance for whose who are concerned
about children who live in a stressful world. Recently (Garmezy, 1983)
in reviewing the literature of children in war, the author took
a backward glance at studies of the adaptation of children in World War II
and a contemporary look at the children of Ireland and Israel. That
literature indicates that even the extraordinary intensity of war fails
to blot out the resiliency of children. And those factors that seem to
play a protective role in other stressful situations find a parallel even
in the extraordinary dislocations, devastation, and dangers precipitated
by wars.

These studies extending from the basic observations of Freud and
Burlingham (1943) and other observers, to the more recent studies in
Israel (Spielberger, Sarason and Milgram, 1982) indicate that the prime
factor in how children will respond to the stress of war is based to a
large extent on how their parents, guardians and other significant adults
have behaved. Such adults provide for the children a representation of
their efficacy and the demonstrable ability to exert control in the midst
of upheaval. From that standpoint the sense of confidence of the adult
community provides a support system of enormous importance to the well-
being of children. Zuckerman-Bareli (1982) has attempted to identify
specific stress-resistance factors in children who have recurrently been
exposed to border incidents in Israel. Citing attributes anchored in the
individual the author notes 'anxiousness' as a 'comprehensive mental
attitude that precedes the actual response to stress'. Other factors
include *age* (the younger, the greater the reservoir of energy), level of
education (for flexibility in problem-solving), sex (a greater emphasis
in the kibbutzim that men are expected to be the defenders of the settle-
ment), and a sense of identification and satisfaction with the community
and its goals. Here too the triad of protective factors referred to
previously appears.

The evidence that resilience in children under stress is a far more
ubiquitous phenomenon than mental health personnel have realized, may be
rooted in the historical concern of the clinician about behavior pathology. The aura of the old lingers on an example of which can be provided by contemporary Ireland.

Morris Fraser (1974) in *Children in Conflict* wrote a poignant description
of the stress that marks the lives of the children of Belfast. His
recital conveys a background to the civil strife that goes far beyond
bullets and bombings:

   'Environment, for a Belfast working-class child, means a decaying
   terrace, a high flat or a concrete housing estate with less than one-
   third the Government recommended playing space. He will mix, play,
   and be educated exclusively with his own religious group, and may

never see a child of the 'other' group, except across a barricade.
His home area is divided from other areas by armed sentries and steel
barriers; he cannot leave this area, and to go out even in his own
street after dusk is to court injury or death. The street is in pitch
darkness at night, carpeted with stones and broken glass, littered
with burnt-out, rusted skeletons that, perhaps a year ago, were cars,
buses, and lorries. His home is overcrowded, his father has a high
chance of being unemployed, and poverty may be acute. He is brought
up with a fear and hatred of members of the other religion that will
last him all his life'. (pp. 40-41)

Despite these external stresses Fraser too has observed those ubiquitous
variations in adaptation that are evident in children whenever they are
exposed to similar traumatic circumstances:

'In Belfast ... the way in which each child reacted to riot stress
seemed to depend on three main factors. There was, first, the degree
of emotional security enjoyed by the child both before and during the
period of acute stress. This related not only to his *own* psychological resources, but also to those of his immediate family.
Secondly, there was the role of the stressful experience itself.
Thirdly, each child's response was idiosyncratic, or unique, depending on his own usual way of responding to new experiences'.
(pp. 99-100)

What will be the outcome for these children exposed to such a long period
of civil strife? An American psychologist, Rona Fields (1977) who
visited Northern Ireland, in a volume, *Society Under Siege*, wrote
despairingly of the future of its children. She wrote of 'psychological
genocide', indicating that in the absence of 'massive rehabilitation
efforts ... the children of Northern Ireland - those who survive physically, those who do not emigrate - will be militaristic automatons,
incapable of participating in their own destiny'. (p. 55)

An Irish psychologist Ken Heskin (1980) in *Northern Ireland: A Psychological Analysis* concluded his volume on this different note:

'The people of Northern Ireland have suffered much in the past decade
but they have come thus far with characteristic human fortitude and
resilience in the face of adversity. Despite the prophets of doom,
the evidence is that societal norms in Northern Ireland have not
deteriorated and will not deteriorate to a level at which peace might
be only marginally better than conflict. There remains in Northern
Ireland a community of people whose strengths and similarities far
outweigh their weaknesses and differences'. (p. 157)

Which view shall we heed? The literature of stress, the adaptive potential of children, their resilience, which is patterned, in part, out of
personal disposition, the nature of their families, and the 'community
of people of strengths and similarities' that provide support for them
would favor Heskin's view. There is little gained by those who cry havoc
while failing to heed the recurrent findings of our research literature
on the ability of children to meet and to conquer adversity.

Acknowledgments

Preparation of this paper was facilitated by research grant support provided by the National Institute of Mental Health, William T. Grant Foundation and a Research Career Award (N.I.M.H., U.S.P.H.S.) to the author.

Dr. Michael Goldstein, U.C.L.A., provided a most helpful exchange of views regarding aspects of several issues presented herein.

References

BEARDSLEE, W. R., KELLER, M. B. and SHAPIRO, R. W. (1979) *Studies of Children of parents with major affective disorders.* Unpublished manuscript. Children's Hospital Medical Centre, Cambridge, Mass.

BENNETT, J. (1959) *Delinquent and Neurotic Children.* New York, Basic Books.

BIERMAN, B. R. and STREETT, P. (1982) Adolescent girls as mothers: Problems in parenting. In I. R. Stuart and C. F. Wells (Eds.), *Pregnancy in Adolescence: Needs, Problems, and Management*, pp. 407-426. New York, Van Nostrand Reinhold Co.

BLEULER, M. (1978) *The Schizophrenic Disorders: Long-term Patient and Family Studies.* New Haven, Yale University Press.

BLOCK, J. (1971) *Lives through Time.* Berkeley, CA, Bancroft Books.

BLOCK, J. H. and BLOCK, J. (1980) The role of ego-control and ego-resiliency in the organization of behavior. In W. A. Collins (Ed.), *Development of Cognition, Affect, and Social Relations: The Minnesota Symposia on Child Psychology*, Vol. 13, pp. 39-101. Hillsdale, N. J., Lawrence Erlbaum Associates.

ELLIS, N. R. (Ed.) (1975) *Aberrant Development in Infancy.* Hillsdale, N. J., Lawrence Erlbaum Associates.

FIELD, T. M. (Ed.) (1979) *Infants Born at Risk: Behavior and Development.* New York, SP Medical and Scientific Books.

FIELD, T. M. (Ed.) (1980) *High-risk Infants and Children: Adult and Peer Interactions.* New York, Academic Press.

FIELDS, R. M. (1977) *Society under Siege: A Psychology of Northern Ireland.* Philadelphia, Temple University Press.

FRASER, M. (1974) *Children in Conflict.* Harmondsworth, Middlesex, Penguin Books.

FREUD, A. and BURLINGHAM, D. T. (1943) *War and Children.* London, Medical War Books.

GARBER, J. and SELIGMAN, M. E. P. (Eds.) (1980) *Human Helplessness: Theory and Applications.* New York, Academic Press.

GARMEZY, N. (1977) On some risks in risk research. *Psychological Medicine*, 7, 1-6.

GARMEZY, N. (1978a) Attentional processes in adult schizophrenia and children at risk. *Journal of Psychiatric Research*, 14, 3-34.

GARMEZY, N. (1978b) Observations on high risk research and premorbid development in schizophrenia. In L. C. Wynne, R. Cromwell, S. Matthysse (Eds.), *Nature of Schizophrenia: New Findings and Future Strategies*, pp. 460-472. New York, John Wiley and Sons.

GARMEZY, N. (1981) Children under stress: Perspectives on antecedents
and correlates of vulnerability and resistance to psychopathology.
In A. I. Rabin, J. Aronoff, A. N. Barclay and R. A. Zucker (Eds.),
Further Explorations in Personality, pp. 196-269. New York, John
Wiley and Sons.
GARMEZY, N. (1983) Stressors of childhood. In N. Garmezy and M. Rutter
(Eds.), *Stress, Coping, and Development in Children*, pp. 43-84.
New York, McGraw-Hill.
GARMEZY, N. and STREITMAN, S. (1974) Children at risk. The search for
the antecedents of schizophrenia. Part I. Conceptual models and
research methods. *Schizophrenia Bulletin*, 1, 14-90.
GLUECK, S. and GLUECK, E. T. (1950) *Unraveling Juvenile Delinquency*.
Cambridge, Mass., Harvard University Press.
GRUENBERG, E. M. (1981) Risk factor research methods. In D. A. Regier
and G. Allen (Eds.), *Risk Factor Research in the Major Mental Dis-
orders*, pp. 8-19. Washington, D.C., U.S. Government Printing Office
(D.H.H.S. Publication No. ADM 81-1068).
HESKIN, K. (1980) *Northern Ireland: A Psychological Analysis*. New York,
Columbia University Press.
HIRSCHI, T. (1969) *Causes of Delinquency*. Berkeley, CA, University of
California Press.
HUTCHINGS, B. and MEDNICK, S. A. (1974) Registered criminality in the
adoptive and biological parents of registered male adoptees. In
S. A. Mednick, F. Schulsinger, J. Higgins and B. Bell (Eds.),
Genetics, Environment and Psychopathology, pp. 215-227. Amsterdam,
North Holland, North Holland/Elsevier Press.
JEKEL, J. F., HARRISON, J. T., BANCROFT, D. R., TYLER, N. C. and
KLERMAN, L. V. (1975) A comparison of the health of index and sub-
sequent babies born to school age mothers. *American Journal of Public
Health*, 65, 370-374.
KENT, M. W. and ROLF, J. (Eds.) (1979) *Primary Prevention of Psycho-
pathology. Vol. III: Social Competence in Children*. Hanover, N. H.,
University Press of New England.
LEFF, J. P. (1976) Schizophrenia and sensitivity to the family environ-
ment. *Schizophrenia Bulletin*, 2, 566-574.
McCORD, W., McCORD, J. and ZOLA, I. K. (1959) *Origins of Crime*.
New York, Columbia University Press.
MEDNICK, S. A. and SCHULSINGER, F. (1968) Some premorbid characteristics
related to breakdown in children with schizophrenic mothers. In
D. Rosenthal and S. S. Kety (Eds.), *The Transmission of Schizophrenia*,
pp. 267-291. Oxford, Pergamon Press.
MEDNICK, S. A. and SCHULSINGER, F. (1970) Factors related to breakdown
in children at high risk for schizophrenia. In M. Roff and
D. F. Ricks (Eds.), *Life History Research in Psychopathology*, Vol. 1,
pp. 51-93. Minneapolis, University of Minnesota Press.
MORRISON, H. L. (1978) The asocial child: A destiny of sociopathy? In
W. H. Reid (Ed.), *The Psychopath: A Comprehensive Study of Antisocial
Disorders and Behaviors*, pp. 22-65. New York, Brunner/Mazcl.
NUECHTERLEIN, K. (1970) *Competent Disadvantaged Children: A Review of
Research*. Unpublished summa cum laude thesis. Minneapolis, University
of Minnesota.

ORVASCHEL, H., WEISSMAN, M. M. and KIDD, K. K. (1980) Children and
   depression: The children of depressed parents; The childhood of
   depressed parents; Depression in children. *Journal of Affective Dis-
   orders*, 2, 1-16.
RACHMAN, S. J. (1978) *Fear and Courage*. San Francisco, Freeman.
RACHMAN, S. J. (1979) The concept of required helpfulness. *Behavior
   Research and Therapy*, 17, 1-6.
RADKE-YARROW, M. and ZAHN-WAXLER, C. (in press) Roots, motives and
   patterns in children's prosocial behavior. In J. Reykowski,
   D. Karylowski and E. Staub (Eds.), *The Development and Maintenance of
   Prosocial Behaviors: International Perspectives* (1984). New York,
   Plenum Press.
RADKE-YARROW, M., CAMPBELL, J. D. and BURTON, R. V. (1970) Recollections
   of childhood: A study of the retrospective method. *Monographs of the
   Society for Research in Child Development*, 35, Serial No. 138.
RADKE-YARROW, M., ZAHN-WAXLER, C. and CHAPMAN, M. (1984) Children's
   prosocial dispositions and behavior. In P. H. Mussen (Ed.),
   Carmichael's Manual of Child Psychology, Vol. 4, 4th ed., pp. 469-
   545. New York, John Wiley and Sons.
REGIER, D. A. and ALLEN, G. (Eds.) (1981) *Risk Factor Research in the
   Major Mental Disorders*. Washington, D.C., Government Printing Office
   (D.H.S. Publication No. ADM 81-1068).
ROBINS, L. N. (1966) *Deviant Children Grown Up*. Baltimore, Williams and
   Wilkins.
RODNICK, E. H., GOLDSTEIN, H. J., DOANE, J. A. and LEWIS, J. M. (1982)
   Association between parent-child transactions and risk for schizo-
   phrenia: Implications for early intervention. In N. Goldstein (Ed.),
   Preventive Intervention in Schizophrenia: Are we Ready?, pp. 156-172.
   Washington, D.C., Government Printing Office (D.H.H.S. Publication
   No. ADM 82-1111).
RUTTER, M. (1977) Family, area and school influences in the genesis of
   conduct disorders. In L. A. Hersov and D. Shaffer (Eds.), *Aggression
   and Antisocial Behaviour in Childhood and Adolescence*, pp. 95-113.
   Oxford, Pergamon Press.
RUTTER, M. (1979) Protective factors in children's responses to stress
   and disadvantage. In M. W. Kent and J. Rolf (Eds.), *Primary Preven-
   tion of Psychopathology, Vol. III: Social Competence in Children*,
   pp. 49-74. Hanover, N. H., University Press of New England.
RUTTER, M., MAUGHAN, B., MORTIMORE, P. and OUSTON, J. (1979) *Fifteen
   Thousand Hours: Secondary Schools and their Effects on Children*.
   Cambridge, Mass., Harvard University Press.
RYAN, G. M. and SCHNEIDER, J. M. (1978) Teenage obstetric complications.
   Clinical Obstetrics and Gynecology, 21, 1191-1197.
SACKER, I. M. and NEUHOFF, S. D. (1982) Medical and psychosocial factors
   in pregnant adolescents. In I. R. Stuart and C. F. Wells (Eds.),
   Pregnancy in Adolescence: Needs, Problems and Management, pp. 107-
   139. New York, Van Nostrand Reinhold Co.
SAMEROFF, A. J. and CHANDLER, M. J. (1975) Reproductive risk and the
   continuum of caretaking casualty. In F. D. Horowitz (Ed.), *Review of
   Child Development*, Vol. IV, pp. 187-244. Chicago, The University of
   Chicago Press.

SAWIN, D. B., HAWKINS, R. C., WALKER, L. O. and PENTICUFF, J. H. (Eds.) (1980) *Exceptional Infant, Vol. 4: Psychosocial Risks in Infant-environment Interactions*. New York, Brunner/Mazel.

SCHWARTZ, J. L. and SCHWARTZ, L. H. (Eds.) (1977) *Vulnerable Infants*. New York, McGraw-Hill Book Company.

SCOTT, K. G., FIELD, T. and ROBERTSON, E. G. (Eds.) (1981) *Teenage Parents and their Offspring*. New York, Grune and Stratton.

SELIGMAN, M. E. P. (1975) *Helplessness: On Depression, Development, and Death*. San Francisco, W. H. Freeman and Company.

SHAFFER, D., PETTIGREW, A., WOLKIND, S. and ZAJICEK, E. (1978) Psychiatric aspects of pregnancy in school girls: A review. *Psychological Medicine*, 8, 119-130.

SPIELBERGER, C. D., SARASON, I. G. and MILGRAM, N. A. (Eds.) (1982) *Stress and Anxiety*, Vol. 8. Washington, D.C., Hemisphere Publishing Corporation.

SUGAR, M. (1976) At-risk factors for the adolescent mother and her infant. *Journal of Youth and Adolescence*, 5, 251-270.

TJOSSEM, T. D. (Ed.) (1976) *Intervention Strategies for High Risk Infants and Young Children*. Baltimore, University Park Press.

VAUGHN, C. E. and LEFF, J. P. (1976a) The influence of family and social factors on the course of psychiatric illness. *British Journal of Psychiatry*, 129, 125-137.

VAUGHN, C. E. and LEFF, J. P. (1976b) The measurement of expressed emotion in the families of psychiatric patients. *British Journal of Social and Clinical Psychology*, 15, 157-165.

WALLERSTEIN, J. S. and KELLY, J. B. (1980) *Surviving the Breakup: How Children and Parents Cope with Divorce*. New York, Basic Books.

WATT, N., ANTHONY, E. J., WYNNE, L. C. and ROLF, J. (Eds.) (in press) *Children at Risk for Schizophrenia: A Longitudinal Perspective*. New York, Cambridge University Press.

WEISNER, T. S. and GALLIMORE, R. (1977) My brother's keeper: Child and sibling caretaking. *Current Anthropology*, 18, 169-190.

WEISSMAN, M. M., PAYKEL, E. S. and KLERMAN, G. L. (1972) The depressed woman as a mother. *Social Psychiatry*, 7, 98-108.

WERNER, E. E. and SMITH, R. S. (1977) *Kauai's Children Come of Age*. Honolulu, University of Hawaii Press.

WERNER, E. E. and SMITH, R. S. (1982) *Vulnerable, but Invincible: A Study of Resilient Children*. New York, McGraw-Hill Book Company.

WERNER, E. E., BIERMAN, J. M. and FRENCH, F. E. (1971) *The Children of Kauai: A Longitudinal Study from the Prenatal Period to Age Ten*. Honolulu, University of Hawaii Press.

WEST, D. (1977) Delinquency. In M. Rutter and L. Hersov (Eds.), *Child Psychiatry: Modern Approaches*, pp. 510-523. Oxford, Blackwell Scientific Publications.

WEST, D. J. and FARRINGTON, D. P. (1973) *Who becomes Delinquent?* London, Heinemann.

WHITING, B. and WHITING, J. W. M. (1975) *Children of Six Cultures*. Cambridge, Harvard University Press.

ZAHN-WAXLER, C. (1981) *The Social-emotional Development of Young Children with a Manic-depressive Parent*. Presentation May 29 to the Board of Scientific Counselors, National Institute of Mental Health, Bethesda, M.D.

ZLATNICK, F. J. and BURMEISTER, L. F. (1977) Low 'gynecologic age': An
  obstetric risk factor. *American Journal of Obstetrics and Gynecology*,
  128, 183-186.
ZUCKERMAN-BARELI, Ch. (1982) The effect of border tension on the adjust-
  ment of kibbutzim and moshavim on the northern border of Israel. In
  C. D. Spielberger, I. G. Sarason and N. A. Milgram (Eds.), *Stress and
  Anxiety*, Vol. 8, pp. 81-91. Washington, D.C., Hemisphere Publishing
  Corp.

Author Index

235

Subject Index

abuse, child
  see child abuse
adjournment procedure
  for truancy 137-40
adolescence
  depression 127,129
adoption 45
affect, positive 15-16
affect, negative
  ex-care mothers 36-7
  mothers 26-7
affection
  mother-child 32-3
affective disorders
  risk factors 215
affectual depression 128,130
aggression
  children 152
agorophobia
  psychiatric treatment 8
Allergic-Tension-Fatigue
  syndrome 95-107
allergy
  food 104-6
altruism 226
anti-depressants 8
anti-social behaviour
  as predictor of
  psychopathology 214-15
antidepressants 131
  response of children to 126
asthma 81-93
  adaptation to 87
  definition 81
  diagnosis 82
  severity rating 83,88
auto-immune antibodies 103

Bayley Scales of Infant
  Development 193-4,197
bedtime routine
  children 158-9
Behavior Screening
  Questionnaire 54-64
behaviour
  see also child behaviour
behaviour changes
  bereaved children 184-5
behaviour problems
  Allergic-Tension-Fatigue
  syndrome 96
  asthmatic children 81-93
  children of depressed
  mothers 4,6-8
  effects of food additives
  106
  infants 208
  pre-school and school entry
  51-64
  regression analysis 58-61
  symptom continuity 55-8
  visually handicapped
  children 73-9
behaviour therapy
  for sleep problems 69-71
Behavioural Screening
  Questionnaire 74,83,85,89
Belfast 227-8
bereavement
  children 179-86
  parents 171-8
  professional support 185
bereavement counselling 171,
  172,173-4,181

243